Praise for *The Healthcare Mandate*

A timely and thoughtful road map for the sustainable future of healthcare.

—MATTI W. PALO JR., MD, board certified orthopedic surgeon

The Healthcare Mandate outlines exciting new paradigm shifts focused on technology with a hopeful call to action via concrete examples and creative anecdotes.

—SCOOTER PLOWMAN, MD, MBA, MHSA,
medical director of digital medicine

In this unprecedented and historic moment of massive upheaval and disruption, there has never been a more imperative time than now for *The Healthcare Mandate*.

—PAULA M. CRONE, DO, Vice President of WesternU Oregon
and Dean of the College of Osteopathic Medicine of the
Pacific-Northwest at Western University of Health Sciences

The Healthcare Mandate addresses the critical intersection and application of healthcare and digital data to illustrate how this can translate into positive patient outcomes while enhancing the patient-centric journey.

—PAUL SETLAK, PharmD, MBA

This book is a timely clarion call to action. Leaders in healthcare need to firmly grasp accelerating change to propel clinical quality and future readiness.

—DANIEL R. WILSON, MD, PhD,
President of Western University of Health Sciences

Nicholas has done an amazing job of capturing the future of health-care—and how new technology innovations will get us there. A must-read for anyone in healthcare.

—JOHN WEATHERSPOON, PhD, JD,
medical researcher and registered patent attorney

The Healthcare Mandate provides a model for how we lean into digital doctor-patient interactions in ways that will clearly improve patient outcomes and enhance this sacred relationship that has devolved in our current sick care environment.

—EDWARD BARNES, MD, FACP, Associate Dean of Academic Innovation and Chief of the Division of Nephrology and Hypertension at the College of Osteopathic Medicine of the Pacific-Northwest at Western University of Health Sciences

The Healthcare Mandate provides specific recommendations on how to significantly influence positive patient outcomes by partnering with our patients in a community setting and putting ourselves in their shoes through constant touch points. These techniques are enabled by the latest connected technologies and represent the Big Shift required to fix healthcare in the modern era. The key insight is linking patient wellbeing to specific targeted innovation.

—RAY POWER, MB BCh, BAO, MICGP, MRCGP, MBA,
Cofounder of the Centric Health Physician Group (Ireland)

The Healthcare Mandate not only shows us why things have to change but how we can do better in the future with the right plan, using tools we have never had before. In a post-Covid world, this could be our last chance to get it right.

—PAUL CARROLL, MBBS, FRACGP, MICGP,
General Practitioner, Churchtown Medical (Ireland)

The
Healthcare
Mandate

The Healthcare Mandate

How to Leverage Disruptive
Innovation to Heal America's
Biggest Industry

Nicholas J. Webb

New York   Chicago   San Francisco   Athens   London   Madrid
Mexico City   Milan   New Delhi   Singapore   Sydney   Toronto

1 2 3 4 5 6 7 8 9   LCR   25 24 23 22 21 20

ISBN   978-1-260-46812-0
MHID   1-260-46812-7

e-ISBN   978-1-260-46813-7
e-MHID   1-260-46813-5

Library of Congress Cataloging-in-Publication Data

Names: Webb, Nicholas J., 1958– author.
Title: The healthcare mandate : how to leverage disruptive innovation to heal America's biggest industry / Nicholas J. Webb.
Description: New York : McGraw-Hill, [2020] | Includes bibliographical references and index.
Identifiers: LCCN 2020015680 (print) | LCCN 2020015681 (ebook) | ISBN 9781260468120 (hardback) | ISBN 9781260468137 (ebook)
Subjects: LCSH: Medical care—United States. | Health care reform—United States. | Medical economics—United States. | Medical innovations— Economic aspects—United States.
Classification: LCC RA395.A3 W425 2020 (print) | LCC RA395.A3 (ebook) | DDC 362.10973—dc23
LC record available at https://lccn.loc.gov/2020015680
LC ebook record available at https://lccn.loc.gov/2020015681

McGraw Hill products are available at special quantity discounts to use as premiums and sales promotions or for use in corporate training programs. To contact a representative, please visit the Contact Us pages at www.mhprofessional.com.

To my amazing wife, Michelle,
and our children, Taylor, Madison, Chase, and Paige

Contents

Preface

During my 40 years in the healthcare industry, I've enjoyed meeting a cross section of the world's healthcare thought leaders. While some have been well-known media and industry personalities, others have been quiet, unassuming people dedicated to making a difference, one patient at a time.

Perhaps the most profound connection I ever made was with Dr. Manly Michaelson. He was not a Nobel Prize laureate, world-renowned surgeon, or even academic royalty. To me, he was much more impressive than all of those: Dr. Michaelson was an old-fashioned family doctor. He served the community of Bellevue, Iowa, a town of just over 2,000 souls—primarily farmers and everyday hardworking families—nestled on the banks of the Mississippi River. Dr. Michaelson, known to friends simply as "Doc," and who died in 2008 at the age of 77, understood the incredible importance of the relationship between the doctor and the patient. He took his role very seriously. He loved his patients, and they loved him. This love was based on his incredible commitment to his patients, not merely as a physician but, more importantly, as a compassionate and loving human.

In those days before specialized medicine, Dr. Michaelson offered a wide range of medical procedures. He set and cast fractured bones, ran his own x-ray machine, delivered babies, repaired lacerations, and even performed tonsillectomies at the old Bellevue Hospital. He routinely made house calls to families in the Bellevue area, and he especially loved caring for children, always arriving equipped with a variety of toys and techniques to make his young constituents laugh.

After he retired—with great reluctance because his health was failing—he gave me two of his doctor's bags. Familiar to anyone of a certain age who remembers when doctors made house calls, these battered black leather bags have become among my most prized possessions. Not because they're of particular value, but because of what they represent: a time and place when the doctor-patient relationship was close, and primary care physicians (although the term hadn't yet been invented) were much more than technicians who diagnosed and treated disease.

The lessons I learned from Dr. Michaelson were revitalized when I met Dr. Ray Power, of Dublin, Ireland. I was speaking at a large conference in Dublin, and at the end of my presentation Dr. Power enthusiastically greeted me. I was startled by the first thing that he said to me: "It's all about the patient!" He went on to tell me that in his career he always felt honored to be in service of patients. As I got to know him, almost every discussion was about his passion to change the conversation about healthcare and how we needed to refocus on the doctor-patient relationship. I also learned from Dr. Power that healthcare is about both science and art and how the beautiful art demonstrated by caring physicians requires the support of a healthcare industry that gets us back to compassionate care fueled by (but not led by) both technology and economics.

While the business of healthcare must still be all about the patient—or, as I redefine "patient" in this book, the "constituent"—I do not advocate returning to the days of family doctors making house calls. Those days are gone. This book is about leaping forward to a new era of doctor-patient closeness in which the doctor and his or her constituents are in constant digital communication. This growing connectivity is just one of the major trends—the Big Shift—that's changing healthcare.

For some, these new developments may seem impractical, far-fetched, or even suggestive of Big Brother. But I believe that if we can forge a bond between high technology and high touch that comes from a human-first approach, these new technologies can be managed to significantly improve the quality of clinical care while allowing for a newly energized focus on compassion and human connection.

Acknowledgments

I would like to acknowledge the technologists, clinicians, researchers, innovators, and educators who have supported the research in this book. Thank you to all my amazing colleagues at Western University of Health Sciences and to my core team at the Center for Innovation—Shawna, Stacy, Jesse, Chris, and Miary. I would also like to thank my colleague and friend Dr. Ray Power for his amazing support and genuine commitment to patient care.

Introduction

In this time of crisis in the healthcare industry, you and every other person in a position of leadership need sharp analysis to identify problems and powerful new ideas to implement change. You need a fresh perspective on how we got ourselves into our current situation, explanations of future trends, and specific action plans to get your organization on track to meet the demands of a changing marketplace.

The language we use to talk about the problems facing the healthcare industry and the solutions to these problems is important. In *The Healthcare Mandate*, you'll note I use the term "marketplace" in the context of the healthcare industry. I'll also talk about "customer experience," another term that's increasingly being applied to the healthcare industry. You'll read about the Big Shift, which can either destroy your organization or act as a lever to propel you into the future. You'll hear very little talk about "patients" but much about "constituents," a broader term that more accurately reflects your changing relationship to the people you serve.

I'll discuss organizational innovation and how any organization in any industry needs to innovate or perish, including healthcare companies. We'll explore the power of technological progress and how digital communications can reshape the doctor-patient relationship.

We all know about the sudden explosion of "lifestyle diseases"—conditions such as obesity, diabetes, and heart disease that are caused, or at least intensified, by the personal choices made by your constituents. How, we ask, can we effectively treat those whose behavior puts them at risk for getting the same disease all over again? The truth is that we're discovering we can't, and throwing money at the problem isn't the answer.

This book begins the conversation about your constituents taking personal responsibility for their own healthcare—not responsibility for diseases over which they have no control, such as hereditary conditions, but responsibility for choices they make that adversely impact their health, thereby raising the cost of healthcare for everyone.

None of the ideas offered in this book are farfetched or imaginary. All of them are operational, in some form, right now. This is a book for today, not some vague time in the future. For example, I talk about connecting every constituent with his or her primary care physician by the use of a digital device to send real-time health data to the physician, who will be alerted if the data suggests a health problem. Impossible? Hardly. At this very moment, millions of people are using wearable health monitoring devices, and implantables are already in use, not only in pets but in humans.

We explore the idea of penalizing constituents who consistently make poor health choices. Crazy? We already do it. If you choose to smoke cigarettes, in many states you will pay more for health and life insurance, and high taxes on cigarettes are designed in part to discourage smoking.

We discuss the question of the personal health data of your constituents. Why would your constituents possibly agree to allow the real-time streaming of their data if they thought it would be sold at a profit to another company? There are people who are working on this problem, and with the help of blockchain technology, your constituents have the ability—right now, today—to assert their ownership of their own personal data.

The Big Shift in healthcare is happening now. This book will help you understand it and leverage its enormous power and potential for the benefit of your constituents and your organization. The future can be either very grim or very bright. You already know which path you want to take, and *The Healthcare Mandate* can help you on your journey.

Ready? Let's get started!

The Healthcare Mandate

Change Is
Happening Now

L et's journey into the not-too-distant future and meet Roberta.

At age 70, Roberta is in very good health. She's happy with her healthcare providers. This group includes not only her primary care physician but a set of stakeholders comprising her employer (yes, she's still working!), health insurer, the local hospital, medical data managers, pharmaceutical companies, even government regulators—anyone with an interest in her wellness. She's so happy with them, she doesn't think about them very much. This is because she doesn't have to. Digitally connected to her, they hover out of sight, like guardian angels, watching over her, day and night. If they detect a health problem on the horizon—a change in her blood chemistry or a variation in the pressure in her eye—her primary care provider sends her a message. If necessary, her primary care provider asks her to come to the clinic for an examination or consultation.

Roberta's *constituent healthcare operating system* (CHOS)—which we'll learn much more about in the pages ahead—is designed to meet the twin goals of *anticipation* and *prevention*. The CHOS's central processing module, which could be located anywhere, captures and stores the steady stream of Roberta's biomedical data, along with her genomic profile, environmental trends, and new medical technologies and discoveries. It cleans the raw data before turning it into actionable information. When necessary, the constituent healthcare operating system responds with a call for appropriate intervention.

This process allows the CHOS to anticipate emerging health problems and prevent them from blossoming into full-fledged disease.

Roberta lives in a culture in which wellness is rewarded. This is not to say that infectious diseases and accidents are ignored; Western medicine has long excelled at defeating viruses and fixing physical damage. But in the system that Roberta is happy to be a part of, the focus is on anticipating and preventing not only infectious diseases but the deadly lifestyle diseases—obesity, diabetes, heart disease, addiction—which, when she was younger, afflicted many other people.

As Roberta goes about her daily life, sometimes she reflects on her current state of health and how it has dramatically improved since she was a young woman. Back then, she was overweight and smoked cigarettes. She had a primary care physician, but he did what most well-meaning doctors do, which was to provide the usual physical exams, note any worrisome personal habits, and give Roberta a pep talk about reducing her weight and quitting smoking.

Then one day Roberta started to have abdominal pain. It was accompanied by a feeling of nervousness, heart palpitations, headaches, and elevated blood pressure. She went to her doctor, who ran the usual blood and urine tests but found nothing unusual. He gave her a blood pressure medication and sent her home.

The symptoms persisted, and soon anxiety and sleeplessness were added to the list. Roberta went back to her doctor, and this time the blood and urine tests included a measurement of the level of her adrenal hormones, which can detect a functional tumor. Roberta was required to provide a 24-hour urine sample, which meant she had to collect her urine for an entire day, so it could be used for laboratory testing.

Her doctor used a dexamethasone-suppression test to check her cortisol levels. They were found to be elevated. More tests followed—first a CAT scan and then a scan designed to detect the presence of metaiodobenzylguanidine, which would—and did—indicate an adrenal tumor.

Then came the staging—the process by which doctors determined the exact location of the tumor, if it were cancerous, if or where the tumor had spread, and whether it was affecting other parts of the body.

Next came surgery. The tumor was larger than five centimeters, so a large incision in her back was needed. Roberta was hospitalized for six days. Once she was sent home, she was told not to lift heavy objects for six weeks. The cost for her adrenal gland surgery was $25,000, which was a middling price, neither the cheapest nor the most expensive.

She made a full recovery. By all accounts, her treatment had been a success, at least by the definition at the time. Costly? Yes, but what else could you do? Those big machines were expensive, and the patient was entitled to treatment to fix her problem, for which her healthcare plan was obliged to pay. By a very slight degree, Roberta's surgery for her adrenal gland tumor contributed to the upward price pressure on healthcare insurance in America. Little by little, dollar by dollar, healthcare costs continued to rise, but with no better outcomes.

At the time, and despite individual success stories like Roberta's, analysts, doctors, insurers, and ordinary citizens were becoming convinced that our healthcare system was not serving patients well. It was a time when a Harris Poll revealed that only 16 percent of US consumers believed health insurers put patients over profits, and only 9 percent thought pharmaceutical and biotechnology companies did. "We are in the midst of a healthcare maelstrom," said Wendy Salomon, vice president of reputation management and public affairs at Nielsen. "Consumers see no safe port, no place where their interests are truly protected—and that lack of consumer trust is reflected in the reputational risk we see across the US healthcare landscape."[1]

To healthcare constituents like Roberta, the flaws were obvious—costs were sky-high and outcomes often poor—but no one had any clear answers. The patients blamed the healthcare providers and insurers, who blamed the government, who blamed the patients. It was like a house on fire, with everybody arguing about how to put it out and no fire department in sight.

Fast-forward to Roberta at age 70. Times have changed! The strategy taken by Roberta and her healthcare providers has been reinvented. They had learned, and were acting upon, two key lessons: treating an emerging disease is better than battling it when it's full-blown, and keeping a person healthy is the best way to reduce that person's rate of disease. It costs much less to prevent disease than to treat it, and not only in direct payments to the healthcare provider but in lost productivity when the patient is out sick. Now the healthcare emphasis is on *anticipation* and *prevention*. Treatment is much lower on the list, and because it comes much earlier in the disease cycle, it's shorter, easier, and cheaper than in years past.

Now, Roberta's hormone levels are closely monitored by the central module of her constituent healthcare operating system. She's grateful that today, if (hypothetically) her CHOS module were to detect a slight but persistent elevation in any one of her key hormones including cortisol, androgens, and aldosterone, the module would send a notice to her primary care physician while simultaneously searching for other anomalies such as high blood pressure and low blood potassium. If found, they would be added to the report.

All of this would happen without Roberta having to do anything. She could live her life knowing that at the very first symptoms, of which she might not even be aware, her medical team would be alerted.

People Dodge Their Doctors

In the old days, the relationship between Roberta and her healthcare providers was dependent on the patient's *motivation to self-report* disease symptoms. The patient first had to notice a problem and then actively seek treatment. If the patient failed at either action, the disease or injury could intensify unchecked.

The way the system worked was this: A person such as Roberta—or anyone else—would go about her daily affairs with no contact with healthcare providers. Then, if Roberta felt sick or noticed something unusual, such as abdominal pain, she would contact her doctor. If the doctor deemed the problem to be an emergency, she might see her doctor quickly, perhaps even the same day. If it was not considered to be an emergency, then she might see her doctor in weeks. Specialists were often booked months in advance. Eventually the problem would be diagnosed. By this time, her condition would have advanced so that she required surgery, and Roberta would receive the treatment she needed.

Even within this imperfect system, by virtue of being proactive, Roberta was the ideal patient. She was her own health monitor, and she responded when she sensed or saw something amiss. This was about as good as it got.

True, it might happen that Roberta could go for a routine checkup while showing no symptoms, be tested, and get flagged for disease. This approach has worked with mammograms and colon cancer tests, which people seem to accept. But those are just two diseases, and the use of such tests by patients is not 100 percent. This method also requires that patients get routine checkups, even when they feel fine. Most people, especially men, don't get regular checkups.

Millions of people are *not* ideal patients. Unlike Roberta, they might be insensitive to the signals their body sends them, fail to recognize a warning sign, or be unwilling to call their doctor. They might wish the problem would go away if they ignored it. They may think they can "battle through" the problem without professional care.

Perhaps the biggest reason why people put off calling their doctor is because they're afraid of the cost. In a national poll of more than 1,300 American adults, 44 percent of respondents said they didn't go to a doctor when they were sick or injured in the previous year because of concerns about cost, and 40 percent said they skipped a recommended medical test or treatment for the same reason. The poll, conducted by NORC at the University of Chicago and the West Health Institute, revealed insights into how the costs of healthcare affected the medical decisions made by respondents. Thirty percent of respondents said over the previous year they had to choose between paying for medical bills and paying for basic necessities like food, heating, or housing. Many said they were not only delaying seeing their doctor but also going without recommended care such as tests and treatments.[2]

Statistically, men are more averse to seeing the doctor than women. Over a two-year period, men are half as likely as women to go to the doctor, according to survey data collected by the US Centers for Disease Control and Prevention. Men are also more than three times as likely to report going more than five years without a visit to a doctor, and more than twice as likely to say that during their adult life, they've *never* had contact with a doctor or health professional.[3]

This massive level of doctor avoidance is not proving to be a very good strategy! Men tend to die earlier than women, and are more likely than women to die from 8 out of the top 10 causes of death in the United States.[4] While researchers believe several factors are involved in men's shorter life spans, a major reason is that men don't go to the doctor as often as women do.

Why not? A survey commissioned by the Orlando Health hospital system provided insight into why many men avoid their doctor. According to the survey results, claims that they are too busy, discomfort with certain physical exams such as prostate checks, and false pride keep them out of the doctor's office. On top of that, many men see asking for help as a sign of weakness. They want to be self-sufficient tough guys. As Orlando Health's Jamin Brahmbhatt, MD, wrote, "Women are much more proactive about their health than men. This may sound harsh, but this complacency is killing us. Far too many men die or experience compromised quality of life because of preventable diseases." He then drew an analogy that many men can understand: "Our bodies are a lot like our cars. We'll take the time to do preventative maintenance on our cars, getting tune-ups and oil changes, but we often don't take the same care of our bodies."[5]

Motor Vehicles Self-Report Damaged Components

Indeed, the comparison to automobiles is worth making.

Since their invention over a century ago, automobiles have been equipped with rudimentary mechanical sensors that provide information about the car while in operation, such as the fuel gauge and oil pressure indicator—for example, when the oil pressure gets too low, the little red light on the dashboard begins blinking, alerting the driver to the problem. The capability of motor vehicles to report on the status of key systems has steadily progressed, and with the advent of digital communications in the 1980s, it took a big leap forward.

As we enter the third decade of the twenty-first century, motor vehicles of all types are becoming increasingly able to diagnose their own mechanical problems and report these to the dealership and even to schedule repairs and order new parts, all without the driver's involvement. Electric automaker Tesla touts its ability to offer cars that "virtually maintain themselves." Using the Internet of Things (IoT), each Tesla vehicle, its service center, and the factory are interconnected in real time, allowing technicians and engineers to work together to identify and resolve issues as they occur. "Within hours," says the company's website, "we can make updates across our entire customer fleet. We are also developing new ways for your Tesla to self-improve. The result is a car that is constantly evolving and improving, allowing you to stay out of the shop and on the road."

With the car's remote diagnostics, the company says that 90 percent of the time it can remotely diagnose an issue and what is needed to repair it. The car's software can be updated by the factory remotely, and if there's a problem, a feature Tesla calls "SmartAlerts" can communicate to the owner what the car needs and walk the owner through a simple fix or connect the owner to the company service team.[6]

Many vehicles are now capable of performing self-diagnostics and reporting the results. Cadillac offers the OnStar system, which among other features checks the vehicle's engine, transmission, antilock brakes, and other key systems to assure the owner that the car is in proper running condition. With OnStar's "Diagnostic Alerts," the owner can receive a monthly diagnostic report. But OnStar is also able to detect future problems; a "Proactive Alert" is sent to the OnStar member when data from the vehicle's systems predicts *potential* issues with key vehicle components, including the battery, fuel pump, fuel pressure sensor, and starter motor.[7]

In 2017, Italian supercar manufacturer Lamborghini announced it had created the world's first "self-healing" sports car. The Terzo Millennio concept car, which translates to "third millennium" in Italian, is equipped with sensors that conduct checks to detect any damage, and then the car can repair itself by filling any crack with nanotubes to prevent the crack from spreading. Created in collaboration with researchers from the Massachusetts Institute of Technology, these body panels will use electricity-storing carbon nanotubes sandwiched between two laminates of carbon fiber. If sensors detect damage to the carbon fiber, micro-channels can generate heat to seal cracks and mitigate the risk of any further damage.[8]

In their paper "An Integrated Self-Diagnosis System for an Autonomous Vehicle Based on an IoT Gateway and Deep Learning," Korean researchers YiNa Jeong and others describe how the cars of the future will be able to diagnose more faults and conditions than ever before, a feature of car ownership dramatically influenced by the IoT.

The authors propose that using information gathered from the sensors within the autonomous vehicle will allow it to diagnose itself and assess the influence between parts by using deep learning, and then the vehicle would inform the driver of the result. The integrated self-diagnosis system would consist of three modules:

1. The first in-vehicle gateway module collects the data from the in-vehicle sensors. This data comes from sources including component sensors, the "black box," and the radar units while

driving. The data control center transfers the data collected through each controller area network (FlexRay), and through the media-oriented systems transport protocol to the on-board diagnostics or actuators.

2. On the basis of the data collected from the in-vehicle sensors, the optimized deep learning module creates the training data set and evaluates the risk of the malfunction of monitored components. It also diagnoses the status of the vehicle's total condition.

3. The third data processing module has an edge-computing-based self-diagnosis service to improve the self-diagnosis speed and reduce the system overhead, while a V2X-based accident notification service informs adjacent vehicles and infrastructures of the self-diagnosis result analyzed by the on-board diagnostics.[9] This last feature allows the vehicle, which may be operating on the street or highway, to notify nearby vehicles of its potential mechanical problem, thereby reducing the risk of an accident.

What works today in cars will soon work with people. Imagine getting into a crowded elevator. As the doors close, you notice that the man next to you is coughing and seems short of breath. Then suddenly you receive a digital warning relayed to you from the man's biomonitor that says, based on his detectable symptoms including a fever, the man is likely to have a case of undiagnosed coronavirus.

But more about that later.

How Roberta Is Plugged into the Digital Healthcare Network

As for Roberta, at age 70 she has never felt better. Her healthcare costs have been dropping, and she feels increasingly empowered to keep herself in optimum health.

Here's how her digital healthcare network system works.

Roberta wears a small medical device in her ear. Hers is one of many available designs of health biomonitors; other people might wear dermal patches or have a tiny device implanted. Roberta's biomonitor looks like a discreet hearing aid, but she's not self-conscious about it because everyone else at her company wears some sort of biomonitor.

Roberta's biomonitor provides a detailed overview of her current health. It takes her four primary vital signs: body temperature, blood pressure, pulse (heart rate), and breathing rate (respiratory rate). It also connects to other body sensors, providing a massive amount of rich predictive data. It detects many of the factors that once had been determined only by blood tests, including the basic metabolic panel, the lipid panel, and various hormones including insulin, cortisol, serotonin, and melanin. It can even—through artificial intelligence and machine learning—know and respond when Roberta is eating or sleeping more or less than usual, is lethargic, or seems unusually active. It can sense when her blood sugar is too high or too low, and even—though she sometimes chafes at this—audibly advise her not to eat too much of the sugary cake served at the office birthday party.

As one component of her constituent healthcare operating system, her biomonitor feeds data to the CHOS module, which captures and stores it, cleans it, turns the raw data into actionable information, and, when necessary, responds with a call for appropriate intervention.

This is not science fiction. It's happening *now*. Medical device wearables are becoming increasingly commonplace—as we'll discuss in greater detail in this book—and a similar biomonitor to Roberta's, while not yet commercially available, has been prototyped and is well within reach. As they describe in their 2019 paper "A Smart Wireless Ear-Worn Device for Cardiovascular and Sweat Parameter Monitoring During Physical Exercise: Design and Performance Results," Bruno Gil, Salzitsa Anastasova, and Guang Z. Yang designed and built an external device worn on the ear that, in clinical tests, measured cardiovascular and sweat parameters during physical exercise. The device itself was worn on the left ear, with a second set of sensors on the right ear. Electrocardiogram bipolar recordings captured the electric potential around both ears. Sweat rate was estimated by the impedance method over one segment of tissue closer to the left ear, complemented by the measurement of the lactate and pH levels using amperiometric and potentiometric sensors, respectively. Together with head acceleration captured by a sensor, the acquired data was sent to a mobile phone via Bluetooth Low Energy, a form of wireless communication, enabling extended periods of signal recording.[10]

To the best knowledge of the authors of the study, this was the first device that combined the measurement of cardiovascular performance with sweat parameters that was fully integrated into a single ear-worn device. While crude in appearance, it clearly demonstrates that with further innovation the ear-worn biomonitor—and many other types—will become increasingly smaller and more powerful.

To return to Roberta in the near future, her health data—which she owns and controls—is collected by her ear-worn biomonitor and sent to the CHOS module. It's stored in the cloud using blockchain technology, where it's both secure and instantaneously available. There it's monitored around the clock and compared against massive data sets that include all current medical literature, demographic data, and her own health history. Any anomalies are instantly detected. If necessary, she's notified and asked to come into the doctor's office for further testing. If appropriate, a tiny pod attached to her body will formulate and administer medication either subcutaneously or directly into her blood system.

Let's say her adrenal tumor reappeared. Because her health was being monitored, when her biomonitor detected a change in her blood level of aldosterone, she immediately went to her doctor. After the diagnosis had been verified, she checked in for surgery. But this time the tumor was still very tiny and the procedure was laparoscopic. She went home the same day, and the cost was $2,500—about one-tenth that of her previous surgery.

Even better, her company—which like most employers paid a portion of her healthcare coverage—offered a program whereby employees who stayed healthy were rewarded with a bonus of $5,000 at the end of the year. The employees qualified based on a set of biomarkers, which included the data accumulated by Roberta's ear-worn sensor and shared with her employer. She could use the extra cash to pay her healthcare premiums, so it was like getting totally free healthcare.

Because Roberta is plugged into a comprehensive digital system that collects, analyzes, and acts upon her healthcare data, when she does get sick, it's caught earlier and treated more quickly and at lower cost.

TAKE ACTION!

- Ensure that your healthcare organization is focused on the shift from diagnosis and treatment of existing diseases to anticipation and prevention of disease in your constituents.
- The automotive industry is showing us that not only can biomonitors report the status of operating systems to the owner—which has been done for years—but can, thanks to the Internet of Things, also report to a central health management center. This lifts the burden of reporting from the patient.
- Consider ways to reward your constituents— employees, for example—for maintaining good health. What people won't do for themselves they will often do for cash. Incentive programs can be powerful motivators for behavioral change.

The Four Historical Stages of Healthcare

You can't envision your future without understanding your past, and you can't know where you're going without knowing where you've been. So let's look back on the four stages of the practice of medicine that, over many centuries, brought us to our current state of disruption. We'll see that each stage has been generally characterized by good, well-meaning people doing the very best they could with the information available to them at the time. And then we'll look ahead to the fifth stage, into which we can collectively journey and which can make the future of healthcare much brighter.

Stage 1: Providing First Aid

From ancient times until the twentieth century—a span of thousands of years—the well-meaning people who attempted to cure or repair others (you could call them "doctors" if you don't mind a very loose definition of the word) were powerless to treat infections and other disease processes. They were able to effect only crude first aid remedies, such as setting broken legs with sticks or using animal hides to control bleeding. Human anatomy could only be discerned from a dead person, and the processes of life—blood circulation, the function of the brain, reproduction—could only be guessed at.

Life was short, but there were a few effective innovations. Amazingly, in the ancient world, a common first-aid procedure was trepanation, a surgical intervention in which a hole was drilled or scraped into the human skull, exposing the dura mater. It was done to treat health problems related to intracranial diseases or release pressured blood buildup from an injury. It's perhaps the oldest surgical procedure for which there is archaeological evidence; at one burial site in France dated to 6500 BCE, 40 out of 120 prehistoric skulls found had trepanation holes. And based on cranial healing, many of these ancient patients survived the procedure![1]

As technology progressed, these would-be doctors began to get more skilled at first aid. Barbers started removing abscessed teeth, and amputations became survivable. During the American Civil War, approximately 60,000 surgeries—roughly three-quarters of all the operations performed during the war—were amputations of injured arms or legs. The operation was intended to prevent deadly complications such as gangrene, but the pressure of the battlefield and the inexperience of many surgeons made it a gruesome business. As Confederate Army surgeon Julian John Chisholm said in 1864, "The limbs of soldiers are in as much danger from the ardor of young surgeons as from the missiles of the enemy."[2]

The "cut first, ask questions later" mentality extended well into the twentieth century. Notorious examples include Dr. Walter Freeman, who from the mid-1930s into the mid-1960s performed over 3,400 lobotomies on his hapless patients. And from 1894, when William S. Halsted published his landmark paper, "The Results of Operations for the Cure of Cancer of the Breast Performed at the Johns Hopkins Hospital from June 1889, to January 1894," until the 1980s, the needless radical mastectomy was the standard treatment for breast cancer.

History shows us that mistakes can be made, and it's not only possible but imperative that healthcare providers learn from those mistakes and continually strive to secure better patient outcomes and improved overall wellness for their constituents.

Stage 2: Conquering Infectious Diseases

Amid the routine butchery, a major leap toward modern medicine was the invention of antibiotics and vaccines, which for the first time could both treat existing microbial infections (antibiotics) and prevent future viral infections (vaccines). Introduced by Edward Jenner in 1796, the first successful vaccine to be developed was for smallpox. He followed up his observation that milkmaids who had previously caught cowpox did not later catch smallpox by showing that inoculated cowpox protected against inoculated smallpox. This was highly significant because it represented our first ability to control disease before it appeared.

Today, we have an unprecedented ability to target and neutralize many deadly viruses and to even eradicate them. For all practical purposes, modern medical science has wiped out smallpox and rinderpest, and with the right public support could eliminate measles, mumps, rubella, lymphatic filariasis, and cysticercosis.[3]

But there's a flip side—a bad one.

As anyone who knows anything about Darwin's laws of natural selection can tell you, if you try to poison a billion individuals—in this case, bacteria—with an antibiotic such as penicillin, it's likely that a few of those bacteria will be genetically impervious to the drug. It won't kill them. As a result, you will have knocked out 99.9 percent of the nasty germs, but 0.1 percent will be alive and kicking. And 0.1 percent of a billion is 1 million. These 1 million survivors will then multiply and thrive, and their billions of offspring will be resistant to the antibiotic.

There's a name for these microscopic survivors—superbugs. One such superbug is *Staphylococcus epidermidis*, related to the better-known and more deadly methicillin-resistant *Staphylococcus aureus* (MRSA). *S. epidermis* is found naturally on human skin and most commonly infects the elderly or patients who have had prosthetic materials implanted, such as catheters and joint replacements. It's resistant to two of the most common antibiotics, often administered in tandem to treat hospital infections. Researchers believe the superbug is spreading rapidly due to the increasing use of antibiotics in intensive care units, and it is even growing increasingly tolerant to alcohol-based disinfectants found in the antiseptic sanitizers used on hospital wards.[4]

As the Centers for Disease Control and Prevention (CDC) reports, antibiotic resistance has become one of the world's most urgent public health problems. Each year in the United States, at least 2 million people are infected with antibiotic-resistant bacteria, and at least 23,000 people die as a result.[5]

Stage 3: The Rise of the Healthcare Industry

As we began to improve on disease control, we also developed a range of surgical procedures and medical devices and saw the advent of the pharmaceutical industry. While the technology was often spectacular, most of these innovations were designed to treat sick people; there was no sense of supporting wellness and prevention, just fixing an emergent problem through post facto intervention. This is an important time in the trajectory toward disruption; and as we now can clearly see, the entire contemporary US healthcare industry has been created by hospitals, healthcare insurers, drug companies, and medical device companies for the purpose of intervening through treatment. And treatment most often means selling patients a product or service to cure their existing disease: a pill, an MRI, an operation. Products and services can be quantified, marketed, recorded in sales ledgers, and profitably billed.

Good advice is much more difficult to market and build into an industry.

As treatments became more expensive, the healthcare insurance industry sprang up to provide a way for consumers to access the massive expansion of healthcare treatments and interventions. The problem was that we created an industry that *rewarded treatments* and *discouraged prevention*, punishing doctors for spending time with patients in an effort to build a preventive healthcare lifestyle. The entire trillion-dollar healthcare ecosystem was designed to treat, treat, treat, while the insurance companies, which needed to make a profit, were vested in deny, deny, deny.

Meanwhile, the patient was increasingly forced to wait for hours to see the specialist, whose bag of tricks contained only treatments—no prevention, no wellness, just treatment.

The national healthcare ecosystem rapidly scaled as more drugs were invented. There were drugs to put you to sleep, and drugs to wake you up, and drugs to address everything from thinning hair to a diminished libido. Who could blame the scientists and researchers for focusing on pharmacological solutions? You do the best you can with the tools you have available, and at the end of the twentieth century and into the next, these efforts produced results.

Faced with a bounty of marketable treatments, consumers began to see healthcare as a birthright, and they demanded more and more pills to cure every ailment.

In the United States, the cost of healthcare has steadily risen. By 2017, it had soared to $3.5 trillion, making healthcare one of the nation's largest industries, gobbling up 17.9 percent of gross domestic product. In comparison, in 1960, healthcare cost $27.2 billion, or just 5 percent of GDP. In 2017, the average person—healthy or sick—spent $10,739 on healthcare. In 1960, the amount was $146. Adjusted for inflation, that's just $1,209 in 2017 dollars.[6]

The high cost of healthcare is an increasingly crushing burden on American families. According to CNBC, a study found that 66.5 percent of all bankruptcies were tied to medical issues, because of either time lost from work or the high costs of care. Each year, an estimated 530,000 families are forced into bankruptcy because of medical issues and bills.[7]

We created modern medicine with the idea of rewarding doctors and companies for treating sick patients. There was no economic model for helping patients *avoid* treatments, getting them to a better place of health, and eliminating the need for healthcare intervention. As a result, healthcare costs have skyrocketed while our overall health—and even longevity, which for centuries had steadily risen—has in many ways declined.

Stage 4: Hyper-Interventional Healthcare Marketing

Direct-to-consumer (DTC) advertising of drugs has been legal in the United States since 1985, but the practice began to accelerate in 1997 when the Food and Drug Administration relaxed a rule obliging companies to offer a detailed list of product side effects in their infomercials. Suddenly, drug companies could offer a spoken summary of side effects and squeeze the summary plus the sales pitch into a one-minute TV commercial.

This, combined with increased scrutiny of how drug companies were persuading doctors to prescribe their products, threw the healthcare ecosystem into high gear, as pharmaceutical companies sought to find new and enticing ways to not merely respond to patients who were sick but to proactively sell patients more treatments. As Lisa M. Schwartz, MD, and Steven Woloshin, MD, wrote in "Medical Marketing in the United States, 1997–2016," in the emerging era of hyper-interventional healthcare, DTC medical marketing exploded, with spending increasing from $17.7 billion to $29.9 billion. DTC advertising for prescription drugs and health services accounted for the most rapid growth, while pharmaceutical company marketing to health professionals represented the most promotional spending.[8]

Today, drug companies routinely advertise drugs on TV with the goal of getting patients to ask for their medicines by name, and the strategy is working. DTC advertising is just one example of how the healthcare ecosystem continues to push for more and more utilization.

There are industry segments selling more and more interventions to consumers, and the trend is at a fever pitch. Medi-spas are springing up to sell you your regular injection of skin smoother. New pharmaceuticals and new medical devices are here to save the day, and their DTC advertising is at an all-time high. Hospitals and clinics are in the game as well, selling their unique and special blend of skill sets to cure your ills.

TAKE ACTION!

- When advocating for change, it's important to avoid blaming individual people for the state of our healthcare system. While it's true that just as in any other industry, the healthcare industry has had its share of bad actors, over the past century the system as a whole has developed through the efforts of well-meaning people using the best information and best tools available.
- We're entering an era of disruptive innovation in both information and tools, including connection architecture, and this is why the time is ripe for healthcare transformation. The old tools have served their purpose, and now it's time to invest in the future.
- Before reaching for the prescription pad, healthcare providers need to focus on helping their constituents improve their lifestyles and try to thwart disease states as soon as possible in the disease cycle.

Two Drivers of Rising Healthcare Costs

Currently in the United States, two significant forces are driving up the cost of healthcare:

1. **Lifestyle diseases.** Data suggests that as much as 80 percent of all healthcare costs are based on the utilization of healthcare by individuals who are eating, smoking, or drugging their way to chronic disease. The overwhelming majority of cases of diabetes, cardiovascular disease, and even cancer are driven by obesity and lifestyle choices.

2. **A mission dedicated to diagnosis and treatment.** The current focus is on economic rewards for treatment intervention, while concurrently ignoring doctors and caregivers who support anticipation, prevention, and overall wellness.

These two forces are closely intertwined. To correct one of them, you also must correct the other.

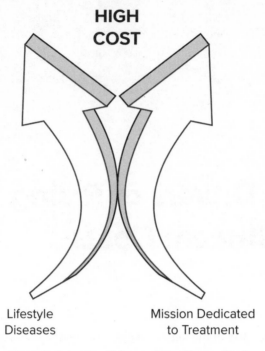

HIGH COST

Lifestyle
Diseases

Mission Dedicated
to Treatment

FIGURE 3.1   **Two Drivers of Healthcare Costs**

We're Good at Diagnosing and Treating Infectious Diseases

During the past century, thanks to the development of vaccinations and antibiotics and to improved methods of personal and public hygiene, the healthcare industry has done an amazing job of combating infectious diseases. A good example of the miracles being wrought by medical research and the pharmaceutical industry is the battle against the human immunodeficiency virus (HIV), which causes acquired immunodeficiency syndrome (AIDS).

When HIV first emerged in the United States in 1981 and patients began dying of AIDS, it quickly became apparent that there was no cure. The virus seemed unkillable. The healthcare industry swung into action, and in 1987, the FDA approved AZT, the first drug designed for the treatment of AIDS. The battle against HIV was tough, and by 2018, about 75 million people had become infected worldwide, and about 32 million people had died from the disease.

Today, there are a host of HIV medicines called antiretroviral therapies. An estimated 38 million people live with HIV, and of them, about 23 million are accessing antiretroviral therapies, up from just 7.7 million in 2010. People are living longer with HIV, and since 2010 AIDS-related mortality has declined by 33 percent.[1]

In March 2019, the anonymous "London patient" became the second person in history to be declared cured of HIV (scientists prefer to call it "long-term remission"). If progress continues to be made, it will be a shining example of what Western medicine has always been good at: identifying a disease with a specific causative agent, attacking the cause, and neutralizing it.

During the past century, we've had such success killing pathogens that the causes of death have changed. In the year 1900, the leading causes of death in the United States were:

1. Pneumonia and flu
2. Tuberculosis
3. "Digestive disease"
4. Heart disease

As Cleveland Clinic pointed out, in 1900 none of the top four causes of death could be effectively treated. There were no antibiotics or vaccines for pneumonia, tuberculosis was poorly understood, and there were few treatments for internal diseases.[2]

In 2019, according to the CDC, the leading causes of death in the United States were:[3]

1. Heart disease
2. Cancer
3. Accidents (unintentional injuries)

4. Chronic lower respiratory diseases
5. Stroke (cerebrovascular diseases)
6. Alzheimer's disease
7. Diabetes
8. Influenza and pneumonia
9. Nephritis, nephrotic syndrome, and nephrosis
10. Intentional self-harm (suicide)

The Rise of Lifestyle Diseases

Thanks to the development of vaccines and antibiotics, infectious diseases have been pushed far down on the list. They have been replaced by "lifestyle diseases," which are defined as those associated with the way a person or group of people live. They may have a genetic component, but genetics is not the primary method of transmission. Lifestyle diseases include atherosclerosis, heart disease, and stroke; osteoporosis; obesity and type 2 diabetes; and diseases associated with smoking and alcohol and drug abuse. Some lifestyle diseases such as Alzheimer's are associated with longevity, while others, such as asthma, bear no relation to age.

The word "lifestyle" needs some qualification. Proponents of a new approach to healthcare do not seek to blame patients for their illnesses. Some diseases attack indiscriminately; for example, if you are bitten by a mosquito carrying yellow fever, you may get infected regardless of how healthy you are. Worldwide, nearly 700 million people get a mosquito-borne illness each year, resulting in over 1 million deaths. While environmental conditions may be a factor, these are not people who got sick because of unhealthy personal habits.

Anyone who is ill should be healed. But if the disease is related to lifestyle, responsible healthcare providers *must insist* upon a new sense of personal responsibility—and then provide the tools to achieve it.

Consider diabetes. Between 1990 and 2010 the number of people living with diabetes tripled, and the number of new cases annually doubled.

Writing for *Population Health Management*, William R. Rowley, MD, and others noted, "The prevalence of diabetes (type 2 diabetes and type 1 diabetes) will increase by 54 percent to more than 54.9 million Americans between 2015 and 2030; annual deaths attributed to diabetes will climb by 38 percent to 385,800; and total annual medical and societal costs related to diabetes will increase 53 percent to more than $622 billion by 2030."[4]

The question is, why?

The short answer: We are eating too much and exercising too little. These are lifestyle problems, not examples of people being attacked by a pathogen.

The solution is no secret. To reduce the impact of prediabetes and type 2 diabetes, the CDC established the National Diabetes Prevention Program (National DPP), which provides the framework for type 2 diabetes prevention efforts in the United States. The National DPP includes an evidence-based, yearlong behavior change program to improve eating habits and increase physical activity to lose a modest amount of weight and significantly reduce the risk of type 2 diabetes.[5]

The science behind the rise in diabetes has long been settled. In one of many similar studies, for 10 years researchers followed 4,883 men and women who were participating in the Cardiovascular Health Study. In their paper "Lifestyle Risk Factors and New-Onset Diabetes Mellitus in Older Adults," Dariush Mozaffarian, MD, and colleagues found that 80 percent of cases of diabetes in the survey population of older adults appeared attributable to four adverse lifestyle factors: low physical activity level, poor dietary habits, smoking, and excessive alcohol use. "If these associations are causal," they wrote, "then 8 in 10 new cases of diabetes might have been prevented if all older adults were in the low-risk group for these lifestyle factors. Adding either not being overweight or not having a high waist circumference, nearly 9 in 10 new cases of diabetes appeared attributable to not being in the low-risk group for these lifestyle factors."[6]

The way to lower your risk of diabetes is clear: exercise, eat a healthy diet, don't smoke, consume alcohol in moderation, and reduce the amount of fat you're carrying.

To be honest, some might quibble with that prescription. Why? Because back in 1970, when diabetes was a relatively rare disease, people smoked plenty of cigarettes and drank plenty of booze. But they got more exercise and they ate less. The rate of obesity was far lower. So you could argue that cigarettes and liquor are not primary drivers of diabetes; the twin causes are junk food and lethargy.

But what drives the treatment policies of the healthcare industry? From the perspective of pharmaceutical companies and hospitals, there's no profit to be made from long-term personal counseling to get people to change their personal habits. It's much more profitable to sell them pills and perform surgeries.

Not surprisingly, the market for diabetes medication is huge. According to the American Diabetes Association, in the United States the direct medical cost of diagnosed diabetes is $237 billion per year. Of that, 30 percent, or $71 billion, goes into the coffers of pharmaceutical companies. Another $36 billion is spent on antidiabetic agents and diabetes supplies. The rest goes to doctors and hospitals.[7]

By way of comparison, $237 billion is roughly equal to the entire gross domestic product of the state of North Carolina or the nation of Portugal. Imagine if the entire economy of North Carolina were earmarked for the treatment of diabetes![8]

Lifestyle Diseases Stubbornly Defy Pharmaceutical Solutions

From the perspective of the pharmaceutical industry, the problem with lifestyle diseases such as diabetes is that they're not caused by viruses or bacteria. There is no germ that infects you with heart disease. There is no virus that gives you cancer. You don't catch Alzheimer's disease or diabetes by getting sneezed on by someone with the condition.

The response by the pharmaceutical industry has been to do what it does best: search for a "druggable" molecule in your body that's associated with the disease. (That's the actual word—"druggable.") When the industry identifies one, then it creates a drug that will do something to that molecule that researchers hope will lessen the effects of the disease.

Prescription drugs designed to control lifestyle diseases can be very expensive. As the *Washington Post* reported, specialty drugs often boast astonishing prices. Therapies for hemophilia are priced at $580,000 to $800,000 a year; a drug designed to treat non-Hodgkin's lymphoma carries a $475,000 price tag.[9] Drug companies have also raised prices for commonly used medications to treat diabetes, high cholesterol, and asthma.

One reason why prescription drugs cost so much is the role of pharmacy benefit managers (PBMs). As Robin Feldman reported for the *Post*, when Medicare introduced prescription drug benefits in 2006, PBMs helped health plans set formularies (the terms on which patients can access drugs) and negotiated prices with drug companies. Health plans pay their PBMs based on the amount of the discount that a PBM can negotiate with individual drug companies. You'd think this would spark competition and enable the PBM to drive prices down. But drug companies responded by raising their prices so they could give a greater discount. Between 2006 and 2014, prices for drugs rose by an average of 57 percent, and prices for drugs with no generic substitutes rose by 142 percent.

Still, you'd think that if these retail prices were deeply discounted, there wouldn't be a problem. But many plans require patients to pay the retail price until they meet their deductible, and other plans require coinsurance, both of which are based on the full price.[10]

You can't blame pharmaceutical companies for competing in the free market of healthcare. New drugs are extremely expensive to develop, and the failure rate is very high. According to a study by Tufts Center for the Study of Drug Development and published in the *Journal of Health Economics*, developing just one new prescription medicine that gains FDA approval is estimated to cost a drugmaker $1.2 billion in out-of-pocket costs, $312 million in post-approval research and development, and $1.4 billion in lost opportunity costs suffered by investors while their cash is tied up in the lengthy R&D process.

While the average time it takes to bring a drug through clinical trials has decreased, the rate of success has gone down to just 12 percent. Developing new drugs is a risky business, and the retail cost of every new drug must also include the costs of the many failures that preceded it.[11]

The Hypertension Industry

A rampant lifestyle disease that's not caused by a virus or bacteria is hypertension, which has evolved into another major US industry.

Let's say you experience headaches, fatigue, and vision problems, and you go to the doctor. Your doctor will run a series of tests, including one for your blood pressure. It's measured with an instrument called a sphygmomanometer and recorded with two numbers: the systolic number, which is the pressure inside your arteries when your heart is pumping, followed by the diastolic number, the pressure inside your arteries when your heart is resting between beats. For example, a normal blood pressure would be recorded as a result lower than 120/80. Readings at or above 120/80 and less than 140/90 are considered prehypertensive, while results consistently at or above 140/90 are considered evidence of high blood pressure, or hypertension.

If the results are in that upper range, your doctor will diagnose your problem as hypertension. The disease increases the risk of coronary heart disease and ischemic heart disease, which are the leading causes of death worldwide.

It's a common condition—globally almost 1.13 billion people suffer from high blood pressure. According to the World Health Organization, globally 22 percent of adults aged over 18 had increased blood pressure, and the CDC says that 70 million American adults are suffering from high blood pressure, with only approximately 52 percent, or half the patient pool, having gotten the condition under control.[12]

Under the current healthcare system in America, the most efficient and profitable way for your doctor to lower your blood pressure level is to write you a prescription.

A Wealth of Prescription Options

In writing your prescription, your doctor can choose among many patented pharmaceuticals. He or she may prescribe these drugs one at a time, over time, and see which one is most effective. He or she may also try combinations of these drugs.

Your doctor might first prescribe a diuretic, designed to make your kidneys remove water and sodium from your body. That decreases the amount of fluid flowing through your blood vessels, which reduces pressure on your vessel walls. There are three types of diuretics: thiazide, loop, and potassium-sparing.

Because they change your blood chemistry, all of them have side effects. They include:[13]

- Altered blood potassium levels. If you take a potassium-sparing diuretic, you can develop too much potassium (hyperkalemia), whereas if you take a thiazide diuretic, you can have too little potassium (hypokalemia).
- Dehydration.
- Dizziness.
- Headaches.
- Impotence.
- Joint disorders (gout).
- Low sodium in your blood (hyponatremia).
- Muscle cramps.

Since hypertension is considered a more serious disease than any of these side effects, pharmaceutical companies encourage doctors and patients to tolerate this drug-induced discomfort in the hope of lowering your high blood pressure.

If diuretics don't work, your doctor may then turn to a medication designed to control hypertension, typically an angiotensin-converting enzyme (ACE) inhibitor. These drugs relax blood vessels by inhibiting the production of a hormone called angiotensin, which narrows blood vessels.

Side effects of ACE inhibitors may include dizziness, headache, drowsiness, diarrhea, low blood pressure, weakness, cough, rash, an abnormal taste (metallic or salty), elevated blood potassium levels, and sexual dysfunction.[14]

Your doctor may prescribe angiotensin II receptor blockers (ARBs). These help relax blood vessels by blocking the action, rather than the production, of angiotensin. Drugs with names ending in "sartan" are ARBs, including valsartan, losartan, and others.

Side effects of ARBs may include headache, fainting, dizziness, fatigue, respiratory symptoms, vomiting, diarrhea, back pain, leg swelling, high potassium levels, and rarely allergic reactions, liver failure, or kidney failure.[15]

Your doctor may also prescribe calcium channel blockers. These inhibit calcium from entering heart and blood vessel muscle cells, which causes the cells to relax. Some calcium channel blockers have the added benefit of slowing your heart rate.

Side effects may include constipation, headache, palpitations, dizziness, rash, drowsiness, flushing, nausea, and swelling in the feet and lower legs.[16]

Your doctor may also prescribe beta blockers, or beta-adrenergic blocking agents. These work by blocking the effects of the hormone epinephrine, also known as adrenaline, causing your heart to beat slower and with less force. Common beta blockers include acebutolol, atenolol, bisoprolol, and many others.

Side effects may include diarrhea, stomach cramps, nausea, vomiting, rash, blurred vision, disorientation, insomnia, hair loss, muscle weakness, muscle cramps, and fatigue.[17]

Pharmaceuticals have their place in the physician's treatment toolbox. But as we see over and over again, a strategy of anticipation and prevention is cheaper and more effective than diagnosis and treatment—and carries fewer negative side effects.

TAKE ACTION!

- Your healthcare organization needs to intensify its investment focus on the rise of lifestyle diseases that cannot be affordably treated with conventional diagnose-and-treat approaches.
- Pharmaceutical companies can play a significant role in anticipating disease, but the use of drugs will be far more effective when combined with the CHOS module and biomonitors.
- If the two drivers of higher healthcare costs are the surge in lifestyle diseases and the traditional industry focus on diagnosis and treatment, then to reverse that trend, healthcare leaders need to realign their organizational priorities to anticipate and prevent lifestyle diseases, which will lower both drivers.

The Role of Homeostasis

Our healthcare system incentivizes responding to patients who are sick, selling them treatments, curing their immediate condition, and sending them home.

To be clear: This business model works brilliantly when you're battling an infectious disease or an injury.

When a person goes to the doctor with a physical problem, whether it be pneumonia or a broken leg, the goal of the doctor is to provide a billable product or service—an antibiotic or a cast on the person's leg—that will return the patient to a condition of normality or, more precisely, homeostasis. Coined in 1930 by the physician Walter Cannon in his book *The Wisdom of the Body*, the term "homeostasis," from the Greek words for "same" and "steady," refers to the processes that living things use to actively maintain stable conditions necessary for survival. For example, in the bloodstream, the human body strives to maintain an average level of water, sugar, salt, oxygen, protein, fat, and countless minerals and hormones. When these levels are disturbed, the body will take steps to return them to their average levels.

Personal Homeostasis

When used to refer to your entire body, your "personal homeostasis" means your baseline level of everyday existence. If you have pneumonia, the bacteria or virus is subdued and your lung function restored. If your leg is broken, it's repaired and returned to service. You are made "normal" again.

This approach is appropriate for mechanical problems caused by an accident or exposure to a pathogen. It assumes that your everyday state of homeostasis is healthy. But what if your "normal" everyday state *contributed* to your condition? Why then would merely repairing today's problem provide a long-term solution?

Let's say you're obese. Research has shown that people who are obese and do not exercise lose bone mass and are at a greater risk for broken bones. But obese people who exercise develop stronger bones. (In fact, *all* people who exercise will strengthen their bones.) So if you are obese and don't exercise, and you break your weakened leg, merely fixing your leg and sending you home will not help. You will still be at a high risk of another fracture.[1]

To lower your risk of returning to the hospital with another broken bone, your doctor should counsel you about changing your eating habits and exercising more. Together, you should act proactively to *change your personal homeostasis* and improve your overall health.

The reality is that while your doctor may give you a speech about your weight as you sit there in the examination room, that will likely be all. Why? Because there's no profit in sustained preventive counseling. Your doctor could bill you for a series of consultations, but because the counseling can't be quantified, the insurance company might question it.

Or let's say you're a cigarette smoker. Your risk of getting pneumonia is higher than that of a nonsmoker.[2] If your doctor gives you antibiotics and cures your pneumonia, she might have returned you to your condition of homeostasis, but to what end? You're probably still a smoker! The better solution would be to encourage you to change your lifestyle and quit smoking, and to work with you to make it happen.

But as before, while your doctor may give you a stern lecture about smoking, unless your doctor can write you a prescription for a smoking cessation drug, nothing more will be done.

Environmental Homeostasis

Thinking more globally, what if you lived in a community with an abundance of cheap fast-food outlets but poor access to fresh, nutritious food? Such places are called "food deserts." Living in a food desert is a cause of poor dietary habits, and it's been identified as one driver of the obesity epidemic. Conversely, people who live near a supermarket are more likely to consume fruits and vegetables and are less likely to be obese.[3] So if you are obese, part of the problem may be that in your neighborhood, the only nutrition you can get is from fast-food joints and the processed junk foods sold at the corner convenience store. Your environment is part of your homeostasis. Call it your "environmental homeostasis." It's big and complex, and over time your body, including your eating habits, has adjusted to it. As long as your environmental homeostasis remains unchanged, making a change in your own body will be more difficult.

Under our current system, there's no profit potential in addressing the problem of poor nutrition in your community. It's cheaper and more profitable to treat you and send you home.

Allostasis

A more nuanced description of the body's natural ability to return to a baseline operating level is allostasis. While homeostasis describes the establishment of an unchanging baseline, allostasis is the active process of adaptation to daily experiences, good or bad. It implies a *range* of baselines for blood pressure, hormone levels, and other key indicators, so that the body can fine-tune itself throughout the day or season of the year.

Some scientists also define "homeostasis" as having the systems essential for life and "allostasis" as maintaining these systems in balance.

A good example of allostasis is the habit of bears to eat voraciously and store fat before the winter hibernation. This behavior would be unhealthy if pursued year-round, but it is essential for survival during the long fasting period of hibernation. In the spring and summer, bears follow their normal eating habits.

In allostasis, the term "overload" refers to the cumulative change in brain and body that, when an individual experiences toxic stress, both physiologically and psychologically, causes dysregulation of the mediators that normally promote adaptation. The result may be disease. To use the example of bears, if the seasonal increase in food intake were to continue, as is often the case with animals in captivity that have sufficient energy reserves, then symptoms of allostatic overload will appear. Abdominal obesity is an example of this condition and is common in animals in zoos, as well as in human beings.

Adverse Childhood Experiences and PTSD

If you're a healthcare professional in a community, the odds are high that you have many "repeat clients." These are people who come to you over and over again for treatment of one condition or another.

If they are inpatients, they stay in the hospital longer than others with the same condition. Your treatment of them seems less effective than for others. Their baseline personal homeostasis is generally more inclined toward illness than good health. They are more frequently obese, feel depressed, smoke cigarettes, or have behavioral issues such as anorexia nervosa or an obsessive-compulsive disorder. In short, they never quite seem to be able to get their lives together.

Among your constituents you may also have military veterans who are plainly suffering from post-traumatic stress disorder (PTSD). You know exactly what their problem is and how they got to where they are today, but aside from prescribing pills and getting them into therapy, there may not be much you can do for them.

A research project conducted by the US health maintenance organization Kaiser Permanente and the Centers for Disease Control and Prevention, the Adverse Childhood Experiences Study (ACE Study) recruited 17,000 participants between 1995 and 1997, many of whom were in long-term follow-up for health outcomes. The study demonstrated an association of adverse childhood experiences (ACEs), also called childhood trauma, with health and social problems across the individual's life span.

The study began when Vincent Felitti, head of Kaiser Permanente's Department of Preventive Medicine in San Diego, wanted to find out why so many obese participants had dropped out of a weight loss program. In the course of his inquiry, he discovered that many of them had experienced childhood sexual abuse.

Felitti's insight came by accident. While interviewing one of the people who had left the program, he asked a series of standard questions: "How much did you weigh when you were born? In first grade? In high school? How old were you when you became sexually active? How much did you weigh when you married?"

"I misspoke," he recalled. "Instead of asking, 'How old were you when you were first sexually active,' I asked, 'How much did you *weigh* when you were first sexually active?' The patient, a woman, answered, 'Forty pounds.'"

On average, this would make her five or six years old.

Felitti assumed he had heard incorrectly, so he asked again. After repeating the same answer, she began sobbing and said, "It was with my father."

This was both disturbing and puzzling. He started asking other patients, and many volunteered stories about childhood sexual abuse. He thought, "This can't be true. Someone would have told me in medical school."

The problem came into sharp focus when Felitti interviewed a woman who had been raped when she was 23 years old. In the year after the attack, she gained over a hundred pounds. "As she was thanking me for asking the question," said Felitti, "she looks down at the carpet, and mutters, 'Overweight is overlooked, and that's the way I need to be.'"[4]

For Many Patients, Obesity Isn't the Problem, It's the Solution

Many people who are obese look at eating not as a problem but as a *solution*. Food offers comfort and a temporary escape and relief from stress, bad memories, shame, or guilt, even when obesity becomes uncomfortable or even life-threatening.

This is one reason why for many millions of overweight people, information about diets, exercise, proper nutrition, and food marketing is irrelevant and will have no effect.

As the study revealed, adverse childhood experiences include:

- Sexual abuse
- Physical abuse
- Emotional abuse
- Physical neglect
- Emotional neglect
- Exposure to domestic violence
- Household substance abuse
- Household mental illness
- Parental separation or divorce
- Incarcerated household member

The number and duration of ACEs suffered by an individual have been strongly associated with adulthood high-risk health behaviors including smoking, alcohol and drug abuse, promiscuity, and obesity. ACEs have also been linked to diseases including depression, heart disease, cancer, chronic lung disease, and shortened life span.

This happens because an ACE, whether manifested as a sudden shock, a long-lasting negative event, or a set of adverse circumstances, can put the body into a permanent state of "fight or flight," with all the physical and hormonal changes that implies. The presence of danger or even severe unpredictability causes the brain to send a message to the glands to release adrenaline and cortisol. Between them, these two hormones effect measurable physiological changes, including increasing the heart rate (which raises blood pressure) and rushing sugar to the bloodstream. When you're attacked by a bear in the woods, these and other effects are positive. But sustained over time, they become negative and even toxic.

For example, in the immune system, short-term stress promotes immune function by enhancing the movement of immune cells to places in the body where they are needed to defend against a pathogen. Once the event is over, the immune system returns to its baseline level. In contrast, chronic stress uses the same hormonal mediators to suppress immune function, causing increased risk of disease.

Imagine two brothers with similar genetic makeup and life experience. They are on parallel "allostatic tracks." Then one brother is repeatedly and mercilessly bullied in school. Even if there is no permanent physical damage, the ACE may alter his biochemistry and set his allostasis on a new and debilitating track (see Figure 4.1).

Continuous and repeated activation of the fight-or-flight response can "burn out" the system, which is not intended to be in constant use. It can alter the structural development of neural networks and the biochemistry of neuroendocrine systems and provoke allostatic overload, the wear and tear on the body and brain that result from being under stress. It can even alter aspects of gene expression, making the changes permanent.

This has a twofold effect: it leaves the body more open to disease, and it steers the patient toward behaviors that ease the inner pain. These behaviors, which are seen as a form of self-therapy, include overeating, self-harm, drug use, and eating disorders such as bulimia. All these dis-

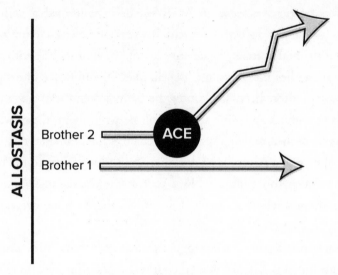

FIGURE 4.1   The Biochemical Effects of an ACE on One Brother

orders have the effect of making the patient *temporarily feel better*. They can be seen as a rational solution when no other solutions are in sight.

The ACE Test

Some doctors are now asking selected patients to take a short test to determine their ACE score. The test consists of 10 simple questions. They include, "Before your 18th birthday, did a parent or other adult in the household often or very often push, grab, slap, or throw something at you? Or ever hit you so hard that you had marks or were injured?" The more of these questions to which the patient answers "yes," the higher the ACE score, with the highest score being 10. Of course, the test misses many factors, does not ask for positive experiences that may help to offset adverse ones, and is only designed for guidance. It doesn't consider diet or genes or whether the patient smoked or drank excessively, to name just a few of the other major influences on health.

Long-term diseases resulting from ACEs are costly not only to the individual but to society as a whole. The Sycamore Institute in Nashville, Tennessee conducted a study entitled "The Economic Cost of ACEs in Tennessee: Medical Costs and Worker Absenteeism from Health Issues Attributed to Adverse Childhood Experiences," which found that among Tennessee adults, ACEs led to an estimated $5.2 billion in direct medical costs and lost productivity from employees who missed work. These costs were associated with eight ACEs-related health outcomes and behaviors, of which cigarette smoking ($2.1 billion) and depression ($923 million) were the most costly. The report concluded: "By affecting our health outcomes and behaviors, ACEs increase healthcare costs in taxpayer-funded programs like TennCare, raise employers' costs for healthcare and productivity loss, and shrink earnings for employees who miss work. Efforts to prevent ACEs and mitigate their effects could potentially reduce those expenses."[5]

The challenge is to intervene as early as possible. "Children do not outgrow the impact of ACEs," said Alicia Lieberman, PhD, who leads one of twenty-five National Child Traumatic Stress Network centers at Zuckerberg San Francisco General Hospital and Trauma Center. "On the contrary, when children are exposed to multiple ACEs, the effect increases such that children get worse over time rather than better—unless we change the conditions."[6]

Imagine how these children could benefit from real-time monitoring of their vital signs, which could alert both the child and his or her caregiver to an approaching physical problem.

TAKE ACTION!

- It does no good to fix a problem without addressing the underlying causes. If you cure sick people of their incidental disease and return them to their previous state of personal homeostasis, they are still sick, and they will quickly get sicker again. Constituents need to be counseled and incentivized to change their personal homeostasis and improve their overall health.
- Likewise, the constituent's "environmental homeostasis" needs to be considered as part of any treatment plan.
- As a nation, we need to move away from treating lifestyle diseases as if they were infectious diseases. They aren't, and treating them as if they were is a waste of money and resources.

The Big Shift

Earlier we met Roberta, who as a young woman was generally unhealthy and who fought a battle against a tumor on her adrenal gland. The surgery was successful but expensive.

Now, at age 70, we find that she's much healthier. The reason for her improved health is the Big Shift: that is, the transformation of our healthcare system from an exclusive focus on diagnosis and treatment to a new investment in anticipation and prevention.

Not only does her ear-worn biomonitor and other sensors actively ascertain and acknowledge the presence of a suspected illness, they make her go to the doctor—which too many people, including many men, are reluctant to do. Her CHOS module actively collects her medical data and sends it to her doctor, representing the most significant change in how we identify and treat disease since the days of Hippocrates.

Even as an unhealthy young woman, Roberta was the ideal patient. She saw her healthcare provider regularly, and when her abdominal discomfort became alarming to her, she went to her doctor. And her doctor did everything right, too—he scheduled the appropriate tests, and when they came back positive, Roberta was scheduled for surgery. The surgeon did a fine job, and the cancer was removed. The price tag was $25,000—about average. By all accounts, hers was a success story. She was an ideal patient at age 30, and at age 70 she's still an ideal patient.

The Big Shift is transforming not only how ideal patients including Roberta receive care but even more profoundly how *difficult* patients receive care. Take a man whom we'll call George. He's 60 years old. Unlike Roberta, he doesn't see a doctor regularly. His company doesn't subscribe to the new digital healthcare network. He doesn't wear a bio-monitor earpiece. He's overweight (he's tried diets but never sticks to one), and he eats too many sugary foods. The last time he visited the family doctor was when he had the flu, when he was 50 years old. At that time she told him he had elevated blood pressure, needed to lose 20 pounds, and was at risk for cardiovascular disease. George had agreed to get more exercise and eat less junk food, but the moment he left the office, he put those resolutions aside. He tells himself that he's too busy in his career to worry about stuff like that. Every morning his wife nags him to get a checkup, but he just nods and says, "Yes, dear," before getting into his car and joining the other commuters on the highway.

Does George always feel good? No. He complains to his wife of tiredness, and sometimes he feels light-headed and short of breath. His feet get swollen, and he sometimes gets chest pains. He just chalks up these symptoms to his hard work at the office, and tells his wife that all he needs is a good vacation spent lying on the beach and playing some golf.

Unbeknown to George, his wife, and his family doctor, George is a walking time bomb. He has coronary artery disease, or atherosclerosis. Before he reaches retirement age, he's going to have a non-ST segment elevation myocardial infarction (NSTEMI). While this type of heart attack doesn't cause major changes on an electrocardiogram, it can be detected through chemical markers in the blood that indicate damage has occurred to the heart muscle. The blood test would show elevated levels of creatine kinase–myocardial band, troponin I, and troponin T. These markers are evidence of possible damage to the heart cells.[1]

In NSTEMI, the blockage may be partial or temporary, so the extent of the damage can seem relatively small. Without monitoring, and with a reluctant patient such as George, he might have such a heart attack and never even go to the hospital. But eventually "the big one" will happen, and his life will hang in the balance as his frantic wife calls 911.

The High Cost of Heart Attacks

Heart attacks are both dangerous and expensive.

According to the CDC, every year about 735,000 Americans have a heart attack. Of these, 525,000 are a first heart attack and 210,000 happen in people who have already had at least one heart attack. About 610,000 Americans die of heart disease in the United States every year—that's one in every four deaths.[2]

Each heart attack hospitalization costs a median of $53,384, while strokes cost $31,218 each. Bypass surgery costs substantially more than a heart attack and stroke, with a median hospital cost of $85,891 to $177,546, according to a study published in *Circulation*. The figures don't factor in additional costs following hospitalization, such as loss of productivity from missing work or ongoing medical care and drugs, which may have further financial consequences.[3]

And if George has a heart attack and survives (for which he and his family will have to pay part of the cost, even with health insurance), he may face a future with less earning power. An important study published in *CMAJ* suggested that people who suffer a heart attack, stroke, or cardiac arrest may be less likely to work afterward, and those who do work may make less money. According to the study, Canadian heart attack survivors still working earned about C$3,834 less, and cardiac arrest survivors about C$11,143 less. Stroke survivors saw the greatest drop, earning about C$13,278 less. Dr. Allan Garland of the University of Manitoba in Winnipeg, the lead author of the study, noted, "These losses in the ability to work and earn were greater for people who had lower income before the events, had more chronic medical disorders, and needed more or longer hospital care for their acute health events."[4]

Imagine if George's family doctor had said to him, "George, you're going to wear this little biomonitor, which will alert us to any imminent or contemporaneous heart problem. Just put it on and go about your business." And then imagine if, to sweeten the deal, George's employer had announced a wellness program that paid cash rewards to employees who met certain health biomarker goals and who wore the biomonitor. Under such circumstances, if George participated in the program, he would take a big step from being a difficult patient to being a good one. He'd improve his health, be more productive, and have a far lower risk of having an expensive and possibly deadly heart attack.

This system can be said to be a *virtuous cycle* (see Figure 5.1):

1. George recognizes he has a problem.
2. George agrees to wear a biometric monitor.
3. George's health improves, and his chances of having a heart attack decrease.
4. Because his employer will save on healthcare costs, George receives a financial reward.

Thus encouraged, George maintains his efforts to live a healthy life.

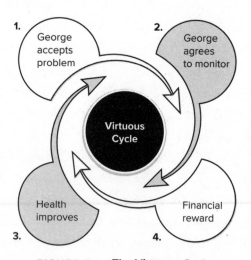

FIGURE 5.1 The Virtuous Cycle

Prevention Is Not a New Idea—
It's Been Done Before!

The newly reinvented healthcare system, of which Roberta is a part, is focused squarely on *anticipation* and *prevention*, as well as prompt treatment when necessary.

But how can that happen? How can a problem as big and cumbersome as healthcare be transformed?

We know it can happen because it's been done before. We've taken a problem, and instead of focusing only on combating the visible damage done when the problem erupts, we've focused more on prevention, which means we then experience instances of damage that are smaller and easier to correct.

Everyone knows the old saying, "An ounce of prevention is worth a pound of cure." It's the basis for the healthcare system that Roberta enjoys in the not-too-distant future.

The maxim was coined by Benjamin Franklin in 1730. But he wasn't writing about healthcare—he was writing about fire prevention.

In that year, the city of Philadelphia suffered a major conflagration. Igniting deep in the timbers of Fishbourn's wharf, a structure on the Delaware River, flames quickly spread to all the stores on the wharf before destroying three homes across the street.

At that time, such incidents were commonplace. With Philadelphia and all the other major American cities full of wooden buildings and people using open flames for cooking, heating, and lighting, uncontrolled fire was a serious problem.

A few days after the fire, Franklin expressed in his newspaper, the *Pennsylvania Gazette*, the need for public education and introduced his famous maxim:

> In the first Place, as an Ounce of Prevention is worth a Pound
> of Cure, I would advise 'em to take care how they suffer
> living Coals in a full Shovel, to be carried out of one Room

into another, or up or down Stairs, unless in a Warming
pan shut; for Scraps of Fire may fall into Chinks and make
no Appearance until Midnight; when your Stairs being in
Flames, you may be forced, (as I once was) to leap out of your
Windows, and hazard your Necks to avoid being oven-roasted.[5]

While to the modern reader the idea of carrying a load of smoldering
coals from one room to another in a shovel may seem insane, at that time
wood and coal were the only means of heating a home, and you needed
to keep the embers glowing through the night. And Franklin was right—
a hot bit of coal or wood, if accidentally lodged in the wooden timbers,
could smolder for hours until erupting into flame.

Franklin realized that in addition to public education, the city
needed the right firefighting tools. Franklin and other activists spurred
the Common Council of Philadelphia to order the latest in firefighting technology from England. Fire hooks, ladders, leather buckets, and
engines (pumps mounted on wheels) were purchased and distributed at
strategic points around the city.

But without people trained in the use of the new equipment and
organized to respond, even the latest technology is useless. A few years
later, again at Franklin's urging, the city organized the colonies' first volunteer fire brigades, to ensure a prompt and organized response to a fire.

The Four Drivers of the Big Shift

Franklin also recognized the need for an organization that could both
exert pressure on building owners to prevent fires and respond financially
after a fire. In 1752, Franklin and other leading citizens of Philadelphia
formed the Philadelphia Contributionship for the Insuring of Houses
from Loss by Fire. It was structured as a mutual insurance organization, providing fire insurance to its members within a limited area in
and around the city. Fire prevention was also paramount. In order to

join the group and receive the benefits of insurance, your building had to undergo inspection, and rates were set based on a risk assessment. Rates could be increased for unsafe practices such as storing combustible materials in your wooden building, and buildings that were deemed to present too great a fire hazard were rejected for coverage.

As a result of these efforts, unlike many other American cities such as Chicago and Charleston, there was never again a major conflagration in Philadelphia.

You can sum it up by saying that Franklin's "ounce of prevention" comprised four drivers (see Figure 5.2), which happen to coincide with the Big Shift:

1. **Education.** Franklin's article in the *Gazette* directly addressed the issue of awareness, and he urged residents to transport hot coals not with an open shovel but with a simple piece of technology—a covered warming pan. If you took the commonsense precaution of using a container with a lid, the embers couldn't fall out, and your house would be safe.

2. **Technology.** For Franklin, this meant having the proper tools to fight fires. In those days, these tools included leather buckets for hauling water, the "engine" or portable pump, long hooks for pulling down burning sections, and ladders.

3. **Human resources.** Training and cooperation are keys to a quick response to a fire. Before the emergence of organized fire brigades, when a fire broke out, whoever happened to be in the area would rush to the scene and do whatever could be done to help. Too often, the result was wasted effort and the spread of the fire. Trained volunteer firefighters were more efficient and more reliable and had greater technical capability.

4. **Government support.** One of the useful things that government can do is make regulations that apply to everyone and that serve to enhance public safety. Since the earliest days of our nation, the adoption of building codes and zoning laws has

gradually reduced the risk and severity of fire. Particularly after the great fire in Chicago in 1871, which destroyed thousands of buildings and left 300 people dead, municipal building codes started addressing the risks of fire in cities. Cities passed regulations outlawing fire hazards including wooden chimneys and mandating the construction of common walls between buildings. Codes were adopted for fire escapes, light and ventilation, water supply, toilets and sanitary drains, and stairs and railings.

A key characteristic of regulations such as building codes is that everyone has to obey them, and therefore no builder can gain an unfair advantage by offering a cheaper price for circumventing them. Everyone competes on a level playing field.

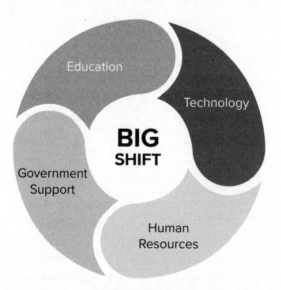

FIGURE 5.2 The Four Drivers of the Big Shift

Education, technology, human resources, and government support, with a focus on *prevention*, proved to be a powerful strategy for reducing the number, size, and cost of fires in the great cities of our nation. It took time, but the approach worked. The same will work for the Big Shift in healthcare.

We Have Many Pounds of Cures . . .

Too bad we cannot yet say the same about our healthcare system. It's too expensive, it's too bureaucratic, and it's not even delivering the primary goal of healthcare, which is to help people live longer.

Instead of an ounce of prevention, we have many pounds of cures. The cumulative result of all that curing isn't very encouraging. While patients and their families pay exorbitant prices for healthcare plans, treatments, and drugs, for the first time in modern history, the life span of the average American is getting *shorter*. Average life expectancy decreased from 78.9 years in 2014 to 78.7 years in 2015, and it decreased again between 2016 and 2017 to 78.6 years. In 2018, it upticked slightly to 78.7 years—still below the 2014 level.[6]

This, despite the fact that the healthcare industry is big and getting bigger. The current GDP of the United States is $19 trillion, of which $3.5 trillion is spent on healthcare, or $10,739 per person. The United States spends more money per person on healthcare than any other nation—the next in spending is Switzerland, which spends $8,009 per person. In 2017, the United States spent 17 percent of its GDP on health consumption, whereas Switzerland devoted 12 percent of its GDP.[7]

And the Swiss get better results for their investment. As of 2019, the average life expectancy in that mountainous, landlocked nation is 82.9 years—well above that of the United States. In fact, in life expectancy, the US ranks forty-eighth—behind Lebanon, Chile, Slovenia, Greece, and Costa Rica.[8]

We spend a lot of money for poor results. To make the situation even more challenging, this orgy of spending is happening in a climate of bewildering disruption. Healthcare is undergoing major disruptions including hyperconsumerization, the power of the crowd, and new economic models. Aging patients, growing populations, the increase in chronic diseases, and exponential advances in innovative but costly digital technologies are destroying old models of healthcare delivery. Healthcare stakeholders—consumers, providers, governments, insurers—are struggling to manage clinical, operational, and financial challenges as the industry grows and is beset by new problems while at the same time seeing exciting new opportunities.

The Big Shift from Patients to Constituents

Despite the expensive healthcare quagmire in which we're caught, there is much hope for a brighter tomorrow.

The first thing that we must do is make an adjustment in our language—specifically, the terms we use to describe the people we serve. Traditionally, doctors had *patients*. These were the people being treated for a disease or condition. The dictionary defines "patient" as a person receiving or registered to receive medical treatment. Other similar terms include sick person, case, sufferer, victim, invalid, or convalescent. A doctor would say, "So-and-so is my patient," implying the person was being treated for a disease or injury.

In the Big Shift, we may keep the word "patient" for such people, but we add the broader term "constituent," which includes the total population of people for whom the healthcare provider is responsible for helping to *stay well*. In other words, the goal is for a healthcare provider—doctor, hospital, healthcare insurer—to assist a group of constituents who are generally healthy. Of those, a much lesser number will be sick or injured and will therefore be patients.

The difference is subtle but important. The goal of healthcare providers should be to proactively help their constituents to stay healthy while, when necessary, providing treatment to those patients who need it. In this book, I'll strive to maintain the distinction between constituents who are healthy versus patients who require medical treatment.

In the coming era of healthcare, we can significantly improve the quality of constituent care by focusing on anticipation and prevention. For the first time in human history, we can do this by leveraging emerging digital technology, which will allow us to create the connection *architecture* upon which the new healthcare system will depend.

I'll talk much more about this in the pages ahead, but we're already seeing a slew of innovations including artificial intelligence, facial AI, genomics, anticipatory healthcare, data-rich wearable technologies, healthcare dashboards, and automated healthcare management systems. Collectively, these innovations will not only treat but *anticipate* disease before it becomes expensive or lethal, significantly improve the efficiency of diagnosis and treatment, emphasize prevention and wellness, and ultimately solve the problems of the dysfunctional healthcare system.

For example, as MedicalDevice-Network.com reported, researchers in Australia have unveiled a new handheld device that examines saliva for biomarkers of heart disease and warns the user via an app, allowing early preventive interventions. The portable diagnostic stick has nano-sensors at its tip to measure the biomarkers. It is designed to predict the risk of heart disease, heart failure, or heart attack. Researchers from RMIT University in Melbourne have partnered with the Innovative Manufacturing Cooperative Research Centre to further research and develop the diagnostic for pilot manufacture. They expect to work with startup ESN Cleer to make the device commercially available by 2021.[9]

But there's the 900-pound gorilla in the room: the profit motive. Everyone knows that healthcare is a big-money business. Many people have gotten very rich by providing treatments and drugs to patients, and these people will resist any effort to change a lucrative system. This is a huge and complex subject, but I will offer a general concept that may ameliorate their concerns.

From a revenue standpoint, the Big Shift in healthcare can include a shift from receiving large individual payments from a pool of sick patients or their insurers to receiving a larger quantity of smaller payments from more constituents. In terms of per capita participation, prevention is a larger industry with more participants than is treatment. Imagine the Big Shift resulting in a 10 percent drop in *treatments*—which for many institutions would be a disaster—but a 50 percent increase in *constituent participation* and the resulting income streams that would be generated (see Figure 5.3).

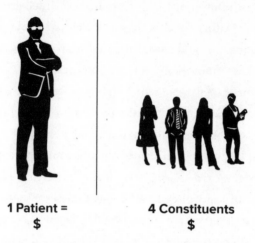

1 Patient =   **4 Constituents**
$**   **$

FIGURE 5.3   **The Big Shift Revenue Model**

Indeed, the Big Shift represents a change to a subscription model of healthcare, in which more constituents like Roberta or her employer will be paying smaller amounts for her to be plugged into the digital healthcare network and receive ongoing health monitoring. Of course, if and when she needs treatment, it will be provided with the same professionalism and dedication to quality as patients receive today; but the Big Shift anticipates that treatments will be earlier in the disease cycle and therefore less costly.

In the pages ahead, we'll dive into the many reasons why, after decades of ballooning healthcare costs and declining mental and physical health, we now have both the tools and the motivation to transform our nation's healthcare system. It's within our power to usher in a new golden age of healthcare in America—all that we need to get started is the personal and political will.

TAKE ACTION!

- Ensure your healthcare organization is ready for the Big Shift, which can be defined as the transformation from the constituent being required to report signs of illness—which even in the case of Roberta, the ideal patient, can be very late in the game—to the active collection of biometric data by the healthcare provider.
- Your constituents like George can become healthier with the use of biomonitors combined with incentives—cash, if necessary—to adopt a healthier lifestyle.
- To accelerate the Big Shift, you can adapt the successful efforts to reduce deadly urban fires by making four investments:
  1. Educate the public.
  2. Acquire and use appropriate technology.
  3. Organize human resources.
  4. Provide government support.
- Economically, it makes more sense to collect less revenue from a larger number of people consistently over time (the subscription model) rather than counting on payments for treatments (the current model).

The Six Steps
of the Big Shift

t's no secret that your constituents—the people in your community or practice for whose health you are responsible—are feeling and behaving more like consumers of a service. They no longer look at healthcare professionals as demigods who deserve to be treated with awe and deference. When they get sick or break a bone, they want prompt, friendly treatment. They want to be in and out of the hospital or doctor's office as quickly as possible after undergoing a safe and effective cure. They don't want to be lectured about their weight or smoking, even though they should be. They want the doctor or nurse practitioner to fix their problem at a reasonable cost and send them home.

In recent years in the industry, there has been increasing awareness of the consumerization of healthcare. Medicine is becoming proactive and is meeting constituents on their own turf, so to speak. As a service that's anticipatory and preventive, it will leverage the unique biology, genomic profile, life history, and environment of constituents to help them stay healthy, assess their probability of developing disease, pinpoint emerging symptoms, and then (if necessary) design appropriate treatments while the disease is easily contained.

The Big Shift represents the increasing *personalization* of medicine— the ability to see and analyze the individual patient's unique behaviors, genetic makeup, and environment to customize the healthcare provider's approach to lifelong wellness.

The Big Shift in healthcare is being driven by technology, in particular the emerging ability to gather a steady stream of real-time measurements on the individual constituent. The challenge will be to take this growing flood of data and turn it into actionable information about health and disease. This new approach is disrupting the existing healthcare industry. It's becoming clear that the business plans of every sector of the healthcare industry are being entirely transformed.

Here are the six steps of the Big Shift.

1. Anticipate

With biomedical sensors monitoring the body's component systems, unusual or unforeseen variations from homeostasis can be detected before either the constituent or caregiver is aware of symptoms. By identifying those changes at the molecular level and combining that data with the constituent's genomic information, medical history, and environmental data, the constituent healthcare operating system module will be able to predict when an anomaly in a biological network represents either a shift toward poor health or progression to disease. As the capabilities of such instruments are improved—as history has shown will be inevitable—the proteins and other components in blood will reveal the health status of every major organ in the body, enabling accurate predictions of disease causation and progression and alerting primary caregivers and specialists to take action.

Anticipation of disease can also be made at the macro-level, by using data to identify and track health trends emerging within a population—for example, a rise in the rate of obesity or the emergence of an infectious disease. This data can be cross-referenced to data from the constituent to identify if he or she is at risk.

2. Identify

Not every anomaly in a constituent's health data stream represents a disease or decline in the quality of the constituent's health. The constituent should not be unduly burdened by "false alarms." If the constituent is notified of a potential problem and then hurries to the doctor, only to discover that the information didn't warrant intervention, then he or she will learn to ignore such messages. A key driver of the Big Shift is our increasing ability to parse data and extract information about a condition that represents a threat to health.

Disease comes from a variety of sources, including communicable diseases (such as HIV/AIDS), noncommunicable lifestyle diseases (diabetes), and psychological diseases with a physical manifestation (anorexia nervosa). With advancing age and/or manifestation of chronic disease and comorbidity, functional and physiologic health will decline. Aging is associated with increases in the likelihood of chronic diseases and comorbidities, thereby intensifying their negative effects on health and well-being.

More quality data means better anticipation and identification. Internal data from the genetic, molecular, cellular, and organ levels provides indicators of early signs of diseases. Genetic data will reveal any predispositions to disease that may align with the internal data. Environmental data, such as the presence of toxins in the soil or water, adds to the mix, as well as allowing the formulation of appropriate public policy and individual screening.

For example, if a constituent's data sensors show elevated levels of arsenic in the body, the central module or "brain" (which I'll describe in the pages ahead) will instantly check for any evidence of pollution in the groundwater or public water supply. Let's say the data sweep reveals news articles describing a local mining operation that has been accused of polluting groundwater with toxins including arsenic. With this evidence, the constituent's primary care physician will contact the constituent, inform the constituent of the data point, and ask from what source the household gets its water. If the constituent replies, "City tap water" (which is known to be safe), then the search for the source needs to continue. If the constituent replies, "From our well," then a plan of action can be drawn up, which will begin with testing the well water while urging the constituent to drink only bottled water.

3. Prevent

The ability to anticipate and identify an emergent disease will in turn make it possible to prevent or minimize the effects of the disease, limit its severity, and lower the cost of treatment. The approach recognizes that individuals respond very differently to drugs and other types of medical interventions, as well as to lifestyle factors such as food, activity, and sleep.

It has long been known that the DNA differences between individuals contribute not only to their unique physical characteristics but also to their differing susceptibility to disease. It's become possible to sequence an individual's genome quickly and inexpensively, providing the healthcare professional with a wealth of information on the susceptibility of the constituent to genetic diseases and aspects of gene expression. Caregivers will be able to take into account how each person's DNA, environmental exposures, and life experiences will influence the person's biological systems. The result will be personalized predictions of disease and personalized responses to disease.

4. Empower

Empowerment has two faces.

One is that your constituents are increasingly accustomed to questioning the medical establishment. They are behaving less like patients and more like consumers. They don't want to sit in the waiting room for an hour. They don't want to call the medical center and be put on hold or sent to voicemail. They have choices—for many medical procedures, they can even go to a foreign country for treatment at a lower cost. In 2016, over 11 million travelers left the United States in search of affordable healthcare. A recent report by Visa and Oxford Economics stated that this figure will grow by up to 25 percent every year for the next decade as the competition among countries for health tourists becomes increasingly intense.

Constituents looking for cosmetic surgery can fly to Brazil. For dentistry, they go to Mexico. Panama, Costa Rica, India, Turkey . . . the list of competitors to US healthcare providers is long. As a healthcare executive, you may have thought that contracting with a medical lab in India to read x-rays at a fraction of the cost you paid the lab in the US was a right reserved for the industry. Guess what? Your constituents are thinking just like you. They're saying, "Why should we pay top dollar for a medical service when we can get the same quality in India?"

The second face is that medicine has a longstanding tradition of taking a top-down approach, whereby an expert diagnoses and treats the individual. This approach may be appropriate when infectious diseases and acute injures are the main health concerns. If you slip a disc in your back, you want to place yourself under the care of a skilled orthopedist. If you get HIV/AIDS, you want the drugs that will defeat the virus. But with chronic lifestyle diseases now being the primary health crisis, the new approach involves the constituent and his or her family actively participating as primary stakeholders in the care being given.

If a patient breaks a leg, it's pretty easy for that patient to follow the doctor's orders and hobble around in a cast. But for a patient who has prediabetes, active participation is key to returning to good health.

With the service of ubiquitous digital devices, constituents will take the lead in collecting their own health-related data. Empowering individuals to interpret the collected data gives them tools for early detection of signs of diseases.

5. Unify

The approach of the heathcare mandate is that the healthcare industry and the unlicensed wellness industry should be *one and the same*. The goal is to *unify* wellness and healthcare, and there are two important reasons for doing this:

1. As a healthcare provider, you need to be involved with your constituents in every aspect of their wellness. You do not want your constituents to be participating in a vast and generally unregulated wellness industry—following diets, taking supplements and medications, listening to wellness gurus—without your participation and oversight.

2. Your constituents are consumers who expect a seamless healthcare experience. They want to come to you and discuss a problem without having to transfer files, produce records, or bring you up to speed on their efforts to stay healthy. They want one-stop wellness/healthcare shopping.

"Healthcare" and "wellness" should be synonymous. They should not represent two different spaces. *Staying healthy* and *being cured of disease* are two sides of the same coin. The same system can, and should, serve both needs.

Consumers don't care what we call it. They just want to live a happy, healthy life. They don't care if the person helping them is in the wellness industry or the healthcare industry. That's a distinction we've created through legislation and tradition.

The healthcare mandate is also the wellness mandate. But for simplicity in discussing the issue, we're using the term "healthcare" to encompass both.

Having said that, looking at the healthcare mandate from the dual points of view of the consumer and the healthcare provider, we need to break down the barriers of the various healthcare/wellness fiefdoms and provide a frictionless consumer experience. Other industries work very hard to do this, and the healthcare industry should also.

In the old days—like the twentieth century—communication between members of a healthcare team was a cumbersome process. If you're old enough, you remember when your patient file was literally exactly that—a bulging file folder full of papers and x-rays. If you went to a specialist, your file had to be copied. Every practitioner had his or her own silo, and it was tough to coordinate efforts.

It was also incredibly easy for patients to go "doctor shopping" to get meds because one doctor had no idea of the patient's history with another.

The advent of digital records changed all that—to a point. Information flows more easily now, and will in the future; but human attitudes are slower to respond. Professionals in the healthcare industry still have the impulse to protect their own turf. Meanwhile, constituents only want results. And for the price they pay, it's understandable they get frustrated with poor service and red tape.

We have the opportunity to change that and to make healthcare as seamless as what the consumer experiences in any other industry.

6. Incentivize

Under our current system there's very little incentive for professional healthcare providers to focus on wellness as opposed to treatment. The big profits are in treatments that require advanced technology and pharmaceuticals, as well as the services of specialists.

The family doctor—who for generations was the frontline healthcare provider and the person who knew the most about the health of a family—is an endangered species. According to MarketWatch, there's significant financial incentive to avoid the traditional vocation of a family doctor. While primary care physicians make between $177,370 and

$231,107 a year, orthopedic surgeons make more than double, between $374,550 and $616,360 a year.

These differences are not just a matter of a doctor wanting to get rich. According to the Association of American Medical Colleges, in 2018 the average student loan debt for four years of medical school, undergraduate studies, and higher education was $196,520. For dental school, it was even higher: $287,331.

Young doctors are under pressure to earn. "With a $197,000 student-loan balance, you would owe $2,212 a month on the standard, 10-year federal repayment plan, assuming a 6.25 percent average interest rate," according to a calculation by the personal finance site NerdWallet.[1]

Primary care physicians must deal with the time and expense of managing their practice. Doctors who leave medical school with significant student debt may opt for the stable income of a job in a hospital, with the prospect of advancement.

As Walter W. Rosser, in his article "The Decline of Family Medicine as a Career Choice," asked: "Why would anyone choose a medical career with an excessive workload, an unclearly defined role, information overload, and the lowest pay? Many specialties have a clear definition of tasks and knowledge requirements and appear to provide more academic opportunities."[2]

In the United States, the per capita supply of primary care physicians is dropping. According to the article "Association of Primary Care Physician Supply with Population Mortality in the United States, 2005–2015," by Sanjay Basu and others, between 2005 and 2015 the per capita supply of primary care physicians decreased from 46.6 per 100,000 population to 41.4 per 100,000 population, with greater losses in rural areas. Because, as the research has shown, primary care physicians are very good at saving lives, there is a negative impact when there are fewer of them. Basu and coauthors found that every 10 additional primary care physicians per 100,000 population produced a 51.5-day increase in life expectancy. In contrast, 10 additional specialist physicians per 100,000 population produced a 19.2-day increase in life expectancy. The positive impact of specialists, who are more expensive than primary care physicians, is less than half that of primary care doctors, who are closer to their constituents and are likely to see them in both sickness and in health.[3]

Too many of the proposed "reinventions" of our healthcare system don't address the daunting question of "Who's going to pay for this?" Until we figure out a way to make the business of constituent wellness as attractive and remunerative as becoming a medical specialist, we're going to be stuck with our current broken system.

Wellness Creates Wealth

The fact is that *wellness creates wealth*. Not for pharmaceutical companies or hospitals, but for society as a whole. To look at one narrow example, studies show that healthy employees are more productive than unhealthy ones, and productivity translates into increased societal wealth. Healthy employees are better at staying focused, handling tasks, and saving their companies money. Enhancing their well-being can lead to drastic improvements in their performance.

As Standdesk.co reported, a study by Brigham Young University (BYU) found that absenteeism is reduced by 27 percent in employees who maintain a good diet and exercise regularly. Companies that invest in wellness get a solid return. For example, SAS (previously called Statistical Analysis Systems) offers programs including recreation centers, swimming pools, and on-site healthcare. It also offers its employees unlimited sick days, but on average, employees only take two per year.

The BYU study found that employees who eat healthier are 25 percent more likely to have increased performance throughout their day. And a study by the World Economic Forum and the Harvard School of Public Health found that employees with healthy habits were 3.1 times more productive than their unhealthy peers.

Exercise releases endorphins through the body, which improve cognitive function, making employees more alert and less likely to have accidents or be mentally disengaged.[4]

Company wellness programs are designed to change the behavioral patterns that can lead to chronic illnesses like asthma, cancer, obesity, heart disease, and diabetes. When employees change their behavior, employers see lower healthcare costs. A study by the University of Louisville found that changing certain unhealthy behaviors decreased the average number of health risks among employees from five or more health risks to zero to three risks. Every dollar invested in a wellness program generated seven dollars in healthcare savings.[5]

Healthy employees are productive employees, but to get the best results, corporate leaders need to ensure that wellness programs are all-encompassing. It's a very simple formula: The more they invest in their employees, the more they get back.

TAKE ACTION!

- Your organization needs to know and invest in the six steps of the Big Shift:
    1. Anticipate
    2. Identify
    3. Prevent
    4. Empower
    5. Unify
    6. Incentivize
- The wellness industry and the healthcare industry will, and should, become one and the same, and healthcare leaders need to plan accordingly. There are two important reasons for doing this: healthcare providers need to be involved with their constituents in every aspect of their wellness, and constituents are consumers who expect a seamless healthcare experience.
- As public policy, we need to encourage future doctors to become primary care physicians who are charged with "case-managing" their constituents.
- Wellness is not only morally good; it's good for business. Wellness creates wealth for society as a whole. Keeping employees healthy is not an unrecoupable expense; in fact, it provides a solid return on investment.

Innovate or Perish

T he healthcare mandate may scare some people. That's to be expected. The industry comprises millions of stakeholders with varying stakes in how it operates. Hospital CEOs, physicians, nurses, specialists, insurance company executives, medical equipment manufacturers, patients, and government legislators and judges all have their individual and professional viewpoints. Some have made fortunes in the game and worry about profitability, while others are paid minimum wage to swab the floors of the hospital wards.

Everyone may have his or her personal opinion about our healthcare system and how to make it better, but there is one ironclad law of business that applies to *every enterprise in any industry.*

Innovate or Perish

A common definition of "innovate" is "to make changes in something established, especially by introducing new methods, ideas, or products."

Let's think about the word "changes." A change can be made in any aspect of your healthcare company: in medical technology, human resources, supply chain, diagnostics, constituent experience, finance.

There is a difference between "change" and "innovate." To innovate goes much deeper. It does not mean make changes gratuitously or simply for the sake of doing something new or novel. To paint your office walls yellow instead of white is not an innovation. To rebrand your healthcare system as being "Patient Centered!" is not an innovation and may do nothing to help the organization grow or, worse, avoid perishing.

Making a change by introducing something new becomes an innovation only when a key condition is met: *the creation of new value that promotes wellness or cures disease.* It's as simple as that.

Tradition Versus Experimentation

Medicine is a unique profession in that it is pulled in opposite directions—forward and back—by two powerful forces.

The first force often leads to innovation paralysis. Because healthcare often deals with matters of life or death, the cost of making a mistake can be very high, including the loss of human life. For this reason, many healthcare professionals are risk averse. They look at the ancient teachings of Hippocrates, who said, "First, do no harm," and they take this as a mandate to be very careful. They want to stick to procedures and systems that are time honored and carry low risk. For them, it's better to err on the side of minimal interference because then you can't be blamed for causing harm.

Ironically, the same play-it-safe approach can drive many physicians to practice "defensive medicine," which means they have a tendency to overestimate the likelihood of "dread risks"—rare but devastating outcomes—rather than make an accurate assessment of actual risk. To protect themselves from legal liability, they schedule batteries of tests that may not be entirely justified and that drive up healthcare costs for everyone.

The second force pulling on the healthcare industry is the deeply rooted knowledge held by every practitioner that medicine is a losing business, in the sense that no person has ever cheated death. Every constituent and patient will eventually die. It is a certainty. The healthcare provider can only hope to extend life, not enable someone to live forever. This grim statistic can be a catalyst for all manner of phony or dangerous treatments that claim to represent a breakthrough and are designed to give people hope when there may be none.

One such unproven and highly dubious "innovation" was the business of cryonics, the low-temperature freezing and storage of a human corpse or severed head, with the speculative hope that resurrection may be possible in the future. The first corpse to be frozen was that of Dr. James Bedford in 1967, and as of 2014, about 250 dead bodies had been cryopreserved in the United States, with 1,500 people having made arrangements for cryopreservation of their corpses. But the economic model of the business is deeply flawed; historically, even the most robust corporations in any industry have only a one-in-a-thousand chance of surviving even one hundred years, not to mention a business built on the concept of the never-ending expense of keeping a corpse frozen for decades or even centuries. As of 2018 most of the early cryonics companies had been shuttered, and their stored corpses thawed and sent back to their distraught families.[1]

It's therefore understandable that healthcare professionals should feel a sense of whiplash between the allure of the traditional image of Marcus Welby—unchanging, with eternal values—and the breathtaking prospects provided by new technologies.

This is precisely why innovation, in all its many forms, must be pursued by an organizational program that is rational, well planned, rigorous, and constantly evaluated. It needs to be a part of every healthcare organization that wants to survive and thrive. As healthcare organizations face unprecedented challenges to improve quality, increase efficiency, improve access, reduce harm, eliminate waste, and lower costs, innovation remains a major mandate. Under our present system, just doing our best or working harder is not enough.

The Three Waves of Change

To leverage change, you first need to understand it. Today, *right now*, we are in the first phase of three successive waves of change sweeping through the healthcare industry (see Figure 7.1).

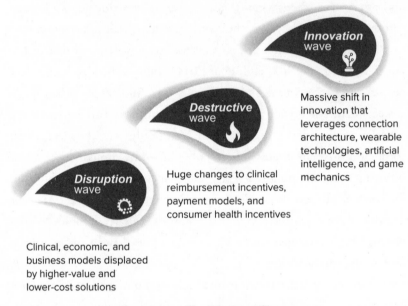

Innovation wave

Massive shift in innovation that leverages connection architecture, wearable technologies, artificial intelligence, and game mechanics

Destructive wave

Huge changes to clinical reimbursement incentives, payment models, and consumer health incentives

Disruption wave

Clinical, economic, and business models displaced by higher-value and lower-cost solutions

FIGURE 7.1   The Waves of Change

Disruption (Now)

During this wave, technology and practices are changing. Clinical, economic, and business models are being displaced by higher-value and lower-cost solutions.

For many organizations, the nature of the disparate change is hard to understand. During this wave, organizations are trying to develop hierarchies of priority and initiatives to square up with a massive disruption that is occurring. This is a strategic inflection point for most organizations, as there are but two paths in this fork in the road:

One path is to postpone your response to disruption and to take a wait-and-see philosophy toward change. This path ensures that progress will pass you by, making it that much more difficult to catch up. It can move any organization into irrelevancy and ultimately bankruptcy.

The other path is to *lean into disruption* and to begin immediately building the systems, methods, tools, and processes necessary to address all the ingredients of the Big Shift. It means making an investment in innovation the same way you'd make an investment in a new warehouse or office building. Just like any other part of your business, innovation needs to be a line item in your annual budget.

Destruction (Through 2025)

This wave is the shipping address for organizations that have ignored massive changes in the marketplace. This wave is where many legacy businesses and models are destroyed and many new enterprises and wealth centers are created.

Blockbuster, Toys "R" Us, Sears, Mattress Firm, Palm, Compaq, Sienna Biopharmaceuticals . . . the list of major US corporations destroyed by waves of change is long.

In the healthcare industry, we'll see massive changes to clinical reimbursement incentives, payment models, and consumer health incentives.

The Innovation Wave (Through 2030 and Beyond)

Innovators in the healthcare space are rapidly creating solutions that concurrently reduce cost and improve the patient's experience, anticipate and predict disease, and add significant value to the healthcare economic ecosystem. It's a period encompassing a massive shift in innovation that leverages connection architecture, wearable technologies, artificial intelligence, and game mechanics.

This period of time is marked by rapid innovation that is big and either disruptive (if you try to ignore it) or an agent of growth (if you harness it).

Hospitals Can, and Do, Go Out of Business

From a business perspective, there's nothing special about hospitals. The fact that they save lives is not relevant to their viability.

Here's a list compiled by Ayla Ellison of *Becker's Hospital Review* of hospitals that had closed in just the first half of 2019:[2]

1. De Queen (Arkansas) Medical Center. Bankrupt.
2. Mercy Hospital El Reno (Oklahoma). Cited financial losses.
3. Providence Hospital (Washington, D.C.). Closed after 158 years of service. Its owner, St. Louis–based Ascension, said it was making investments in other types of services, including telehealth, care coordination, home care, and community-based behavioral healthcare.
4. Belmont Community Hospital (Ohio). Hospital officials cited a decline in patient volume and financial strain.
5. Kentuckiana Medical Center (Indiana). Bankrupt.
6. Horton Community Hospital (Kansas). Bankrupt.
7. Georgiana Medical Center (Alabama). Owner Ivy Creek Healthcare cited growing costs and cuts to reimbursement.
8. Cumberland River Hospital (Tennessee). Financial challenges, declining reimbursements, and lower patient volumes.
9. UPMC Pinnacle (Pennsylvania). Consolidation with sister hospital.
10. Oswego Community Hospital and its two affiliated clinics (Kansas). Bankrupt.

Note that none of these hospitals cited the reason for closing as "too many patients dying" or "incompetent doctors." It's almost always financial, which means lack of revenues and/or declining utilization.

If you were to look deeper, the underlying reason could be "failure to innovate."

The Three Levels of Innovation

Innovations come in every size and shape and from many sources. They have many levels of impact on an organization, from minimal to massive. In simplified form, here are the three levels of innovation:

1. Incremental

You've probably heard of how the Japanese carmaker Toyota built up its expertise in the practice of slow, steady innovation. Toyota calls it "kaizen," or "continuous improvement," based on a sustained organizational effort to identify and implement small improvements, each of which adds more value in the eyes of the customer. In an interview with *Harvard Business Review*, Katsuaki Watanabe of Toyota said, "There is no genius in our company. We just do whatever we believe is right, trying every day to improve every little bit and piece. But when seventy years of very small improvements accumulate, they become a revolution."[3]

Incremental innovations need not be visible to your constituent. They can happen anywhere, from the operating room to the database where patient medical records are stored and shared. They can come from any source, including frontline employees, patients, and even social media. To capture and leverage new ideas, every healthcare organization needs an innovation operating system (IOS) and an innovation pipeline, which I'll talk much more about in the pages ahead.

2. Breakthrough

A breakthrough innovation is a game changer that makes an immediate difference to your constituents or the organization.

In the field of medical technology, breakthrough innovations are made on a regular basis. For example, cancer immunotherapy (or biologic therapy, or immuno-oncology) uses the body's own immune system to fight cancer. Immunotherapy "educates" the immune system to recognize and attack specific cancer cells, boosts immune cells to help them eliminate cancer, and provides the body with additional components to enhance the immune response.[4]

Breakthrough innovations don't have to directly involve the patient. For example, digital x-ray imaging was a breakthrough innovation. This eliminated film processing, allowing the images to be viewed just minutes after exposure via computer networks and to be seen by many people at once, in many different places. This made it possible, for example, for x-rays taken in the United States to be read overnight by technicians in India and at a relatively low cost.

Another breakthrough innovation was electronic medical records (EMRs) technology, a vast improvement over paper records. It allowed the storage of more information, permitted more than one person to use a patient's chart, and facilitated the rapid transfer of records to healthcare providers who needed them. EMRs boosted patient safety and improved the efficiency of a practice or hospital. The federal government recognized the technology's importance with the American Reinvestment & Recovery Act, enacted in 2009, which included the Health Information Technology for Economic and Clinical Health (HITECH) Act. The HITECH Act featured the concept of "electronic health records—meaningful use," proposing the meaningful use of interoperable electronic health records throughout the US healthcare delivery system as a critical national goal.[5]

3. Disruptive

A disruptive innovation is one that alters an entire industry. Sometimes a disruptive innovation is immediately recognized. In the early part of the twenty-first century, the emergence of fast and inexpensive DNA sequencing changed the healthcare industry. As *Science News* noted in 2018, affordable, rapid DNA sequencing caused a "revolution in medicine and healthcare globally." In the previous decade, the cost of reading an individual's DNA sequence plummeted from hundreds of millions of dollars to a few hundred. Genomics drove a paradigm shift in health practices and outcomes, ushering in a new era of precision healthcare in which prevention strategies, treatments, and health advice could reach the right person at the right time.[6]

The example of DNA sequencing underscores a common misconception about innovation: that it has to be a "bolt from the blue," something unforeseen to the industry, like the first Apple Macintosh computer. This is often far from the truth. For example, DNA was first discovered in 1869, and the first full DNA genome sequenced was that of bacteriophage φX174 in 1977. Thanks to the Human Genome Project, the human genome was nearly 100 percent mapped by 2003, at a cost of $2.7 billion. By 2006—just three years later—the cost had decreased to $300,000, and by 2016 it had fallen to $1,000.[7]

Sometimes disruptive innovations are controversial. Such was the case with the Patient Protection and Affordable Care Act (ACA), signed into law by President Obama in 2010. Representing the largest overhaul of the US healthcare system since the 1960s, conservative politicians have consistently opposed the ACA and have vowed to repeal it.

An Innovation Program Needs to Be More Than Just a Band-Aid

The number one reason why innovation efforts fail, and produce no benefits for the organization, is because the effort is half-hearted. It's a placebo, a Band-Aid, a bumper sticker.

You'd think that of all people, doctors would understand the importance of making a comprehensive, thorough, long-lasting effort to reach a desired state. After all, when a patient has cancer, you know that you need to get that cancer 100 percent out of the body, and half-hearted measures won't do the job.

Doctors know that if an obese patient needs to go on a diet to lose weight, the program has to be structured, long-lasting, and with a component of accountability. Otherwise it will fail.

Healthcare officials know that to eradicate measles from a population, you cannot inoculate a third of the individuals or even half. To achieve herd immunity for measles, at least 95 percent of the population must be vaccinated.

Every healthcare organization needs an innovation operating system. Think of it as similar to a computer operating system, in that the goal of the system is to *run the machine*. When creating an IOS for a healthcare organization, you need to get a solid level of commitment from the very top. The support shown must be consistent with leadership's expectation in terms of outcomes and overall costs. Once you understand the true level of commitment, you can build a custom IOS, as you will need continued leadership sponsorship to succeed.

Define Your Innovation Goals

Every hospital or healthcare organization uses metrics to measure success. They may include average length of stay, patient satisfaction, physician performance, patient readmission rate, and others. Goals are set and performance measured against them.

Innovation goals are no different. They need to be understandable, relevant to your organization, and, most importantly, *measurable* and *attainable*. Here are just a few examples:

- Track how many ideas per month your employees—doctors, staff, administrators—are submitting.
- Mandate that a percentage of annual revenues must come from new devices, processes, or services. This is often called the "innovation sales rate."
- Measure the success of individual innovation projects (from concept to implementation) and new business development programs.
- Calculate the risk-adjusted net present value of the innovation pipeline and the return on investment in that pipeline, which we'll discuss next.

The Innovation Pipeline

To establish a long-term, secure, and viable innovation operating system, you need to make clear exactly how the process works, from the first glimmer of a new idea through its evaluation, acceptance, deployment, and review.

This is your innovation pipeline.

You start with the strategic case. You have to know why you're innovating and what you hope to get out of it. The strategic case is at the very core of the innovation process. Remember, every proposed new idea—a new device, process, service—must fulfill this definition of innovation: *the creation of new value that promotes wellness or cures disease.*

Your innovation pipeline will consist of five steps (see Figure 7.2). At every stage, you need to have gatekeepers who review every idea and take one of three actions: Discard the idea, pass it along to the next level, or send it to a subject-matter expert for further review.

The steps are:

1. **Identify.** New ideas come from many sources—employees, the lab, patients, social media, external partners. This is the "widest end" of the innovation pipeline. Here, virtually every new idea can enter, no matter how crazy or outlandish.

2. **Capture.** This is where ideas are first filtered. Is the idea properly described? Can we own it? Ideas that don't fit any criteria are deleted. Those with potential proceed to the next step.

3. **Validate.** Does the idea work for us, and will it be an innovation that brings value? This is where you decide which ideas to invest in. They get the proverbial green light.

4. **Develop.** Chosen ideas will require an investment to make them operable. Some will be developed quickly, while others will require significant investment and time.

5. **Deploy.** A new idea is an expense until it's put into action, at which time it can begin to add value. Deployment also includes

periodic evaluation to confirm the innovation's performance. At any stage from 1 through 5, an idea or project can be shelved if it fails to prove its utility.

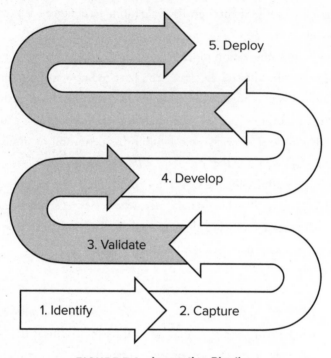

FIGURE 7.2   Innovation Pipeline

Sameness Is Your Frenemy

In our personal lives, it's nice to have traditions and a familiar routine. You live in your neighborhood, eat at your favorite restaurants, and see your old friends. As you go through the day, you don't have to constantly adjust to your environment or waste time trying to figure out where to go for basic necessities.

In business, a certain level of sameness is necessary, in the form of efficient systems. There could be no manufacturing, no supermarkets, no hospitals without systems designed to replicate the same event over and over again. Especially in the healthcare industry, when your people are performing routine tasks, you expect consistency and accuracy. You need to know they are executing the proper procedures and sticking to the protocol. Sloppiness and improvisation can cost lives.

Given that in some contexts sameness can be your friend, it's understandable that there can be a powerful impulse to resist change, because change means disruption. It means new training, new expense, new risk.

That's why it's even more important for healthcare leaders to get out of their comfort zones and champion innovation. It may take energy to do it, but the alternative is slow decline and institutional death. When we're talking about maintaining a competitive edge, striving for better and better outcomes, and refocusing our efforts from treatment to prevention, sameness is our "frenemy." It's good to have systems, but an avoidance of innovation and change means trouble. Sameness is the friend who will stab you in the back.

Disruption is about the introduction of forces and ideas that are different, or as I call it, "differentness." The nature of differentness is fast and big; yet most organizations in healthcare are committed to legacy, or more simply, sameness. When faced with rapid change, too many organizations respond by doubling down on sameness. This can be a fatal choice.

Create a Culture of Innovation

To be successful, a program of institutional innovation needs to meet a set of five simple conditions.

1. Innovation Must Be Endorsed and Supported from the Top Down

Innovation means change, and frontline healthcare workers are not going to experiment or improvise on their patients. But they do have new ideas, and they need to know there is a system in place for submitting their ideas and having them evaluated. This is the innovation pipeline, and it can only be created by top leadership.

2. Innovation Must Be Woven into the Fabric of the Organization

It's tempting to set up an innovation center or lab and then say, "OK, innovate!" This strategy is doomed to fail. Healthcare leaders need to follow the lead of Toyota, which actively solicits ideas from all workers at all levels and has a robust pipeline process. Managers at Toyota keep track of the number of suggestions made by employees during the year. Over a 35-year period, Toyota's culture of innovation increased the number of annual suggestions from 1 per 10 employees to 480 per 10 employees. This high rate of participation is a direct result of the company instilling in every employee the necessity and value of new ideas.[8]

3. "Hackathons" Work if They Are Taken Seriously and Are Regularly Scheduled

For example, as part of its annual conference in Orlando, Florida, the American Nursing Association hosts a massive hackathon in which nurses compete for cash funding for their ideas. In 2019, the ANA Innovation Awards recognized "exemplary nurse-led innovation that improves patient safety and outcomes." The individual nurse and nurse-led team award recipients received monetary prizes of $25,000 and $50,000, respectively. These funds are meant to provide support in translational research, development, prototyping, production, testing, and the implementation of their products over the following year.

The individual winner was Kathleen Puri, MSN, RN, who invented "Fitsi," a bedside caddy allowing patients to easily clean their own hands and access and store their personal items, such as cell phones and glasses.

The group winners were Michael Wang, MBA, MSN, RN, and Paul Coyne, DNP, MBA, MSF, RN, AGPCNP-BC, who designed "iN," a wall-mounted device placed directly behind the patient's bed that uses computer vision to detect potential risks to patients while simultaneously aggregating data from electronic health records and medical devices. Through predictive algorithms, iN can help staff mitigate the risk of medical errors, assess patient workloads, and enhance staffing.[9]

ANA hosts this hackathon every year, and it's well funded and publicized. That's the only way to do it.

4. Innovation Programs Must Be Well Funded

While companies like Toyota take advantage of the "free" ideas submitted by employees, the automaker has a fully funded innovation pipeline for processing those ideas, as well as a formal R&D program. Consistent innovation requires investment in both time and money, and it needs to be included in the budget like any other expense. According to Statista, in 2018, at a spending level of $22.6 billion, Amazon spent the most on research and development. Alphabet (Google), Volkswagen, Samsung, and Intel rounded out the top five of companies with the highest R&D spending.[10]

5. Innovation Needs to Be a Part of the Strategic Plan

Too many innovation programs are half-hearted in the sense that they're seen as an "extra," which if they produce new ideas, then they're good, but if they fail to produce new ideas, that's OK too. No! The most innovative companies have a new product or new service revenue stream built into their budget.

At manufacturing giant 3M, engineers and scientists can spend up to 15 percent of their time pursuing projects of their own choice, free to develop unexpected, breakthrough innovations that have the potential to create value for the customer. For example, a group of employees in the infection-prevention division used their innovation time to pursue wirelessly connected electronic stethoscopes. As a result, in 2012, 3M introduced the first electronic stethoscope with Bluetooth technology that allowed doctors to listen to patients' heart and lung sounds as they went on rounds, while seamlessly transferring the data to software programs for deeper analysis.

At 3M, innovation isn't just encouraged; it's mandated. Under the "Thirty Percent Rule," 30 percent of each division's revenues must come from products introduced within the previous four years. This is tracked rigorously, and employee bonuses are based on successful achievement of this goal.[11]

The Three Steps to Innovation Success

If your company has no permanent innovation strategy or program, it's time to take action! I've broken down innovation success into three steps. Follow them and make your organization an innovation leader.

1. **Conduct an innovation readiness assessment.** You need to do this to determine if your people understand what it means to innovate and how they can contribute to the effort. To succeed at this first step, the number one element necessary in your company culture is *trust.* You're going to be asking people to stretch their minds, go above and beyond the minimum, and then turn over their ideas to their peers and managers. This takes time and trust to develop. You also need to ensure that awareness of the effort is spread throughout the organization.

2. **Develop a comprehensive innovation plan and road map.** You cannot leave innovation to chance; you need to plan for it the same way you plan for any other program. Decide what types of innovations are the most important for your organization, and seek them out. Set goals for the number of new ideas and participation. Determine your budget or investment and a goal for return.

3. **Deploy with depth, consistency, and scalability.** Always start small and let the program grow organically. Nothing is worse than announcing an innovation program with fanfare and then watching it underperform (which it will) and then collapse when the chief financial officer gets fed up and pulls the plug. Use an agile approach: design a small innovation pipeline and keep nurturing it as it grows. Over time, draw more and more people into it. Celebrate successes and reward contributions.

TAKE ACTION!

- Innovation is *the creation of new value that promotes wellness or cures disease.* Your organization needs to make innovation a part of its daily operations or else risk falling behind.
- The three levels of innovation are incremental, breakthrough, and disruptive. All add value to your organization. Incremental innovation is something that any organization can plan for and incorporate into its everyday strategy.
- Every healthcare organization needs an innovation operating system. It's similar to a computer operating system in that the goal of the system is to *run the machine.*
- You need to make innovation goals understandable, relevant to your organization, and, most importantly, *measurable* and *attainable.*

Technological Innovation Propels the Big Shift

T he American healthcare system is designed in such a way that when a patient is treated, every player makes money: the doctor, the hospital, the drug company, the insurer. Consequently, there is little financial incentive to *prevent* illness. There's no profit in it. So the patient keeps paying more in direct costs, insurance costs, and prescription drug costs.

Healthcare eats up a sizable chunk of the typical American household budget. According to the US Bureau of Labor Statistics, in 2017 the average American household had an operating budget of $60,060. Of that, $4,928 was spent on healthcare. That's about 8 percent of the entire household budget for a year.

What if there were a way to maintain the profit motive that's baked into the American healthcare system—indeed, the American way of life—while steering it in the direction of wellness and prevention rather than treatment after the fact?

To attack the twin problems of (1) a dysfunctional mission that provides economic rewards for treatment intervention while concurrently punishing doctors and caregivers for supporting prevention and wellness and (2) the chronic disease epidemic that is driven almost exclusively by lifestyle, we need to develop a system with solutions to those problems: (1) a mission focused on early detection and prevention rather than treatment after the fact and (2) incentives for patients to improve their personal homeostasis.

Remember, with a constituent like Roberta, who as a young woman was the ideal patient in terms of how she approached the diagnosis and treatment of her adrenal gland tumor, the existing healthcare system worked to fix her problem, but at a high cost. This was because her tumor was detected only after she had reported her symptoms and had gone through all the usual testing. By the time she had symptoms, the tumor required surgical intervention at a cost of $25,000. Years later, thanks to her biomonitor, the recurring tumor was detected *before* she felt any symptoms and was removed at a cost of only $2,500 and with far lower risk. The ideal patient was matched with the ideal healthcare system.

Meanwhile, for a problem constituent like George, the benefits are even more pronounced. Equipped with a biomonitor and incentivized at work to reach his personal health goals, his overall health is improving. And at the first sign of a problem with his heart, he can be whisked to the hospital for treatment, even if he himself doesn't recognize his symptoms.

The Exploding Health/Medical Wearables Market

Many serious conditions are typically asymptomatic for months or even years. Given the accelerating rate of technological innovation, it doesn't take a great leap of the imagination to envision wearable technology that can identify cancer, cardiovascular conditions, diabetes, and other chronic conditions well before requiring serious intervention. The farther down the disease process that individuals are diagnosed, the fewer options that are available to the patient, and the third-party providers will need to pay a lot more money. Ongoing wearable technologies that use artificial intelligence and dashboard reporting will be one of the major ways in which we improve the quality of patient healthcare.

The worldwide market for wearable health/medical devices, now inclusive of wireless headphones with smart assistants, is growing rapidly. Driving that growth is the continued proliferation of watches, ear-worn devices, and wristbands, as well as further adoption in the healthcare segment. In 2023, the wearables market will be worth over $30 billion, according to industry analyst firm CCS Insight.[1]

Looking ahead, the market is expected to reach 279 million units by the end of 2023, with a compound annual growth rate of 8.9 percent.[2]

"The rise of smart assistants on wearables, both wrist-worn and ear-worn, is a trend worth watching," said Jitesh Ubrani, research manager for IDC's mobile device trackers. "Though still in its infancy, the integration of these assistants with wearables opens up new use cases, from allowing these devices to tie into the smart home to making the devices more proactive at urging users to live healthier or more productive lives."[3]

Constantly collecting important constituent data while also giving constituents the ability to self-monitor, wearables will play an important role in the emerging field of digital health.

Here are just a few examples of devices that are on the market. Given the rate of innovation, we can safely assume it won't be long before these are superseded by a new generation and then a new one after that, each one smaller and more powerful than the last.

- **Apple Watch.** It's no surprise that Apple is positioned at the top, with the first smartwatch with a built-in electrocardiogram feature. The ECG app can record your heartbeat and rhythm using the electrical heart sensor on the watch, and then check the recording for atrial fibrillation (AFib), a form of irregular heart rhythm. The ECG app records an electrocardiogram and checks the electrical pulses to get the heart rate and see if the upper and lower chambers of the heart are in rhythm. If they're out of rhythm, that could be AFib.[4]

- **Asthma alerts.** A GPS-enabled sensor made by Propellor Health can track the weather and pollutants in the air, as well as track inhaler use and the areas of the city where air pollution is at its worst. It then sends out alerts, helping wearers cut down on rescue inhaler use.
- **iTBra.** Developed by Cyrcadia Health, the device uses dual breast patches worn as a bra insert. They monitor circadian metabolic changes in heat that correlate to accelerated cellular activity common in breast tumors.
- **KardiaMobile and KardiaBand.** Atrial fibrillation, an irregular heartbeat triggered by chaotic electrical signals, is the most common serious heart rhythm disorder and is associated with a heightened risk of stroke. With these mobile devices, users can give themselves an ECG.
- **L'Oreal UV Sense.** This battery-free sensor just nine millimeters in diameter and two millimeters thick can be worn on the thumbnail for up to two weeks to measure UV exposure.
- **Aira.** To help the blind navigate, this subscription service combines wearable eyeglasses with a remote human "concierge" who, while watching a monitor, guides blind and low-vision users with everyday tasks.
- **Owlet.** Worn on an infant's foot, this smart sock uses pulse oximetry to measure oxygen levels and heartbeat and continuously provides real-time data via Bluetooth and a smartphone app.
- **TempTraq.** Another baby wearable, this is a 48-hour, single-use stick-on patch, worn under the arm, that provides continuous real-time temperature feedback to a mobile device.[5]
- **BodyNET.** This "body area sensor network" looks like a Band-Aid. When placed on the participant's elbows and knees, it detects the stretching and contracting of the skin, which corresponds to the muscles flexed. The device can monitor people with sleep problems and heart conditions.[6]

- **Spire Health Tag.** Attached to a person's undergarments and pajamas, the device can measure stress levels by monitoring breathing and heart rate. It sends data to a smartphone, which gives recommendations, such as breathing exercises, to improve the user's sleep and reduce stress.[7]

It's not a stretch of the imagination to say that what we can produce today, and even what we can safely predict for the near future, will in the years ahead seem quaint and crude. Wearables represent a tremendous advance over what was possible just a decade ago. But both the speed and intensity of innovation are accelerating, and the *connection architecture* linking increasingly miniaturized sensors with data processors will become more complex and, at the same time, more invisible.

Implantable Devices

Do you know the significance of the date October 8, 1958? Or the name Arne H. W. Larsson?

On that day, Larsson, a Swedish engineer, received the first battery-powered implanted heart pacemaker. Because Larsson was plagued by fainting spells, his wife implored Dr. Ake Senning, a heart surgeon, and Dr. Rune Elmquist, an engineer at Elema-Schonander electronics company, to test their new device, made with silicon transistors, on her husband.

After trying a model that quickly failed, Dr. Senning then implanted the only backup unit, one with batteries that had to be recharged every few hours. The pacemaker worked, on and off, for three years.

Subsequently, Mr. Larsson underwent 25 procedures to replace pacemakers that had failed for various reasons and to receive newer devices that were smaller, smarter, safer, and more durable and versatile. He died in 2001 at the age of 86—of melanoma skin cancer.

Today an estimated 3 million people, including about 1.5 million Americans, from newborns to centenarians, now use pacemakers.[8]

As they become increasingly miniaturized, implantable medical devices are proliferating.

Way back in 2013—a lifetime ago in medical innovation—scientists at the École Polytechnique Fédérale de Lausanne in Switzerland announced the development of a subcutaneous chip containing five sensors, which could analyze the patient's blood and detect up to five proteins and organic acids simultaneously. With a tiny radio transmitter, it then sent the results to a doctor.

"In a general sense, our system has enormous potential in cases where the evolution of a pathology needs to be monitored or the tolerance to a treatment tested," said Giovanni de Micheli, one of the chief scientists involved in the chip's development.[9]

A subcutaneous loop recorder is a type of heart-monitoring device that records your heart rhythm continuously. It's smaller than a key or a thumb drive, and it's implanted just beneath the skin of the chest. It stays in place for up to three years.[10]

The Confirm Rx ICM (insertable cardiac monitor) from Abbott Laboratories is an implantable device that continuously tracks a patient's heart rhythms and sends the data to a smartphone app via Bluetooth. Encrypted data from the device is coordinated by the myMerlin mobile app before being sent from the patient's phone to a physician at predetermined intervals.[11]

Researchers at the University of Illinois—working with colleagues in Singapore—embedded flat, flexible, stretchable electronic sensors into temporary "tattoos." These microelectronics, which are thinner than a human hair and applied with water, can withstand wrinkling, bending, and twisting of the skin. They can provide irritation-free monitoring of electric signals produced by the heart, brain, and muscles.[12]

Injectable medical devices are here.

Back in 1966, the science fiction film *Fantastic Voyage* imagined the miniaturization of a research vessel—with human crew—to microscopic size. The tiny submarine was injected into the bloodstream of an injured scientist, with the goal of repairing a life-threatening blood clot in his brain. In typical Hollywood fashion, intrigue and action were the hallmarks of the film, which ended with the dramatic escape of the crew through a tear duct in one of the patient's eyes.

For such a device to work, which includes crossing the blood-brain barrier, it would need to be smaller than most molecules, so that's a pretty tall order. But to circulate freely in the bloodstream? It would need to be able to pass through the capillaries, which are only about 7 microns in diameter. By comparison, the average human hair is 100 microns.

Impossible? Remember that in 1968 the most advanced small computer was the Apollo Guidance Computer (AGC). Designed by scientists and engineers at MIT's Instrumentation Laboratory, AGC was the culmination of years of work to reduce the size of the Apollo spacecraft computer from seven refrigerators side by side to a compact unit weighing 70 pounds and taking up a volume of less than one cubic foot.[13]

In 2018—just 50 years later—researchers at the University of Michigan unveiled the next-generation Michigan Micro Mote. Smaller than a grain of rice, it was a precision temperature sensor that could report temperatures in clusters of cells with an error of about 0.1 degree Celsius. It could, for instance, measure the temperature of tumors and conduct other cancer studies, monitor oil reservoirs, or conduct audio or visual surveillance.

In July 2019, medical technology company Biotronik received FDA clearance for its injectable cardiac monitor, the Biomonitor III. It's intended to provide information on suspected arrhythmia or unexplained syncope and allow quick diagnosis and appropriate treatment. The cardiac monitor comes with an app that provides information on system diagnostics and enables patients to annotate symptoms.[14]

The pace of innovation is accelerating, and one can hardly imagine the shrinking size and growing power of computers we will produce by the year 2068. It's a virtual certainty that by that time, we will have computers small enough to be placed nearly anywhere in the human body, providing real-time data on key bodily processes.

Medical Imaging Reveals the Body

Another way to appreciate the breathtaking rate of change in medical technology is by looking at medical imaging. For hundreds of thousands of years, we humans lived on earth without the ability to divine the secrets of the interior workings of our own bodies. Then in 1895, the first x-rays were taken by Wilhelm Conrad Roentgen, a professor at Wuerzburg University in Germany. This was the first time in human history that doctors could safely and reliably look inside a living human being.

The x-ray was the only imaging tool available until 1942, when neurologist Karl Dussik, attempting to detect brain tumors, transmitted an ultrasound beam through the human skull. The technology quickly became widespread, most notably in obstetrics.

In 1970, Raymond Damadian, a medical doctor and research scientist, discovered that magnetic resonance was an effective imaging tool for medical diagnosis. He found that different kinds of animal tissue emitted response signals that vary in length, and that cancerous tissue emitted response signals that lasted much longer than noncancerous tissue. By 1977, Dr. Damadian had built the first whole-body MRI scanner, which he dubbed the "Indomitable."

In 1972, computer technology entered the medical field with Sir Godfrey Hounsfield's invention of the axial tomography machine, which we now know as the CT machine. His device took x-rays from different angles, which were then put together to create an image.

From 1895 to 1972, scientists made more progress in seeing inside the body than in the previous hundred thousand years.

The pace of innovation accelerated. With the advent of the digital era, the focus of invention shifted to data: how to collect, store, analyze, and disseminate it in increasingly vast quantities. Moore's law—

the prediction in 1965 that there would be a doubling of transistors in a chip every two years—has proved to be valid. There has been a doubling every five years of the number of mobile devices connected via the Internet, leading to 50 billion in 2020. Much of the exponential growth of the Internet of Things (advanced interconnectivity between systems and services) comprises sensors of all types, used in a wide range of industries from manufacturing and food production to human health.[15]

By 2020, the auto industry alone is estimated to have installed 22 billion sensors in vehicles, with as many as 200 in each vehicle.[16]

Sensors are not only becoming increasingly miniaturized; they are also becoming "bioresorbable," which means they dissolve over time inside the living tissue. Researchers at the University of Illinois at Urbana-Champaign developed "implantable, multifunctional silicon sensors for the brain," for which all the constituent materials naturally resorb via hydrolysis and/or metabolic action, eliminating the need for extraction.[17]

Smart Constituent Data Monitoring and Leveraging

In the emerging healthcare universe wherein real-time personal and community healthcare data is captured, processed, and stored, the use of smart constituent data (SCD) will take the form of an evolving relationship between the constituent and his or her doctor, characterized by two stages.

Phase I will be data collection, purely for the purpose of identifying disease processes early in the disease process curve so as to reduce cost and save lives.

Phase II will leverage game mechanics, social engagement, and other tools to significantly change constituent behaviors and reduce the causality of disease.

Constituent data will be protected by leveraging blockchain and other emerging technologies.

Ultimately, constituents will be happier and healthier; and as a result of working with their SCD monitoring and primary care physician, they will circumvent life-threatening situations. Ultimately the system will help them make better choices. Hospitals and clinics will leverage command centers that connect to the constituent's PDR system to provide safe and efficacious care without medical mix-ups and exposure to common patient safety concerns.

This is the future of wearable technologies.

Of course, cost will be an issue. (Isn't it always?)

Initially, wearable technologies need to be made available at no cost, especially to underserved communities. However, in order to access governmental and insurance programs in the future, patients will be required to be monitored, as this significantly reduces the cost of delivery.

In recent history, constituents have not been required to meet specific biomarkers to access affordable and convenient healthcare. In the future, their access and costs associated with healthcare will be directly linked to a range of biomarkers that determine their risk profile to insurance companies and the government.

TAKE ACTION!

- Support the development of a healthcare system with two primary features:
  1. A mission focused on anticipation and prevention rather than treatment after the fact
  2. Incentives for constituents to improve their personal homeostasis
- Take steps to ensure your constituents are mentally prepared to wear health-monitoring devices that can provide early alerts for many common diseases. Wearable technologies that use artificial intelligence and dashboard reporting will be one of the major ways in which we improve the quality of patient healthcare.
- Wearables are a rapidly growing industry. You need to ensure that your healthcare organization is a part of this Big Shift and is not falling behind the curve.

Digital Disruption and the Storming of the Gates

I n 2000, at the height of what we might call the Era of Manufacturing, our friend Roberta was a young woman. In her world, conventional medical technology was well developed. Her local hospital and the local eye clinic both offered a wealth of sophisticated diagnostic tools representing the pinnacle of scientific achievement. These included x-ray machines, MRI machines, sphygmomanometers, ophthalmoscopes, electrocardiographs, heart rate monitors, breathing rate monitors, ultra-sounds, medication pumps, and many more wondrous devices.

When Roberta felt her abdominal pain, she had to go to the hospital to be examined and diagnosed. The Internet, with its dial-up modems, was not part of the system. There was no low-cost DNA sequencing.

While manufacturing had long been outsourced to offshore locations such as China, and call centers were being set up in places like the Philippines and India, the digital revolution had not yet affected medical data and analysis.

At that time, the healthcare industry controlled the *means of production*. The industry was the exclusive gatekeeper to medical technology, simply because the machines had a physical presence in a particular location. To access them, you had to show up in person.

The Music Industry Experienced Massive Digital Disruption

The healthcare industry's privileged position of being the technological gatekeeper is analogous to the conditions that the music industry had once enjoyed but that were quickly destroyed. Before the advent of the digital MP3 file, record companies owned the means of production. If a musician wanted to make a record, he or she had to sign up with one of the major labels, because only the labels had the financial and logistical wherewithal to manufacture vinyl LPs. It costs tens of thousands of dollars to record, manufacture, and distribute—by truck—physical record albums. Piracy was impractical and expensive; at home you could tape an album and then arrange to press your own vinyl "bootleg" record, but it was a costly process. In effect, the big record labels—Sony, Columbia, Elektra, and others—were the gatekeepers to the industry, and they profited handsomely.

Meanwhile, the other providers of services to artists—managers, booking agents, merchandise sellers, venue owners—operated in coordination with each other, but from within their own silos. The booking agent who arranged live performances had no business relationship with the record company. The venues in which the artist performed were not owned or operated by the label or the booking agent. When an artist released an album and went on tour, the income streams were separate, and it was up to the artist's manager to coordinate the various stakeholders. The record company made its income strictly on record sales, and the venue made its income only from ticket sales. Data necessary to coordinate a multimillion-dollar marketing campaign or tour was sent by fax from one office to another.

At the dawn of the twenty-first century, this traditional structure was challenged. The advent of the digital music file, which anyone could send over the Internet, destroyed the technological monopoly enjoyed by the record companies. In 2001, Napster was founded as a pioneering peer-to-peer file-sharing Internet service that provided software designed to allow users to exchange digital audio files, typically audio songs, encoded in MP3 format. Now anyone could buy a Nirvana LP, copy it, and distribute it to friends for free.

In 2007, the British rock band Radiohead announced it had left its corporate label and would sell its new album, *In Rainbows*, directly to fans, online, as a digital download. It even gave its fans the option to name their own price. "The traditional business model had been ruined by the Internet," Gareth Grundy, deputy editor of *Q* music magazine, told Reuters. "The industry is still trying to work out what on earth the new model or models should be, and this is just one option."

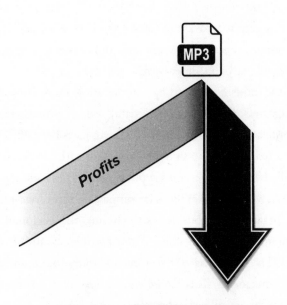

FIGURE 9.1   **The Music Industry**

The recording industry was decimated (see Figure 9.1). In 2000, before Napster, the biggest-selling physical LP was *No Strings Attached* by NSYNC. It sold a staggering 9.94 million copies. Almost overnight, control of the means of production was wrested from the big record companies, and that total was never reached again. As the industry fragmented, sales—and revenues—collapsed. By 2006, the typical bestselling LP sold less than 4 million copies. In 2013, the bestselling album, Justin Timberlake's *The 20/20 Experience*, sold a paltry 2.4 million copies. In 2018, the leader was Drake's *Scorpion*, with 3.9 million sold, including sales from streaming services.

In terms of revenue, the US recorded music industry hit a peak in 1999, with a total of $14.6 billion in all formats. The next year the decline began, and by 2015 it had hit a low of $6.7 billion.[1]

Think about what would happen if the revenues of the established healthcare industry were cut in half within a period of five years. Impossible? That's what record company executives thought in the 1990s.

Artists quickly learned that the big money was in playing concerts, not in selling records. What had once been a valuable product—a recorded song, pressed onto vinyl and sold in stores—became nearly worthless because any consumer could copy it and give it away to friends.

The music industry adapted by consolidating and by breaking down traditional barriers. Record companies and concert promoters started to integrate more services into their contracts. In October 2007, Madonna left Warner Bros. Records to sign a 10-year deal with Live Nation, which had originally been strictly a concert promoter. As *Billboard* reported, the sweeping deal, worth $120 million, encompassed "all of Madonna's future music and music-related businesses, including the exploitation of the Madonna brand, new studio albums, touring, merchandising, fan clubs/web sites, DVDs, music-related television and film projects and associated sponsorship agreements. This model will address all of Madonna's music ventures as a total entity for the first time in her career."[2]

The next year, Live Nation signed a similar deal, reportedly worth $150 million, with Jay-Z. The contract gave Live Nation participation in Jay-Z's tours, albums, publishing, and other rights.[3] This was the biggest of many such "360-degree" deals, in which the partnering organization—whether a record company or concert promoter—assumed control over a substantial part of an artist's creative output.

If you want to get a glimpse of the future of the healthcare industry, just talk to any record company executives who were around during the first decade of the twenty-first century. They will tell you about the massive disruption that no one saw coming and how they had to reinvent their business models.

Your Constituents Have Direct Access to Diagnostic Tools

Not only has the Internet made recorded music easy to access and trade—thus lowering its market value—it has also made an increasing number of medical diagnostic tests, once available only in the doctor's office, accessible to any constituent from just about anywhere.

23andMe

In 2017, the US Food and Drug Administration gave the retail genetics giant permission to sell its genetic tests and accompanying health risk reports for 10 different diseases directly to consumers. This meant that, for the first time, Americans wouldn't need a prescription to receive plain-English medical reports about their chances of developing diseases including Alzheimer's, Parkinson's, celiac disease, and other disorders based on analyses of their genetic makeup.

"The FDA has embraced innovation and has empowered people by authorizing direct access to this information," said 23andMe cofounder and CEO Anne Wojcicki in a statement. "It is a significant step forward for 23andMe and for the adoption of personal genetics."

The decision made 23andMe the first company in the United States that could provide such health reports to consumers without a prescription.[4]

This represents the first trickle of what will soon become a torrent. As Drs. George J. Annas and Sherman Elias wrote in their article "23andMe and the FDA," within the next decade or even sooner, "a majority of health plans will make it easy for their members to have their entire genomes sequenced and linked to their electronic health records and will provide software to help people interrogate their own genomes, with or without the help of their physicians or a genetic counselor supplied by the health plan."[5]

Today, dozens of companies currently offer direct-to-consumer genetic tests for a variety of purposes. Such tests are marketed directly to customers via television, print advertisements, or the Internet, and the tests can be bought online or in stores. Customers send a DNA sample to the company and then receive their results by logging onto a secure website or getting a written report. The system provides constituents access to their genetic information without involving a health insurance company or healthcare provider in the process.[6]

Symptomate.com

This website offers your constituents what is described as a short, safe, and anonymous health checkup. Let's say that Roberta tries the checkup. After asking for her age and gender, the website shows her an anatomical drawing of a woman and asks her to indicate the part of the body that is bothering her (she says her knees), the symptoms (stiffness, pain during movement) she is having, and some other questions. At the end, the website tells her that she should seek prompt medical attention and that her symptoms suggested knee osteoarthritis.[7]

Symptomate is owned and operated by Infermedica Sp. z o.o., a company registered and based in Poland. The company is not in the business of healthcare but of data mining. As its terms of use make perfectly clear, "Symptomate must be assured that it has the right to use the content that is posted to its Site by its Users. Such content may include, but is not limited to, the arrangement of data that you upload about yourself (such as your name, email address, physical attributes, etc.). Whenever submitting content to our website, you agree that you are granting us a non-exclusive, universal, perpetual, irrevocable, sublicensable, commercial and non-commercial right to use, distribute, sell, publish, and otherwise make use of the content that you submit to us."[8]

WebMD

This popular site offers a similar self-diagnosis. After entering various symptoms (this time Roberta said it was a headache), the site advised her that she might be suffering from tension headache or hypertension.

As for the information the user inputs into any of WebMD's services, data mining is part of the company's business plan. As the site's privacy policy states clearly, "We may share your information with our subsidiaries, affiliates and companies acquired by or merged with us and our affiliates."[9]

Essilor.com

Essilor International S.A. is a French-based international ophthalmic optics company that designs, manufactures, and markets lenses to correct or protect eyesight. The world's largest manufacturer of ophthalmic lenses, the company created Varilux, the world's first progressive lens that corrects presbyopia and allows clear vision in the wearer's near, intermediate, and far vision.

On the website, you can take an online vision test. As the website carefully points out, "Vision tests . . . do not replace the eye exams that evaluate ocular motility, visual fields, eye structures and the fundus."

Users take a series of vision tests on their computer or other device, and if a problem is detected, related information is offered. The website seeks not to supplant ophthalmologists, but to drive business toward them. It's a sophisticated lead-generating platform.

The company considers innovation to be a vital part of its identity. As the website says, "Visual health needs are changing. Our industry is today challenged by major societal trends such as aging populations, new digital behaviors, the emergence of middle classes and the purchasing abilities of low-income consumers in high growth countries. With over €200 million each year devoted to research and development, 45 percent of the products we market today were created less than three years ago."[10]

Babylon Health

The website of this London-based company is very forthright: "Babylon is a digital healthcare provider on a mission to put an accessible and affordable health service in the hands of every person on earth."[11]

The company's core product is a digital healthcare app using a mixture of artificial intelligence (AI) and video and text consultations with doctors and specialists. The long-range plan is to move to full diagnosis by AI. Dr. Ali Parsa, founder and CEO of Babylon, said in a statement: "Cutting edge artificial intelligence together with ever increasing advances in medicine means that the promise of global good health is nearer than most people realize. Babylon scientists predict that *we will shortly be able to diagnose and foresee personal health issues better than doctors*, but this is about machines and medics co-operating, not competing" (emphasis added).[12]

Investors like it. In January 2016, Babylon raised $25 million in funding from its Series A round, which at the time was the most funding raised for a digital health venture in Europe. In April 2017, it raised a further $60 million to develop its artificial intelligence capabilities.[13]

In the healthcare industry, AI, which I'll talk about more in the pages ahead, is an increasingly disruptive force. As the consulting and research firm Frost & Sullivan reported, the need for both deep data mining and clear decision-making has put AI-enabled solutions at the forefront of the healthcare revolution. Their analysis estimates market earned revenues of $6.6 billion in 2021 at a compound annual growth rate of 40 percent.[14]

A Lab in a Smartphone

Two University of Illinois researchers developed a camera that could vastly improve the mobile health (or mHealth) diagnostic capabilities of a smartphone. Funded by a National Science Foundation grant, UI professors Brian Cunningham and John Dallesasse created a "science camera" that can conduct optical spectronoscopy. The technology creates and then disseminates LED light through a linear variable filter, enabling the user to read liquid- or paper-based medical tests.

Fitted into a smartphone, the technology could allow users to conduct a wide variety of medical tests that previously have been limited to the clinic or lab, enabling them to test themselves for poor nutrition, cardiac health, sepsis, cancer, pregnancy, drugs, hormones, infectious diseases, and more. As Eric Wicklund wrote for mHealthIntelligence, "A smartphone could be used to test for and begin treatment of diseases like hepatitis, malaria, HIV/AIDS, even Zika and Ebola in remote locations."[15]

Smartphone Microscopes

Smartphone microscopes can be purchased as attachments to smartphones, costing roughly $85 each.

Researchers at the University of Texas Health Science Center at Houston have reported using smartphone microscopes to diagnose non-melanoma skin cancers with about 90 percent accuracy and melanomas with about 60 percent accuracy.[16]

Self-Diagnosis on the Internet

It's become increasingly common for your constituents to seek medical advice online before they call their primary care physician. As board-certified internist Dana Corriel, MD, who refers to this phenomenon as "Google University," told Byrdie.com, "I would estimate that in a typical full day of seeing patients, about a third have searched the internet looking for answers by the time they see me. . . . Think of the steps involved in getting a proper diagnosis. You spend time trying to make an appointment, accommodate your schedule for it, spend the time on travel, and this before any of the aggravating factors involved in dealing with the office visit itself. . . . It's sometimes just easier for a person to Google their symptom."[17]

This produces huge challenges for healthcare providers:

- While the Internet is full of good information, it's equally loaded with dangerous nonsense. For example, a persistent cough can be a symptom of a common cold or lung cancer. People who have a cough can go online and either panic because they become convinced they have cancer when it's just a cold, or tell themselves it's just a cold when, in fact, an x-ray would reveal lung cancer. When your constituents take action based on incomplete information, the results can be damaging to their health.

- Constituents are increasingly going to their doctors with preconceived ideas about their supposed illness and how it should be treated. While it's good to have an informed and engaged patient, one of the most important steps in making an accurate diagnosis is to keep an open mind and not jump to conclusions. Sometimes a headache is just a headache, but every once in a while it's really a tumor, and the physician needs to be willing to recognize it.

  Pharmaceutical companies aren't helping. Too many television and print ads describe a disease and then say, "Ask your doctor if Drug X is right for you." They want the constituent to go to the doctor and say, "I have these various symptoms, and I believe I might need Drug X."

  Such circumstances counter the desired goal of every healthcare professional, which is to make the practice of medicine more personalized. By blanketing the airwaves with generalized ads for drugs, the effect is to make medicine more of a bulk commodity, where you advertise a disease, assemble a population of prospective customers, and sell them the drug.

- Cyberchondria is the unfounded escalation of concerns about common symptomology based on the constituent's search for information online. It can range from a temporary neurotic excess to adjunct hypochondria. Among many healthcare practitioners, cyberchondria is a growing concern, as patients can now research and discover symptoms of a rare disease, become convinced they have it, and manifest a state of medical anxiety.

- Online symptom checkers tend to be overly cautious, encouraging users to seek professional care for situations where staying at home might be reasonable. This tendency toward conservative advice— no doubt driven by the desire to avoid legal liability—encourages people to seek unnecessary care, which drives up costs.

SmileDirectClub

Getting braces on your teeth used to be a significant event in the life of a young person. You'd go to the orthodontist, where you'd be x-rayed and fitted for metal braces; when you went to school the next day, you were given the honorary nickname of "metal mouth" or "brace face." You had to go to an orthodontist because he or she controlled the means of production: braces were highly specialized devices that required technology available only from the dentist.

The advent of 3-D printing changed that. To make the initial impression of their teeth, customers can either visit their local mall and go to a "SmileShop" for a scan, or they can use a remote impression kit. The company says the impressions are reviewed by a duly licensed dentist or orthodontist before a set of molds is created. The customer receives a preview image of what his or her realigned teeth will look like. If he or she approves, then SmileDirectClub sends a supply of graduating clear plastic liners. Dentists monitor the customer's progress by looking at selfies the customer sends over the Internet. After six months, on average, the treatment is concluded.

The current price is $1,895, compared with $5,000 to $8,000 for a traditional orthodontist using the industry-leading Invisalign system created by Align Technology Inc.

Seeing the writing on the wall, the American Association of Orthodontists, which represents 19,000 members in the United States and abroad, filed complaints with 36 state dental boards, alleging that SmileDirectClub violated regulatory standards. "I don't think the diagnosis can happen with three clicks," Hera Kim-Berman, a clinical assistant professor at the University of Michigan's department of orthodontics and pediatric dentistry and the program director of orthodontic graduate training, told *Bloomberg News*. "These companies treat them as consumers, as clients, and that's really the major difference."[18]

The global orthodontics market is worth fighting for: including traditional braces, it's projected to increase from $1.5 billion in 2016 to $2.6 billion by 2023, according to Allied Market Research.[19]

CrowdMed: Diagnosis by the Crowd

The community funding of product development projects through sites such as GoFundMe has become ubiquitous.

How about the diagnosing of disease?

On CrowdMed.com, users can post their case with the CrowdMed community by answering the online questionnaire that covers their medical history, current symptoms, and personal story. Then, as the website says, "Medical detectives lend their unique sets of expertise to work together and provide patients with information to solve their case." Then, based on the information provided by the community, the customer receives a report with the top diagnostic and solution suggestions to take to their physician for testing.

So the hapless primary care provider is put into the position of seeing patients come to their appointments armed with a diagnosis provided by a bunch of strangers on the Internet.

To be fair, CrowdMed pitches itself as the solution of last resort when regular doctors have failed to diagnose a set of symptoms presented by a patient. On a TED Talk, executive chairman Jared Heyman explained that the average CrowdMed customer had been sick for eight years, seen eight doctors, and incurred more than $50,000 in medical expenses (presumably related to the person's mystery illness). He said that half these patients reported that the crowd successfully brought them closer to a correct diagnosis or cure.[20]

Except for the disruptive threat to orthodontists posed by companies such as SmileDirectClub, you could argue that, individually, none of these examples is particularly disruptive to the massive healthcare industry. That could be true. But storm clouds are on the horizon. Remember the fate of the music industry. In 1982, the first digital compact disc (CD) was marketed. It was a recording from 1979 of Claudio Arrau performing Chopin waltzes. It was a curiosity, but the curiosity quickly became the industry standard. For the next 20 years, CDs were actually a huge boon to the music industry, as fans clamored to buy old recordings by their favorite artists. In 1992, *ABBA Gold*, a greatest hits collection by the Swedish band, sold a record 4 million CDs. For the label, PolyGram, it was practically pure profit.[21]

But while record company executives quaffed their champagne in celebration of record revenues from sales of CDs, they didn't realize the same digital technology that made CDs possible would be their Achilles' heel. When you download a CD onto your computer, you get a digital file. As soon as the Internet became capable of quickly transmitting files that were five megabytes in size—the typical three-minute song—the game was over. The Huns had stormed the castle and taken the means of production—the technology monopoly—away from the royals huddled within. Music industry revenues plunged, and people wondered whether the industry could even survive.

The healthcare industry is vastly more complex than the music industry, but the digital revolution will soon be at the castle gates. Will you be ready?

TAKE ACTION!

- Do not be complacent. Do not believe that because there is something "special" or even "holy" about the healthcare industry, that it's immune from massive disruption. It's not immune. People—your constituents—will seek comfort and healing from wherever they can get it, including from the Internet.

- WebMD is owned by a company called Internet Brands, based in El Segundo, California. During 2015, the most recent year for which data is available, WebMD reached more unique visitors each month than any other leading private or government healthcare website, making it the leading health publisher in the United States. In the fourth quarter of 2016, WebMD recorded an average of 179.5 million unique users per month and 3.63 billion page views per quarter.[22]

  The question is, what is your healthcare organization doing to capture a chunk of this market? Like it or not, this is the wave of the future, and you can either ride it or be wiped out.

  Ask yourself, "Is my healthcare company allowing my constituents to seek out WebMD? Is WebMD building its brand loyalty among consumers while we sit by and watch?"

  Disruption often goes unrecognized. In the early 2000s, Blockbuster video rentals failed to acknowledge the disruption posed by the Netflix mail model until it was too late. Instead of dismissing sites such as WebMD, ask yourself how your organization can meet the needs of those constituents.

The Constituent as a Consumer

For some caregivers, calling the constituent or patient a "consumer" is considered profanity. It's offensive to their sensibilities because for centuries they've enjoyed the professional ability to have a *doctor-centered delivery model*.

This means that the service provided by the physician is so mysterious and vital that the patient—the consumer—should feel grateful to receive it and should be willing to tolerate delays and high prices to get it. The naysayers who claim we shouldn't call our constituents "consumers" try to justify this bold proclamation with a barrage of unconvincing rhetoric. This is because they're accustomed to making their patients wait for an hour to see them and then charging them for the privilege.

It's analogous to buying an exotic sports car. If you walked into your local Bentley dealer and said you wanted to buy a new $500,000 Bacalar, the dealer would tell you that you could have your car in a year. You'd accept this because the car is custom built, and, well, it's a Bentley.

On the other hand, suppose you walked into your local Ford dealer and said you wanted a new $30,000 F-150 pickup truck. If the dealer said you could have your truck in a year, you'd reply, "Are you insane? It's a pickup truck! I want to drive it off the lot today!"

For generations, doctors have been like Bentley dealers. The problem is that their constituents—healthcare consumers—are beginning to think of them as Ford dealers. And you know what? If you're just trying to get from point A to point B, a Ford is as good as a Bentley.

Whether an organization is providing healthcare services or selling motor vehicles, customer service (also called consumer service or constituent service, or CX for short) is critically important. In the healthcare industry, the days of assuming that the delivery of safe and efficacious care justifies any unpleasant consumer experience are over. Each and every year, your organization's constituents will be given more choices, and they will continue to make the choices that deliver the highest transparent value and experience.

Will this negatively impact the quality of care? There's a good argument that improving patient insights and designing better patient journeys will deliver safer and more efficacious care than the old-fashioned model. As a chief innovation officer and adjunct professor at a health science university, I'm a staunch advocate for the amazing doctors we educate. But the argument that we shouldn't call healthcare constituents and patients "consumers" for some clinical reason is absurd. In fact, some of the best universities in the world are now teaching their medical students methods that improve the quality of the human experience, not just clinical care.

Consumers Choose the Best Experience

There is a movement toward the term "patient experience" (PX), as many healthcare providers remain uncomfortable with the term "customer" or "consumer." In fact, I was told by one primary care physician that the term "consumer" is disrespectful to the patient. The truth of the matter is, this particular physician was more concerned that the term was disrespectful to *him*. He went on to tell me that he is a learned physician, not a counter person at McDonald's.

I take a lot of heat for this assertion, but I must say he is dead wrong. Studies show that while patients have virtually no way of determining clinical efficacy, they're experts on knowing what their *experience* was like. As the economic models rapidly change, consumers will select the best experience, as they have no idea in most cases what is the best clinical delivery.

In the work I do with drug companies, pharmaceutical firms, and major hospital systems, I see that this shift to the delivery of healthcare as a "consumer product" is meeting much resistance. Be that as it may, in my consulting practice we have a simple policy: if an executive can't call a patient a consumer, we can't help that executive. It is said that words matter, and the term "consumer" changes the philosophic vantage point to allow the cultural shift to occur.

The "Uberfication" of Healthcare Delivery

The term "uberfication" speaks to the Uber phenomenon. Founded in 2009, this San Francisco–based company has nearly destroyed the traditional taxicab industry. Using self-employed freelance drivers, Uber created a new system whereby passengers use an app to order a ride, at which time they are quoted the fare. Uber uses a "dynamic pricing model," in which prices for the same route vary based on the supply and demand for rides at the time the ride is requested. So if you want to ride from Times Square to Wall Street at rush hour, it's going to cost you more than if you ordered your ride on a quiet Sunday morning.

Uber didn't reinvent the *vehicle*. It reinvented the business model and eliminated the middleman—the taxi company and dispatcher. Customers deal directly with the driver, while the corporate parent hovers, unseen, in the background.

You can call these interactions *moments of transportation*. Similarly, Apple reinvented moments of the machine, Amazon reinvented moments of merchandise, Spotify reinvented moments of music, and Netflix reinvented moments of movies.

One of the big changes in healthcare will be the reinvention of *moments of medicine.*

The agility of the Uber business model, which was made possible by advanced digital communications and data processing, has made these moments of urban mobility much more immediate. As an analogy, a moment in healthcare would be moving from a constituent making an appointment for an annual physical checkup to experiencing real-time health monitoring. It circumvents the need for the constituent to report a health issue during an available window of time. It means the intermediary is being eliminated. Intelligent apps, wearables, and other personal devices enable constituents to measure vital signs and send that information remotely to their healthcare professionals. They don't need the traditional healthcare framework.

This uberfication of healthcare is a strong indication that smart apps and devices are scaling to a point where we can see changes in everyday life. Instead of calling the doctor and setting an appointment for a time in the future, people now have other options: Doctor on Demand, TalkSession, Twine Health, and One Medical are just a few digital health startups that are leading the way in providing consumers direct access to doctors through their smartphones. If you're not familiar with these companies, here's snapshot of what they offer.

Doctor on Demand says it is "rethinking the way you receive care. . . . Our approach to care is all about breaking down the walls of an office and supporting your health wherever you are. Our US-based, board-certified physicians and licensed psychiatrists and psychologists are available on your schedule."[1] The company claims to be able to provide services in urgent care, behavioral health, preventive health, and chronic care.

The "telemedicine" company is really a referral service, and the website carefully notes, "Doctor On Demand, Inc. does not itself provide any physician, mental health, or other healthcare provider services."

Founded in 2013 by Melissa Thompson, TalkSession is another referral service, one dedicated to making mental healthcare accessible through remote therapy sessions between mental healthcare providers and patients. Thompson's innovative approach to remote therapy won her a prestigious position in GE & Startup Health Academy's Entrepreneurship Program as a "healthcare transformer," as well as a Life Sciences Award from the respected Springboard Enterprises accelerator for women-founded healthcare ventures.[2]

Bought by Fitbit in 2018, software company Twine Health has developed an innovative health coaching platform that empowers people to achieve better health outcomes and helps health systems, health plans, and workplace health providers lower healthcare costs. A HIPAA-compliant connected health platform, the service helps constituents manage their chronic conditions, including diabetes and hypertension, and facilitates lifestyle interventions, including weight loss and smoking cessation, by making it easy for care teams of providers, coaches, friends, and family to collaborate on care plans.[3]

One Medical seeks to blend the delivery of virtual services with nationwide bricks-and-mortar locations and a monthly membership revenue model. As of late 2019, the company operated over 70 offices in 9 major markets across the country. In addition to a direct-to-consumer membership model, One Medical contracts with nearly 6,000 companies to provide One Medical health benefits to their employees, including access to primary care providers at offices near where they work, as well as 24/7 access to virtual care.

If you're a traditional bricks-and-mortar healthcare provider, think of yourself as being in the taxicab business. One Medical is striving to be like Uber and pluck your fare off the sidewalk long before you arrive. You can complain that Uber drivers are less qualified than your taxi drivers, but consumers—patients, if you prefer—don't care as long as they get to their destination.

Why the Healthcare Industry Is Different

It's true that healthcare constituents are increasingly feeling and acting like consumers. But as Olubanke Babalola pointed out in his research paper "Consumers and Their Demand for Healthcare," in the healthcare industry the relationship between the consumer and the provider is unlike that in any other industry. Uniquely, healthcare is:

1. **Highly personalized.** Every consumer is chemically, structurally, and emotionally different from the next one. An approach or treatment that works for one person may not necessarily work for another.

2. **Relatively inflexible in provider choice.** Especially for those who are low income or uninsured, people don't usually "shop around" for a doctor, and treatment has to be provided to patients in places like the emergency room regardless of patients' ability to pay.

3. **Paid by third parties.** Healthcare professionals are rarely paid directly by their patients; payment usually comes from government or insurance companies.

4. **An investment.** The money that constituents spend on being healthy today will also benefit them in the future.

5. **Inelastic in its demand.** If constituents are sick and require medical care, they will purchase healthcare services at almost any price, even if it means going into debt.

6. **Not fungible.** It is not possible to swap either "good health" or treatments between constituents. For instance, constituent A, who is nearsighted, cannot exchange that condition with constituent B, who is farsighted. But if they want to trade automobiles, it's no problem.

7. **A market where you cannot "test" the service before buying.** For instance, if Susan is thinking of purchasing a new dishwasher, the company offering this product can give her a 30-day

free trial period. In healthcare, this type of offer is not possible. A patient cannot have a 30-day trial for a new heart valve. If the surgery is less than successful and no malpractice is indicated, there can be no refund and no recourse.[4]

The Framework of Consumer Experience Innovation

Today, disruptive innovators are looking to destroy the old-fashioned friction-laden patient experience with fast, beautiful, and economical alternatives. Healthcare professionals need to start looking at healthcare delivery through the eyes of their constituents, and ask, "What do they want? And what's stopping us from giving it to them? Why should an upstart company undercut our business model, slowly eroding our constituent base?"

In healthcare, consumer experience innovation is the process of collaborating with patient-facing stakeholders to gain insights into how to improve their experience. This includes, but is certainly not limited to, the reduction of friction and wait times, more scheduling options, flexible office visits, blended experiences that include telemedicine and clinic visits, and improved patient engagement.

Historically, much of healthcare has focused on developing clinical and surgical solutions with little thought to the human experience. This was because patients had little choice in who would treat them and how; despite naïve assertions to the contrary by some politicians, when consumers are looking for a doctor to cure their disease, it's extremely difficult to "shop around" for the best provider. People used to say, "Oh, after getting a diagnosis from your doctor, you should always get a second opinion." But a 2010 Gallup poll found that 70 percent of Americans don't feel the need to check for a second opinion or do additional research.[5] The poll said this was because patients felt confident in the accuracy of their doctor's advice, but everyone knows it's a pain in the neck to find a second doctor, get an appointment, and then get your health insurer to pay for it.

Over time, this reality transitioned into an experience in many hospitals and clinics that was akin to visiting the department of motor vehicles. Patients would wait for an hour to see a doctor and would have to fill out the same form for the umpteenth time. In fact, in many hospitals and clinics, patients were treated as if the caregiver were doing them a favor to see them. This problem was exacerbated by a dysfunctional system that punished caregivers for spending time with their patients. The net result was a disastrous experience that also in many cases adversely impacted the quality of patient clinical care.

The healthcare industry began to realize it was losing patients to far more beautiful clinical models. So what did people in the industry do? They implemented what I consider a "swipe" at resolving the problem. That is, they started developing patient experience programs designed to improve the patient's experience when compared with historical healthcare human experiences. Although well meaning, many of these programs were nothing more than bumper stickers and slogans.

A constituent is someone for whom you are responsible. A patient is someone you are treating for a disease. Every healthcare provider should have many more constituents than patients.

In a time of hyperconsumerism, you must realize that you are now competing with Amazon, Apple, Google, and thousands of other consumer experts, and that means you need to go to a completely new level. In my book *What Customers Crave*, I identified three things that you need to do to master consumer experience design:

1. You need to accept the fact that your constituents have no way of judging clinical efficacy.
2. You need to recognize that constituents judge you based on their experience, and they also rate you on social and digital platforms, not based on clinical care but on human experience.

3. You also must identify the range of customers that you serve through consumer personification, and develop thoughtful journey maps to ensure that you're delivering exceptional experiences across all touchpoints.

The Patient Consumerization Maturity Model

The best organizations in healthcare today are transitioning beyond improving the patient experience to creating a holistic and thoughtful constituent experience design. They have moved through three clearly defined levels (see Figure 10.1):

1. **The lowest level.** This is the world of autocratic, doctor-centered patient experiences. The customer experience most closely resembles a visit to the department of motor vehicles.

2. **The middle.** The healthcare provider has some awareness of the necessity to compete for patients and satisfy them the same way any other company would seek to satisfy its customers. But it's an incremental approach toward patient experience, coupled with a lack of acceptance of true hyperconsumerization, so it's still not on par with other service industries.

3. **The top.** Here we find friction-free, relevant, and customized constituent experiences that blend the physical and digital channels. Concurrently, the healthcare organization is moving decisively from a hard focus on diagnosis and treatment to include more resources devoted to anticipation and prevention.

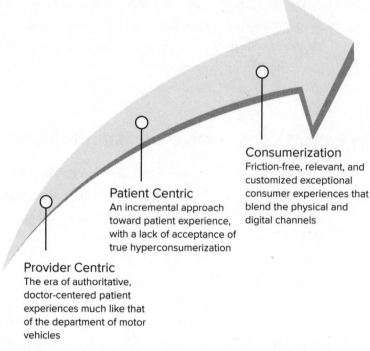

Consumerization
Friction-free, relevant, and customized exceptional consumer experiences that blend the physical and digital channels

Patient Centric
An incremental approach toward patient experience, with a lack of acceptance of true hyperconsumerization

Provider Centric
The era of authoritative, doctor-centered patient experiences much like that of the department of motor vehicles

FIGURE 10.1 The Patient Consumerization Maturity Model

Constituent Personification

If a healthcare organization insists on treating its constituents as the beneficiaries of a rare and mysterious service that they should happily stand in line to receive, that healthcare organization has every right to do so. It also has the right to see its constituent base slowly shrink, as more agile providers give the constituents what they want, which is unfettered access to quality healthcare with a focus on wellness. It does no good to complain about the poor choices constituents make. It would be more useful to provide *better* service than the upstarts.

Our current healthcare industry tends to deliver one-size-fits-all care to a monolithic patient. This is perhaps no more true than in the pharmaceutical industry, which deals in volume percentages in large populations. In addition to being erroneously lumped together, patients have also suffered from the opposite assault and have been segmented and pigeonholed by some very disturbing demographics and factors. Some healthcare practices cynically divide their patients according to how they pay their bills—in other words, uninsured self-payers (the worst), Medicaid (better), and private insurance (the gold mine).

In a mistaken effort to provide better customer service, some industries like to group customers according to preconceived demographics. They believe that baby boomers are somehow different from the so-called millennials, and that rich people behave differently from middle-class consumers, and that Republican customers have different expectations than Democrats.

In reality, when thinking about how your constituents access and use your healthcare services, the best way to identify the various constituents you serve is to break them up into constituent personas based on what they *dislike* and what they *like*. And guess what? This usually has *nothing to do* with their demographic basket.

Anyone who has ever operated a retail store can tell you that when customers walk through the door, you have no way of knowing what they expect until you interact with them. Some customers—whether aged 30 or 80—are like heat-seeking missiles. They want to get in, do their business, and get out. Others are chatty. They want to get a personal feeling for the store and the product. Others need guidance and ask a lot of questions.

These different types each expect their interactions with the store to conform to what they have in mind. If it doesn't, they'll go elsewhere.

And yes, there are those rare, easygoing people who have no objection to sitting and waiting for service. But don't count on there being many of them!

The Importance of Positive Touchpoints

In terms of the experience your constituents expect, it's becoming increasingly important to meet them on their own turf, so to speak. And every interaction with your constituents must be frictionless and positive, meaning it must leave them happy to proceed with the next interaction. These interactions are called touchpoints.

A touchpoint is any contact your constituent has with the healthcare organization or medical staff. Generally speaking, there are five levels of touchpoints. Together, they make up the constituent journey.

1. The Pretouch Moment

This comes before any actual interaction with the organization. Here, the constituent develops an awareness of your brand or service and is thinking about contacting you. What your potential constituent thinks about the organization, and imagines will happen when he or she interacts with it, is very important. One persona type may see your organization as being tough and no-nonsense—and is pleased with that—while another may see it as a warm, caring place where every question is answered.

Both viewpoints must be correct. For example, on your website, make available all the information that anyone would need, but also clearly mark the buttons that will take the focused visitor directly to the sign-up page.

2. The First Touch

This is exactly what it sounds like: the first interaction between your brand and your potential constituent. It could be digital, nondigital, or both. The prospect might fill out an information form on the website or pick up the phone and call. The variety of your constituent types will determine how you design the range of those first touchpoints.

One of the masters of the first touch is Domino's Pizza. (If you object to your healthcare organization being compared with a pizza delivery service that has been ranked number one in its industry for several decades, then I urge you to rethink your relationship with your constituents.) You can order a Domino's pizza through:

- Google Home
- Facebook Messenger
- Domino's.com
- Text message
- Twitter
- Domino's Zero Click app
- Amazon Alexa
- Samsung smart TV
- Ford Sync Applink in Ford cars
- Many smartwatches including Apple Watch and Pebble Smartwatch
- Siri
- Mobile and iPad apps
- Conventional telephone
- In-person contact—walking into the store

A very important touchpoint is when the constituent feels ill and calls the doctor. In the old days, if the receptionist—who was always on lunch break from noon until one o'clock and was therefore unavailable—told the caller that the first opening was in two weeks, the caller would probably say, "OK, I'll take it." This was because constituents rarely changed doctors. You had your primary care physician, and unless he or she did something really terrible, you stuck with that doctor.

How many ways can your constituents access your services? By calling on the phone and hoping to connect to your receptionist?

3. The Core Touchpoint

This is when your constituents are actually engaging with your service.

They are talking to a doctor on the phone, sitting in the waiting room, seeing the nurse practitioner, or being examined or treated by the doctor.

Suffice it to say, there are many difficult moments when the skill and professionalism of the healthcare provider must shine through. It goes without saying that sometimes doctors and nurses need to deliver very bad news. They need to tell a patient he or she has a serious disease, or even tell a family a loved one has died. It's when you can rightly say, "We're not just selling pizza here," and you'd be right.

But there are also countless interactions that are relatively innocuous, such as when the constituent arrives and is convinced he or she has cancer when it's just a head cold. In such cases, healthcare providers need to balance their duty to inform against the constituent personas and their expectations.

4. The Follow-Up Touches

In healthcare, follow-up is often very important. The patient leaves the hospital or clinic having undergone a procedure. The patient may have a prescription for medication or instructions to return to have stitches removed. The patient may need physical therapy or a second procedure. Or perhaps the patient may need to be informed of the results of tests.

While the rules of medical ethics control much of how and what is communicated, the rules of commerce dictate how patients will feel about their interactions with their healthcare providers. In every case, patients need to be treated like constituents whose health and well-being are an ongoing concern of their healthcare providers.

5. The Perpetual Touch

This newly emerging touchpoint will resemble the relationship that consumers have with utility companies—their electric company or phone company.

As your constituents become increasingly connected via digital devices to 24/7 health monitors, the touch will be never-ending. It will require ongoing maintenance and careful attention to the constituent experience. The constituents, their data, and their expectations will need to be handled with the utmost tact and sensitivity. The rewards for proactively pursuing better health—losing weight, quitting smoking, getting more exercise—must be significant.

Because of the emerging hyperconnectivity via mobile devices, constituents are experiencing the world in a blended way. In other words, their smartphone is rapidly becoming their "physician in their pocket," and they leverage it throughout the day to enhance their health and wellness. The healthcare ecosystem is rapidly building a maturity model around how to blend the digital engagement with the physical engagement of the patient, thereby providing enhanced care and better human experiences.

Thanks to digital technology, the traditional series of discrete touches will turn into a continuous relationship, which can, and should, produce better health and lower costs. But if constituents become unhappy, they will do what consumers do: If they can, they will ditch their utility—cable company or phone service—and get another. If they can't change, they will fume and complain.

Don't Count on Constituent Loyalty

Today, constituents have less loyalty. Unless they're forced by their health plan to deal only with their primary care physician, they're likely to go online and get their own diagnosis or find another doctor. Patients are increasingly impatient. You can face reality and deal with it, or you can retreat into sameness and let the world pass you by.

TAKE ACTION!

There are three very straightforward steps that healthcare organizations can take to build out an exceptional constituent experience (CX).

1. **CX readiness assessment.** The readiness assessment should ask tough questions about the systems, methods, processes, tools, technologies, training, and culture. In my work, we look at about 60

different key indicators through a scorecard process. It's shocking to me how many organizations deploy on constituent experience without first doing an accurate diagnosis. As a healthcare professional, you don't need to be told that the best treatment plan begins with an accurate diagnosis.

2. **Comprehensive CX road map.** Once you've identified resource and other gaps, you will be ready to build out your CX road map that includes everything necessary to create a positive constituent experience. This includes internal branding, executive and team training, improved patient insights, and the creation of an engagement strategy in a wide range of new innovations that will set your healthcare organization apart in both the quality of clinical care and the quality of human experience. Keep in mind that there is no better way to grow a healthcare organization and to improve quality of work life than through a properly deployed CX plan.

3. **CX road map deployment.** When it comes to the deployment of their constituent experience plan, most organizations never pull out of the driveway. Like any strategic initiative, CX plans require deployment with great prejudice, scalability, and sustainability. We're talking about a cultural shift, and that takes time. Build comprehensive success measurements and report them across the enterprise regularly.

The Constituent Healthcare Operating System

The Healthcare Mandate does not call for our current healthcare system to be needlessly or arbitrarily changed for the sake of change. Nor does it call for our current healthcare system to be reengineered to satisfy the whims of one political interest group or another. Instead, it calls for the transformation of our struggling healthcare system to be based on *reality*: specifically, the reality of technological innovation, rampant lifestyle diseases, and the massive change in how our constituents view the healthcare system.

Our current healthcare system has been built on the premise that as free citizens we have the right to do whatever we want to our bodies, and if we get sick, we can go to the doctor and be healed. This time-honored tradition dates from the days when our behavior was *self-limited by our circumstances*. By this I mean there were literally fewer opportunities for each of us to engage in unhealthy habits.

To explore this change, let's go back to 1970.

As Jeanine Bentley wrote in the 2017 USDA report "US Trends in Food Availability and a Dietary Assessment of Loss-Adjusted Food Availability, 1970–2014," in recent decades Americans have had access to more and more food, and we're consuming it in greater quantities than ever before in human history. Since 1970, the obesity rate in the United States has almost tripled for adults and more than tripled for children and adolescents. Growing concern over poor dietary habits and physical inactivity impacting the health of the American population has focused attention on the quantity and quality of food Americans eat.

Table 11.1 presents a comparison of the number and type of calories consumed by the average American per day in 1970 and, 34 years later, in 2014.[1] In calories consumed, there's an increase of over 20 percent.

FOOD TYPE	CALORIES, 1970	CALORIES, 2014
Fruits and vegetables	197	211
Grains	409	525
Added fats and oils	337	562
Meat, eggs, and nuts	506	513
Added sugar and sweeteners	333	366
Total	1,782	2,177

TABLE 11.1   Type and Number of Calories Consumed in 1970 and 2014

In some situations, consuming more calories is not a problem because active people need a lot of energy. On a race day, the typical marathon runner needs to consume as much as 2,500 calories in addition to those needed to sustain life, meaning some runners should eat 5,000 calories a day. An elite cyclist might consume 8,000 calories a day or more on a long-distance ride. Olympic swimmer Michael Phelps reported that when training, he ate as much as 12,000 calories a day. Anyone who works outside and walks or performs labor is going to need more calories than the recommended average intake.

The problem is that while Americans are *eating more*, most of us are *moving less*. In "Trends in Sedentary Behavior Among the US Population, 2001–2016," Lin Yang, PhD, and others found that most Americans spend at least two hours a day watching television or videos, and they are becoming more sedentary as they devote more remaining free time to sitting in front of computers.[2]

The fundamental nature of work has changed, from hands-on labor to sitting in an office. Between 2000 and 2010, US manufacturing employment plummeted by a third, as nearly 6 million American factory workers lost their jobs. As anyone who has worked in a factory knows, it's labor you typically do standing up, burning calories. We're doing a lot less of that these days.

"As our daily life demands less physical activity," said lead study author Lin Yang of the University of Calgary to Reuters, "we accumulate sedentary time from sitting at school and work, from motorized transport, watching TV, computer use, and so on," all of which may be driving recent increases in total sitting time.[3]

And back in 1970, the worst bad habits most middle-class people had were smoking and drinking. Today, we have deadly opioids. Researchers say the number of individuals using illicit opioids is projected to increase by 61 percent by 2025—from 0.93 million in 2015 to 1.50 million just 10 years later. And between 2016 and 2025, the number of individuals in the United States projected to die from opioid overdose is 700,400, with 80 percent of the deaths attributable to illicit opioids.[4]

For society, obesity and opioid addiction and death are costly. If you become obese and suffer resulting health problems, you will pay a price, but your neighbors will pay also. Obesity may prove to be one of humankind's worst and most expensive maladies. Research by McKinsey & Company suggests the impact of obesity on global GDP is $2.1 trillion, only slightly less that of smoking and the combined classification of armed violence, war, and terrorism.[5]

For over a century, we've done a good job of attacking infectious diseases and fixing mechanical problems. We can give you a new heart if you need one, and we can craft a new set of legs or hands. These play to our traditional skills. But sadly, we have not been very effective at combating lifestyle diseases, which are extremely complex and often do not have a clearly identifiable cause. Despite years of research, we still do not know the exact cause of Alzheimer's disease, nor do we have a cure, although we all hope that one will be found. It's unclear why so many people overeat and develop obesity, along with all its attendant complications, including diabetes, sleep disorders, joint problems, and heart conditions. Unlike infectious diseases, lifestyle diseases seem to involve the mind and the body equally.

In the healthcare industry, there is growing awareness that lifestyle diseases need to be approached differently from infectious diseases and mechanical problems. But to date, this growing awareness has not translated into focused national action. In many ways, we are behind the curve.

The bottom line is that the rise of lifestyle diseases, which are generally self-inflicted and drain enormous wealth from society, belies the assertion, "It ain't nobody's business what I do with my body." It becomes your neighbor's business when you ask your neighbor to help pay for the disease you have caused by your personal habits.

Amid the healthcare crisis we're now facing, there's good news: We now have the capability to collect and leverage vast amounts of digital data about the day-to-day health of each one of our 330 million citizens. This is a good thing.

The challenge—our *mandate*—is to reinvent our healthcare system to leverage these new technologies in the service of enhancing the wellness of our constituents, as well as treating them when they become our patients. The linchpin of the reinvented healthcare system will be the constituent healthcare operating system (CHOS).

The Five Steps of the CHOS

The future of constituent care will be driven by the five-step constituent healthcare operating system, to which every individual constituent will be connected. These are the five steps:

1. Capture and store data.
2. Cleanse data.
3. Turn data into information.
4. Respond with appropriate intervention.
5. Drive behavioral change.

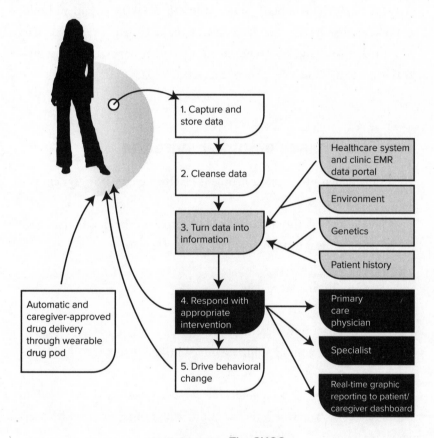

FIGURE 11.1   The CHOS

This operating system—largely automated in its first four steps—will improve our ability to anticipate and predict medical conditions and diseases early on in the disease process. In fact, this approach will provide significant patient and societal benefits to include longer life, healthier life, and lower costs of treatment.

In its simplest terms, each one of our constituents is producing health-related data 24/7. The problem is that heretofore we have not captured this rich flow of data and then interconnected it to external data networks, predictive analytics, the learning machine, and artificial intelligence to *automate* the process of identifying disease processes early while proactively leveraging game mechanics, social engagement, and other methods to drive better states of health. Looking at patient health as an *operating system* that leverages onboard patient biomarker data with predictive analytics, environment, and other data sets will catapult healthcare to a whole new level of successful impact.

The Two Phases of Implementation

The implementation of the constituent healthcare operating system will happen in two phases.

Phase I, anticipatory healthcare, will consist of the first four steps of the constituent healthcare operating system. They are:

1. Capture and store data.
2. Cleanse data.
3. Turn data into information.
4. Respond with appropriate intervention.

In this chapter and Chapter 12, we will focus on these first four steps. Phase II, behavioral intervention, will consist of the fifth step, which we'll discuss in Chapter 13.

Phase I is expressly for the purpose of collecting a variety of biosignals to help identify disease processes early. Continuous patient monitoring will also be used for clinical trials, next-generation wellness, and the management of chronic disease. The first phase will also provide far richer data and graphic dashboard reporting for both patient and caregiver.

In Phase I, our task will be to create the network of digital connectivity linking each constituent to a smart digital network that will anticipate and prevent disease.

This idea is not new, nor should it be seen as revolutionary. In this book we've discussed many examples—from motor vehicles to supply chains—of networks of passive digital sensors connected to the Internet of Things, with the goal of monitoring a set of key indicators and ensuring that information is available to stakeholders and decision makers. For example, the soft drink dispensing machine in a typical hospital lobby can monitor the level of its inventory, know which beverage cans are cold and which ones are warm, and automatically order inventory to restock itself. In the pharmacy, radio frequency identification (RFID) technology has created the ability to automate the entire pharmaceuticals supply chain of storage, use, and inspection, thereby reducing required human labor and streamlining routine processes that previously needed to be conducted on paper. It can reduce risk arising from similar drug names or dosage amount and dosage type, and it can eliminate shortages of stock and facilitate the recall of problem drugs. Overall, digital information technology strengthens drug management and ensures that medicines are prepared and provided accurately.

Within the pharmaceutical industry, the application diversity of RFID has led a wide range of end users—from drug manufacturers and drug wholesalers to hospitals and clinics—to embrace it. A 2019 study by Future Market Insights reported that drug manufacturers, which are particularly concerned with ensuring the authenticity of their products in the market, account for significant investment in RFID technology. In the wake of the rising prevalence of counterfeit drugs, efforts by the Food and Drug Administration, in collaboration with pharmaceutical suppliers, to maintain a secure drug supply have spurred the pharmaceutical industry to use RFID in combination with the electronic product code for real-time tracking, tracing, and authentication of drugs.[6]

In the twentieth century, these applications—and many more—of digital technology would have seemed like science fiction. But today, they have become routine.

As far as our constituents are concerned, in Phase I we ask them to become accustomed to wearing a device on their person that will monitor their vital signs and provide their primary care physician with health information. For many constituents, this will not be much of a stretch. People are becoming increasingly accustomed to wearable technologies; according to Stastista.com, in 2019 approximately 56.7 million people in the United States—that's nearly 20 percent of the population—used some sort of wearable technology device. By 2022, the number is expected to rise to 67 million.[7] And that's without any legislated incentive to do so—these are people who choose to use them for their own reasons.

It's time we leverage our vast and growing digital data capabilities to help our constituents enjoy longer and healthier lives.

TAKE ACTION!

- The challenge—our mandate—is to reinvent our healthcare system to leverage emerging digital technologies in the service of enhancing the wellness of our constituents, as well as treating them when they become our patients.
- Healthcare organizations must prepare for the inevitability of the comprehensive digital interconnection of constituents, healthcare providers, and insurers.
- The implementation of the constituent healthcare operating system must be done in two phases. They cannot happen simultaneously; they need to be put into place consecutively through the combined efforts of all stakeholders.

Phase I of Implementation of the CHOS: Anticipatory Healthcare

Let's take a closer look at the first four steps of the constituent health operating system.

1. Capture and Store Data

Our ability to capture and store data is increasing exponentially.

Earlier in the book I mentioned Moore's law, the observation that the number of transistors in a dense integrated circuit doubles about every two years. Gordon Moore, the cofounder of Fairchild Semiconductor and CEO of Intel, made the prediction in a 1965 paper, in which he projected that this rate of growth would continue for at least another decade. In 1975, revisiting his prediction, he affirmed his forecast of doubling every two years, a compound annual growth rate. For several decades, Moore's prediction has proved accurate, and the semiconductor industry has used it to guide long-term planning and set targets for research and development.

Globally, the amount of stored digital data keeps increasing. According to Statista.com, in 2015 the world stored an estimated 171 exabytes of data. (An exabyte is 1 million terabytes, or about 1 billion gigabytes.) By 2017, that amount had doubled to 397 exabytes. By 2020, it will be 985 exabytes, and just one year later it will reach 1,327 exabytes. That would be an eightfold growth in just five years.[1]

In 2018—in the world of digital data, practically a lifetime ago!—International Data Corporation (IDC) released a report on the ever-expanding datasphere, which is what it calls the collective world's data. In "Data Age 2025," IDC predicted that by 2025 the collective sum of the world's data would grow from 33 zettabytes to 175 zettabytes, for a compounded annual growth rate of 61 percent. (A zettabyte is 1,000 exabytes. To get an idea of just how much data that is, a 1-zettabyte hard drive could store more than 34 trillion 3-minute MP3s of your favorite music artists.)[2]

Here's another data point to give you a sense of scale. In 2010, engineers at Google tried to figure out the data storage requirement for every book ever published. First, they estimated the total number of books ever published at 129 million. Then they assumed an average of 70,000 words per book, requiring 6 bytes of memory for each word, plus a space. After crunching the numbers, they calculated that to digitally preserve the text of every book ever published, you'd need 54.18 terabytes. There are 1 million terabytes in just 1 exabyte. So to preserve the text of every book ever written, we're talking about a minuscule fraction of the world's data power.[3]

Is this data isolated in its own gigantic silo and therefore difficult to use, or is it connected to human activity? In fact, the actions of individual people are directly linked to the relentless growth of new data. "The Digitization of the World" report, by IDC, states, "More than five billion consumers interact with data every day. By 2025, that number will be six billion, or 75 percent of the world's population. In 2025, each connected person will have at least one data interaction every 18 seconds. Many of these interactions are because of the billions of IoT devices connected across the globe, which are expected to create over 90ZB of data in 2025."[4]

Speaking of the Internet of Things, this web of interconnected mechanical and digital machines, computing devices, people, objects, and animals, each of which is provided a unique identifier and the ability to transfer data over a network without requiring human-to-human or human-to-computer interaction, is also growing. It represents the migration of analog functions to monitor and manage the physical world to digital functions involving communications and software telemetry. As IDC reports, the number of sensors (such as the pulse rate sensor in your smartwatch) that track, monitor, or feed data to a network is more than 50 billion, with scientists talking about trillion-sensor networks by 2024.

Of course, not all those sensors and other gadgets are actually wired and communicating on the Internet, but by 2020, this number will grow to 30 billion connected devices.[5] The total human population of the world is now 7.7 billion people, so we're talking about four or five Internet-connected devices or sensors for every person on earth.

We will soon have the capacity to digitally monitor the key vital signs of every person in the United States. This is not farfetched. Today, the collection and storage of human constituent data is in its infancy. This data is mostly a range of biomarkers, including but not limited to core body temperature, EEG, ECG, blood pressure, pulse oximetry, pulse rate, and data that can be gleaned through continuous blood chemistry monitoring. In the near future, the 24/7 patient data flow will include genomics, environmental, historical health, current interventions and medicines, care history, insurance status, and a vast array of data that lives across both the patient and the healthcare ecosystem.

The volume of healthcare data is growing at an astonishing rate (see Figure 12.1): 153 exabytes were produced in 2013 and an estimated 2,314 exabytes will be produced in 2020, equal to an overall rate of increase of at least 48 percent annually.[6]

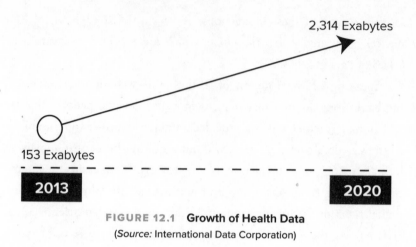

FIGURE 12.1 **Growth of Health Data**
(*Source:* International Data Corporation)

2. Cleanse Data

Just because you can collect huge amounts of data doesn't mean that all of it will be reliable or in the correct form to be processed with other data from other sources.

Also referred to as data scrubbing, data cleansing is the process of detecting dirty data (data that is incorrect, out of date, redundant, incomplete, or formatted incorrectly) and then removing and/or correcting the data.

In the context of healthcare, where the very lives of constituents may be at stake, it's especially important to verify the accuracy of data and the conclusions that are made from multiple data sources. Data cleansing is necessary to bring consistency to different sets of data that have been merged from separate sources; the cleansing may involve consolidating data within a database by removing inconsistent data and duplicates, and reindexing existing data in order to achieve the most accurate and concise database.

To verify the accuracy and completeness of the data, the CHOS module will leverage artificial intelligence and other standardized methods.

It is important to recognize that any resulting insights will have the same quality—good or bad—as the raw data initially provided. As the old computer saying goes, "Garbage in, garbage out." It's analogous to teaching people about a new topic, such as the history of heart pacemakers, and then asking them to write an essay about the subject. If you provide them with outdated or inaccurate source materials, the report they write will perpetuate those same errors. The same goes for artificially intelligent systems; the analytics and conclusions are only as good as the quality of the information provided.

Because the data for a constituent will be gathered from multiple sources, including internal, immediately external, and global, the various originating systems must be *interoperable*. Among its other benefits, interoperability helps to ensure that systems can "talk" and "understand" one another, meaning that data can be shared between different software platforms while retaining its original meaning.

As KHN.org reported, a lack of interoperability has hampered our current healthcare system. Years ago, healthcare experts welcomed the advent of electronic health records (EHRs), and expected the records to inhabit a seamlessly networked system that could instantly share the patients' computerized medical histories with doctors and hospitals anywhere in the country. Unfortunately, the EHR universe is far from ideal, largely because officials allowed hundreds of competing firms to sell medical records software unable to exchange information.[7]

According to GHX, a healthcare business and data automation company, leaders of healthcare organizations often blame inaccurate data for their inability to deliver accountable and informed care. The massive amount of data generated by healthcare IT systems only adds to the substantial challenges for ensuring accuracy.

GHX has found:[8]

- Each month, bad data contributes to over 2 million transactional errors.

- Each month, 192,000 edits or corrections must be made to hospital databases.
- On average, each year manufacturers make changes to one-third of the over 30 million medical-surgical products on the market in the United States.

Compliance is also an issue. It's important to report accurate information to state and federal government agencies. With the requirements of the Centers for Medicare and Medicaid Services' Open Payments reporting, where inaccuracies can result in fines and damaged relationships, data transparency is very important for physicians, patients, and life sciences organizations alike.[9]

At this stage in the evolution of the use of digital healthcare data, it appears that the challenge of collecting data can be easily met. The challenge of ensuring it's reliable and interoperable will be more difficult for the CHOS module to surmount, but with a focus on relentless innovation it can be done.

3. Turn Data into Information

Having aggregated disparate raw data sources for a constituent into a flowing stream of good data, the CHOS module must then transform the *data* into *information*.

Good data consists of raw, unorganized facts that lack context.

When data is processed, organized, structured, or presented in a given context so as to make it useful, it becomes information.

For example, let's say a constituent, whom we'll call Susan, wears a device that streams her vitals in real time. The data reveals that at six o'clock on most nights, she experiences an elevated heart rate and breathing rate, and her adrenaline surges. The elevated numbers last for an hour, until seven o'clock, when they subside back to homeostasis.

A similar pattern is noted in the morning, from nine o'clock until ten, although not as pronounced.

What does this mean?

We cannot be sure. Without context, the data is not information.

The CHOS module will evaluate all the many complex data signals to draw diagnostic and screening conclusions that will be dispatched to both the patient and caregivers. The continuous monitoring of patient data provides for smaller data signals over a period of time to identify potential health risks. The data evaluation will also result in specific action items that are communicated to the caregiver and the patient so as to seek the proper level of intervention.

To take the next step in determining the meaning of Susan's elevated vitals from six to seven o'clock, Susan's CHOS module first looks for any other vital signs that are elevated during that time. It discovers some other signs during that hour—breathing rate, adrenaline, perspiration, pupil dilation, blood oxygen levels—also change from the normal afternoon/evening baseline.

So clearly, Susan is doing *something* during that hour.

Let's propose two possible scenarios. At this point, the CHOS module has not made an attempt to analyze either of them. They are just for hypothetical discussion.

1. From six until seven, Susan goes to the gym to work out. Sometimes at the gym she plays competitive racquetball. She enjoys it and is happy to have the opportunity to stay fit. Then she takes a pleasant five-minute drive home, after rush hour has subsided.

2. From six until seven, Susan takes the subway home. The trains—her route requires one change, with a wait on the platform—are often very crowded and smelly, and there are delays. When she arrives at her apartment, it takes her a few minutes to "de-stress" with a glass of wine.

Clearly, when viewed in context, under the first scenario Susan's elevated numbers would be a good thing, because they're the result of pleasurable and healthy exercise. In the second scenario, her numbers would be a bad thing, because they are the result of stress.

This is the difference between data and information.

In Susan's CHOS module, the data bundle is then passed along to the next gate, which is her daily schedule. There it is matched with her physical movements, and the CHOS module determines that from six until seven o'clock, Susan rides the subway home. This means that her body is relatively inactive. She is either standing or sitting, with no physical exertion. Therefore the elevated vitals must be caused by some form of environmental stress—something she experiences on the subway ride.

She also rides the subway in the morning, from nine to ten o'clock. But this is after the morning rush hour has subsided, and her stress levels are lower.

Now the CHOS module has a chunk of information that consists of a set of facts and a correlation: Susan experiences elevated vitals at the same time she is riding the subway. Is this proof of a cause and effect? Possibly. The CHOS module also notes that on Saturday and Sunday, she shows no predictable elevations of those same vital signs. On these days, Susan is not riding the subway to and from work—more evidence that the subway is the cause of her stress.

The CHOS module must complete its investigation and look for any other recurring activities that Susan does between the hours of six and seven on weekdays. The CHOS notes that Susan's cell phone use is heavy during these times, which may add to her stress.

4. Respond with Appropriate Intervention

Having collected data from the real-time data flow, cleaned the data, and then transformed the data into meaningful information, the

CHOS module now must deliver that information to the appropriate stakeholders.

There are three critical pieces to this step.

1. Triage

The CHOS module has identified an area of concern in Susan's daily data flow: the elevated stress level that correlates with her trips on the subway after work.

The first question the CHOS module will ask itself is, "How should this finding be ranked on the scale of urgency?" There are various color-coded triage scales; here, for example, a scale of one, two, or three could be used, with one being "situation to watch" (green), two being "imminent health hazard, should see the doctor" (yellow), and three being "life-threatening emergency requiring immediate action" (red).

In this case, Susan's stress would be assigned to level one—a situation to watch and possibly remedy.

Let's say Susan showed signs of an atrial fibrillation, with an irregular and fast heartbeat. While not an emergency, it requires medical attention, putting it at level two.

If the real-time data flow from Susan showed a disturbance in her brainwaves, heart stoppage, or cessation of breathing, the report would escalate to level three, which requires immediate lifesaving action.

2. Notify the Appropriate Stakeholders

The circle of stakeholders to be notified would widen with the escalation from level one to level three.

At level one, the appropriate stakeholders to notify would be Susan and her primary care physician. Together, they can determine next steps.

At level two, the appropriate stakeholders to notify would be Susan, her primary care physician, and the relevant specialist—in this case, a cardiologist. The CHOS module might even proactively make an appointment for Susan to see the cardiologist as soon as possible, and it might also alert her healthcare insurer.

At level three, notification would be extended to emergency medical responders as well as to the emergency room of the hospital to which she would be taken.

3. Monitor the Case

Remember, even if Susan is at level three and is seriously injured or unconscious, the data flow continues. For her CHOS module, the job isn't finished. As it tracks her vitals, it will patch in the relevant stakeholders who need to see the real-time data coming from her brain and body.

For example, let's say Susan's CHOS module senses that she's in a public place and suddenly she has stopped moving. This lasts for several seconds. The CHOS module notes that her breathing is normal but her blood pressure is dropping and her brainwave activity is abnormal. It also notes that her accelerometer has registered a sharp impact. After 30 seconds, during which these unusual data points have not improved, the CHOS module notifies the EMTs, who are 10 minutes away, of the level three alert and the address. The EMTs click open the alert and can see Susan's vitals in real time. They are on the way, with two minutes elapsed since Susan's CHOS module detected a problem. Then a 911 call alert is relayed to them, which states that there has been a car accident at the specified address, and a pedestrian has been hit.

The EMTs arrive at the scene 10½ minutes after the accident. They already know Susan's identity, her description (female, age 40, weight 150 pounds), and her medical history (doesn't smoke, had a benign tumor removed, is allergic to penicillin). They know her current vitals: steady breathing, dropping blood pressure that suggests bleeding, and the lack of high-frequency oscillation in the brain EEG that suggests the person is unconscious.

When saving the life of an accident victim or anyone else suffering with a medical emergency, time and knowledge are critically important—and the CHOS module delivers both.

Let's go back to Susan's original problem, which was her elevated stress during her long commute on the subway. This is a nonemergency, level one condition. But that doesn't mean it can be ignored. If Susan fails to take action, or if the condition persists, her CHOS module will remind both her and her primary care physician about the problem. If she's eligible for a good health bonus from her employer, her employer may eventually be notified as well.

This latter step may be difficult for some constituents to accept. We live in a culture that values each individual's right to privacy and in which it's no crime to be sick or to have unhealthy habits. But we also have persistent beliefs that every person should be self-sufficient and should not need "the group" to lean on.

We are beginning to learn a new perspective: that we are stronger, yet every bit as free, when we work together as trusted teammates.

TAKE ACTION!

- Phase I, early anticipatory healthcare, will be implemented expressly for the purpose of collecting biosignals to help identify disease processes and then responding appropriately. It will consist of the first four steps of the constituent healthcare operating system:
  1. Capture and store data.
  2. Cleanse data.
  3. Turn data into information.
  4. Respond with appropriate intervention.
- In Phase I, the task of creating the network of digital connectivity linking each constituent to a smart digital network to anticipate and prevent disease is not a revolutionary idea. With committed leadership, it can be undertaken today.
- In Phase I, you ask your constituents to become accustomed to wearing a device on their person that will monitor their vital signs and provide their primary care physician with health information.
- Each person's CHOS module needs to be empowered to proactively issue health notifications, which, depending on the triage level, will be sent to the appropriate stakeholders.

Phase II of Implementation of the CHOS: Behavioral Intervention

Phase II of the implementation of the CHOS on a mass scale consists of the fifth step of the constituent healthcare operating system—that is, *drive behavioral change*.

This is when the Big Shift transforms from a largely *passive* program in which constituents are asked to do little other than cooperate into an *active* campaign in which constituents are asked to *alter what they do every day.*

They will be asked to modify their behavior (if necesessary) based on one or more of the following criteria:

1. Their genetic background suggests they can avoid or lower the risk of certain genetic diseases by altering their behavior. For example, a group of genetic conditions called inborn errors of metabolism results from genetic changes that prevent the production of specific enzymes. Treatment sometimes includes dietary changes, because limiting certain substances in the diet can help prevent the buildup of potentially toxic substances that are normally broken down by the enzyme.[1]

2. Their external environment suggests a future health problem, for instance, if sensors detect exposure to toxic chemicals such as pesticides.

3. Their mental health record indicates that certain behaviors, such as drinking alcohol in excess, may correlate to an increased risk of self-harm. For example, constituents who live with PTSD may need to be careful about engaging in "triggering" behaviors.

4. Their internal data suggests ongoing or potential damage from their personal behavior, such as an elevated risk of heart attack brought about by a sedentary lifestyle or cigarette smoking.

Persuading Constituents

In such cases, the constituents—who at this point do not yet exhibit symptoms of disease—need to be asked to take action to lower their risk of disease.

For a few, a request is all it will take. They will be easily convinced it's in their best interest to improve their behavior, and they will do so without further prodding.

However, the vast majority of constituents, I predict, will say yes to their doctor, make a half-hearted effort to improve, and eventually return to their comfort zone. People want to feel good about themselves, and unfortunately that often means going for the short-term solution: the extra doughnut at breakfast or the cigarette with their coffee.

These constituents—most of the population—will need an incentive to comply, which I'll discuss in the pages ahead.

As we learned with Benjamin Franklin and the public campaign to reduce the risk of fires in Philadelphia, public education is a key component. Healthcare leaders should not assume that just because we say something true, people are going to accept and embrace it. As we know from watching the often toxic dialogue in the political realm, people will choose to believe what they believe, and if you want to change minds, you need to be persuasive. Through the various social media platforms and traditional media channels, we need to state our case and back it up with examples that show history is on our side.

If we ask our constituents to alter their behavior and accept a limitation on their perceived right to harm themselves, we can point to the fact that millions of Americans routinely allow themselves to be injected with a medication designed not to cure an existing disease but to *prevent* the possibility of contracting a disease *in the future.*

The vast majority of people understand and agree with the basic facts: From the dawn of human existence, infectious diseases have been deadly and costly. In 541–542 CE, the Plague of Justinian is thought to have killed 25 million people in Europe, or half the population. In 1346–1353, the Black Plague killed as many as 200 million, wiping out one-third of the population. The 1918 influenza pandemic killed as many as 50 million around the world. The HIV/AIDS pandemic that began in 1976 has killed over 35 million.[2]

Smallpox (variola) was one of the many deadly scourges that from ancient times decimated whole populations. The earliest evidence of smallpox skin lesions has been found on the faces of mummies from the eighteenth and twentieth Egyptian dynasties and in the well-preserved mummy of Pharaoh Ramses V, who died in 1157 BCE.[3]

Smallpox epidemics occurred in ancient China, Egypt, and India and later in the Roman Empire. The ancient Chinese noted that smallpox was "a disease that affects an individual only once in a lifetime," thus giving the first clue that survivors had become inoculated.[4]

There is no cure for smallpox. As the Centers for Disease Control and Prevention states, "While some antiviral drugs may help treat it or prevent the smallpox disease from getting worse, there is no treatment for it that has been proven effective in people sick with the disease."[5]

Because there is no cure for smallpox, a disease that is extremely costly to human society, *the only way to control it is with anticipation and prevention.* There is simply no other approach that works.

While the prophylactic benefits of exposure to low-dose smallpox had long been noted, it was not until 1796 that Edward Jenner invented a method to protect against smallpox, which involved taking material from a blister of someone infected with cowpox, the milder bovine variety of the disease, and inoculating it into another person's skin. This was called arm-to-arm inoculation. Over the years, vaccines were developed and improved, until at the end of the 1960s, the World Health Organization could propose that the disease should—and could—be wiped out. At that time, smallpox was still endemic in Africa and Asia. Vaccination campaigns, surveillance, and prevention measures were created to contain epidemic hotspots and to better inform affected populations.

Mandatory Vaccinations Work!

The eradication of smallpox could not have been accomplished without state-sponsored, mandatory vaccinations. The right of a few to say no to inoculations was overruled by the greater public interest in limiting and eventually wiping out the disease.

In his book *Pox: An American History*, Michael Willrich revealed how the smallpox epidemic of 1898–1904 represented a turning point in disease control superseding the individual's right to avoid vaccinations. He cited an article from the archives of *The New York Times* discussing a 1901 smallpox vaccination raid in New York, when in the dead of night 250 government health agents arrived at a Little Italy tenement house and set about vaccinating everyone they could find.

"There were scenes of policemen holding down men in their night robes while vaccinators began their work on their arms," Willrich told NPR's Terry Gross. "Inspectors were going room to room looking for children with smallpox. And when they found them, they were literally tearing babes from their mothers' arms to take them to the city pesthouse." (Often used for forcible quarantine, a pesthouse was a place where people with smallpox, typhoid fever, and other communicable diseases prevalent at the time were sent, and where they often died.)

The Little Italy vaccination raid was not an isolated incident. As the smallpox epidemic swept across the nation, health officials ordered mandatory vaccinations in schools, in factories, and on railroads.[6]

In 1905, the authority of the government in the United States was affirmed by the Supreme Court. Pastor Henning Jacobson, of Cambridge, Massachusetts, resisted mandatory vaccinations for smallpox. While many of his fellow citizens were happy to take a vaccine for smallpox, Jacobson was alarmed by the idea of being stabbed by a needle and having cowpox injected under his skin. He refused the vaccine, stating it was an "invasion of his liberty." He was prosecuted and fined $5. His appeal rose to the Supreme Court, which ruled, "The state may be justified in restricting individual liberty . . . under the pressure of great dangers to the safety of the general public." And "There are manifold restraints to which each person is necessarily subject for the common good."[7]

The campaign to eradicate smallpox was successful, and the last known natural case was in Somalia in 1977. Three years later, the disease was declared eradicated. Today, samples of the virus exist in only two secure locations: the Centers for Disease Control and Prevention in Atlanta, Georgia, and the State Research Center of Virology and Biotechnology (VECTOR Institute) in Koltsovo, Russia.

Many other diseases have been controlled by state-sponsored inoculation programs.

Tetanus is a serious disease caused by the *Clostridium tetani* bacteria. A toxin produced by the bacteria affects the function of the nerves and leads to severe muscle spasms in the abdomen, neck, stomach, and extremities. In 30 percent of cases, it's fatal. Vaccination is the only way to protect against tetanus. In the United States, widespread immunization has made it a rare disease.

Diphtheria is an infection caused by the bacterium *Corynebacterium diphtheriae*. Symptoms include a sore throat and fever, with a gray or white patch in the throat that can block the airway and create a barking cough. The neck may swell in part due to enlarged lymph nodes. Due to widespread vaccination, it is rare in the developed world, but it could reemerge if vaccination rates decrease.

Pertussis (whooping cough) is a highly contagious respiratory tract infection. Deaths associated with whooping cough are rare; they most commonly occur in infants. The most effective way to prevent whooping cough is with the pertussis vaccine.

In the United States, a combination booster vaccine, called Tdap, protects against tetanus, diphtheria, and pertussis.

This review has been provided to remind skeptics of two facts:

1. With great success we have used the strategy of anticipation and prevention against these and other infectious diseases.
2. When the danger is compelling, society as a whole has, within reason, every right to compel individual citizens to give up a small portion of their rights elucidated under the Fourteenth Amendment, which says in part, "No state shall make or enforce any law which shall abridge the privileges or immunities of citizens of the United States; nor shall any state deprive any person of life, liberty, or property, without due process of law; nor deny to any person within its jurisdiction the equal protection of the laws."

Anti-Vaxxers

Phase II of the Big Shift, and its mission to achieve greater good for the most people, will encounter resistance resembling the "anti-vaxxer" movement of the past several decades.

Anti-vaxxers need no introduction; they have been active since the nineteenth century. The most recent manifestation of the movement has been the allegation that vaccines cause autism, itself a poorly understood disease. Numerous studies have debunked this assertion. In 2019, the results of a massive study in Denmark again confirmed the lack of causality. The study tracked 657,461 children born in Denmark from 1999 through December 31, 2010, with follow-ups from one year of age until August 2013. As "Measles, Mumps, Rubella Vaccination and Autism: A Nationwide Cohort Study" by Anders Hviid and others found, in their own words, "MMR vaccination does not increase the risk for autism, does not trigger autism in susceptible children, and is not associated with clustering of autism cases after vaccination."[8]

Some parents campaign against vaccinations because they've heard about the incredibly unlikely scenario of their children developing a life-threatening reaction. But the truth is that the rate of adverse vaccine reactions is extremely low. As Eun Hee Chung wrote in "Vaccine Allergies," researchers have reported that "the average rate for immediate type reactions in children and adolescents is 0.22 per 100,000 doses of vaccinations." That translates to about 1 bad reaction per 450,000 doses. Another group of researchers, Bohlke et al., found that reported cases of potential anaphylaxis after vaccination amount to even fewer—0.065 per 100,000 given doses of vaccines, or 1 per 1.6 million.[9]

Despite the scientific proof of the effectiveness and safety of vaccines, there are many who hold fast to their belief that vaccines are the *cause* of their problems, not *protection against them*. Thus the argument becomes one based on emotion, not fact. Citing studies and statistics doesn't matter to them, because they will point to one case of a suspected bad reaction to a vaccine and say, "See the damage done? One injured child is one too many." It's pointless to remind them of the *millions* of children saved by vaccines because none of them is that one child who was harmed.

We need to understand this emotion. As parents, there is simply nothing more precious to us than our children. In my experience, I've found that parents concerned about vaccinations tend to be extremely thoughtful and caring. Contrary to popular belief, they are not "nut jobs"; rather, they are concerned parents who, in my view, are suffering from "selective statistical analysis." It's easy to suggest that vaccines are dangerous because that position requires no effort, and it shifts the blame away from the parent onto unknown, nameless medical bureaucrats.

Given the emotions involved, it can be difficult to address the real statistical risks to children that exist across a variety of scenarios—for example, the chances of developing a chronic disease as a result of poor parental dietary and health modeling. Healthcare professionals know that one-third of the children born today will die early because their parents didn't teach them to eat properly. In its National Diabetes Statistics Report, 2017, the CDC reported that an estimated 30.3 million people of all ages—or 9.4 percent of the US population—had diabetes in 2015. An estimated 33.9 percent of US adults aged 18 years or older (84.1 million people) had prediabetes in 2015, based on their fasting glucose or A1C level. Nearly half (48.3 percent) of adults aged 65 years or older had prediabetes. The number one risk factor for diabetes? Being overweight or obese, and 87.5 percent of adults were defined as having a body mass index of 25 kg/m² or higher. It was the seventh leading cause of death in the United States.[10]

Meanwhile, the rate of death or serious illness from vaccinations of all types is so low as to be statistically negligible.

When talking about vaccinations, healthcare professionals know that while the best strategy is to calmly and patiently explain the reality of how vaccinations have saved millions of lives, many constituents will be driven by emotion and will not be persuaded. It will be the same with the Big Shift. We know that logically, the adoption of the CHOS on a mass scale should be inevitable simply because it will bring the most benefit to the most people. There is no question that connecting every person to a module that monitors the person's health, combined with a proactive campaign to improve individual health-related behavior, will lower rates of disease and extend life. The logic is unassailable. The challenge is to introduce it to healthcare constituents in such a way that it will not arouse reflexive resistance and will lead to broad acceptance.

Benjamin Franklin's System:
An Ounce of Prevention

As we recall from the successful campaign to reduce the risk of fire in Philadelphia, Benjamin Franklin's recommendations focused on four action areas:

1. **Educate the public.** This is the responsibility of every stakeholder in the healthcare industry: policy makers, drug companies, healthcare networks, medical technology companies, hospitals, and frontline caregivers.

2. **Acquire and use proper technology.** The Big Shift would not be possible without innovation in digital technology, massive amounts of data processing, artificial intelligence, and increasingly miniaturized and powerful devices.

3. **Organize resources.** The effort to shift our emphasis from diagnosis and treatment to anticipation and prevention requires the coordinated efforts of every stakeholder. Once the tipping point is reached, those organizations that are not keeping up with the pace of innovation will find themselves slipping further and further behind.

4. **Provide government support.** Just as it is in the case of vaccinations, the efforts of the healthcare industry to convince its constituents to improve their overall health must be backed up by the authority of the federal government. No other entity can reach as deeply into every community—urban and rural, rich and poor—to educate, encourage, and, if necessary, compel people to do the right thing for themselves.

Incentives and Penalties Worked to Cut Down Cigarette Smoking

Phase II will be built on a set of incentives and penalties that will gradually convince the majority of Americans to participate in a grand campaign to make every person in the nation as healthy as can be.

A good analogy is the decades-long campaign to get people to quit smoking.

In January 1964, the US surgeon general published the report "Smoking and Health," which linked smoking cigarettes with a variety of detrimental health effects, including lung and laryngeal cancer, heart disease, and chronic bronchitis.

At that time, roughly 42 percent—nearly half!—of adult Americans smoked. It was a normal part of everyday life. You could buy cigarettes from vending machines. You could smoke at work, in restaurants and bars, and on airplane flights. Tobacco use was glamorously portrayed in the movies and on TV and was advertised in every magazine and on billboards along the highways.[11]

From that moment on, the government used the tools at its disposal to educate the public and discourage smoking.

Just one year after publication of the report, Congress passed the Federal Cigarette Labeling and Advertising Act of 1965, which required warning labels on cigarette packages. It was followed by numerous anti-smoking measures over the following four decades, including the gradual elimination of smoking in most public buildings and workplaces in the United States.

As the American Heart Association reported, the decline in smoking was the result of a combination of cigarette price increases, anti-smoking campaigns, smoke-free laws, and access to cessation programs, all of which were aided by health advocacy groups. "These interventions really de-normalized tobacco use," said Brian King, deputy director for research translation in the CDC's Office on Smoking and Health.[12]

Smokers paid more for life insurance: according to NerdWallet research, they paid an average of $1,455 in 2019 and $1,071 more every year for term life insurance, respectively, than those who were smoke-free. And in most of the country, smokers paid about 351 percent more for life insurance than nonsmokers.[13]

The coordinated effort has worked. By 2018, cigarette smoking among US adults had reached an all-time low of 13.7 percent. "This marked decline in cigarette smoking is the achievement of a consistent and coordinated effort by the public health community and our many partners," said CDC director Robert R. Redfield, MD. "Yet, our work is far from over. The health benefits of quitting smoking are significant, and we are committed to educating Americans about the steps they can take to become tobacco-free."[14]

Two-Tier Healthcare

In regard to cigarette smoking, we now have a de facto two-tier health system, with smokers paying more across the board than nonsmokers. The Big Shift will use this model to encourage participation in the CHOS and discourage nonparticipation. Put simply, there will be two tiers:

1. Affordable with CHOS monitoring and behavior coaching
2. Expensive with no CHOS monitoring or behavior coaching

Constituents will be able to make their choice. They can take a step forward into the Big Shift and pay less, or they can choose to stay in the old system and pay much more.

TAKE ACTION!

- Phase II is the implementation of the CHOS on a mass scale, which includes the fifth step of the constituent healthcare operating system: drive behavioral change, in which constituents may be asked to modify their behavior based on certain health criteria.
- Constituents who object may respond to a program of education that highlights the undeniable success that mandatory vaccinations—which continue to this day—have had in eradicating smallpox, tetanus, diphtheria, and other deadly diseases.
- Leverage the experience gained by Benjamin Franklin's four action areas:
  1. Educate the public.
  2. Acquire and use proper technology.
  3. Organize resources.
  4. Provide government support.
- Build Phase II on a set of incentives and penalties that will gradually convince your constituents to take better care of their health. Such an approach has worked with the anti-smoking campaign.
- We will have a two-tier health system, resembling the one in many states where smokers pay more across the board than nonsmokers.

The Challenge of COVID-19

Wuhan, the capital of Hubei province, China, is home to over 11 million people. On December 31, 2019, health authorities in this sprawling city became aware of a cluster of cases of pneumonia with an unknown origin. In early January 2020, they launched an investigation. Through meticulous contact tracing—the same way it's been done for over a century—they discovered the primary origin of the outbreak at the Huanan Seafood Wholesale Market, an open-air "wet market" selling fish, fresh meat, live animals, produce, and other perishable goods.

As more information emerged, the source of the new virus, identified as "severe acute respiratory syndrome coronavirus 2," or SARS-CoV-2, became diffuse. The *South China Morning Post* reported that a 55-year-old from Hubei province could have been the first person to contract the disease on November 17, 2019. The earliest reported symptoms occurred on December 1, 2019, in a person with no known connection to the Huanan Seafood Wholesale Market or the other 40 individuals in the first cluster. Further investigations revealed that two-thirds of the early cases were found to have no connection to the market.[1]

On December 31, 2019, the Wuhan health authorities issued an epidemiological alert. Suspected cases with fever and dry cough were transferred to a designated hospital. On January 1, 2020, the authorities shut down the Huanan market.

From specimens taken from the lower respiratory tracts of patients, a novel coronavirus, SARS-CoV-2, was isolated. A diagnostic test for this virus was soon developed. Of 59 suspected cases, 41 patients were confirmed infected with SARS-CoV-2.[2]

On January 11, Chinese state media reported the first known death from an illness caused by the virus—a 61-year-old man who was a customer at the Huanan market.[3]

The next day, the Chinese government shared the genetic sequence of the novel coronavirus for countries to use in developing specific diagnostic kits. The virus was particularly alarming because it was a new virus that had never before been seen in humans. While it was clearly contagious, there was no knowledge about its behavior. Unlike other forms of influenza, there was no vaccine and no known immunity.

The disease spread with astonishing speed. On January 13, the first case was reported in Thailand. Two days later, it appeared in Japan, and on January 20, in South Korea. The very next day, the first case was reported in the United States: A man in his thirties who was a resident of Snohomish County, Washington State, developed symptoms after returning from a trip to the region around Wuhan where the outbreak began.[4]

The World Health Organization (WHO) coordinated a response and provided guidance. In its "Situation Report" of January 20, the organization stated, "WHO is working with our networks of researchers and other experts to coordinate global work on surveillance, epidemiology, modeling, diagnostics, clinical care and treatment, and other ways to identify and manage the disease, and limit onward transmission."[5]

On January 23, Chinese authorities isolated Wuhan by canceling planes and trains leaving the city and suspending buses, subways, and ferries within it. But the response of the Chinese government was far from perfect. In early January, the authorities reprimanded Dr. Li Wenliang, who tried to sound the alarm that the small cluster of infections could spin out of control, and forced him to sign a statement denouncing his warning as an unfounded and illegal rumor. He himself caught the virus and died on February 10.

The virus quickly spread to Iran, Italy, France, and Brazil. Soon nearly every industrialized nation was reporting cases. According to WHO, by March 15, the virus had infected 157,500 people in nearly every corner of the globe, with 5,735 deaths. In some areas the rate of new infection was doubling every six days.

By mid-April, the number of infected people worldwide had reached 2.3 million, with 34,000 deaths.[6]

The cost of economic disruption was projected to be very high. *Bloomberg News* put the possible global losses at $2.7 trillion.[7] S&P Global analysts predicted the pandemic could cost US health insurers $90 billion in medical claims, with roughly 50 million insured Americans contracting the new coronavirus. They projected that under a severe pandemic, the number of people needing hospitalization could spiral to nearly 8 million nationally, which would overwhelm the nation's hospital system.[8]

Identifying the Disease

COVID-19 is the name of the disease caused by the SARS-CoV-2 virus. The virus is spread primarily between people who are in close contact with one another (within about six feet) through respiratory droplets produced when an infected person coughs or sneezes.[9] The incubation period ranges from 1 to 14 days, most commonly around 5 days. This means that someone could be infected by the virus and not show any symptoms for an average of 5 days.[10]

For patients who show symptoms, according to the CDC, there are three primary symptoms:

1. Fever
2. Cough
3. Shortness of breath

Emergency warning signs include:[11]

1. Difficulty breathing or shortness of breath
2. Persistent pain or pressure in the chest
3. New confusion or inability to arouse
4. Bluish lips or face

COVID-19 is an infection of the lower respiratory tract, which means that most of the symptoms are seen and felt in the chest and lungs. It's unlike the common cold that creates an infection of the upper respiratory tract, typified by sore throat, runny nose, and sinus congestion. Most deaths from COVID-19 are caused by acute respiratory distress syndrome (ARDS), which causes infected lungs to fill with fluid and makes breathing difficult. Unlike pneumonia, which is a bacterial infection, ARDS is not treatable with antibiotics.

The Best Response in Early 2020

As the virus spread around the world, it became clear that of all the nations affected, South Korea organized and executed the most effective response. There were several reasons for this. As ProPublica reported, following the 2015 outbreak of the Middle East respiratory syndrome (MERS) that killed 38 people in South Korea and severely damaged the country's economy, the government of South Korea analyzed the poor results of its containment effort. The government found that a lack of tests had prompted sick people to go from hospital to hospital seeking diagnosis and treatment. As a result, nearly half the people who got the disease were exposed at hospitals.[12]

In response, and to prepare for the next outbreak of a viral disease, South Korea ramped up its ability to design and manufacture tests. When COVID-19 struck, South Korea was prepared, and it quickly rolled out a massive testing program that included drive-through test stations. Drive-through testing, which the US was slow to embrace, involved a healthcare worker first asking the driver to fill out some paperwork and then taking throat and nasal swabs. The swabs were sent to a lab, from which results were returned in about a day. While it could be done on a large scale, in terms of disease identification and control, it was still fundamentally the same system that's been in use for over a century: you identify which person is infected, track down the person's contacts, and quarantine those people. Or as it's known, you "trace, test, and treat." (Unfortunately, drive-through testing was not feasible in many big cities like New York, where many residents do not own cars.)

Within days of the first outbreak, the nation of 51.47 million was testing 15,000 people a day. By mid-March, South Korea had tested a quarter of a million people. It was the world's most aggressive testing program. In contrast, according to the CDC, at the same time, the United States, with a population of 330 million, had tested only 15,000 people in total. By last count, South Korea was testing 700 times as many people per capita as the United States.

Of the American effort, Marc Lipsitch, director of the Center for Communicable Disease Dynamics at Harvard University's School of Public Health, said on March 13, "I think we're flying almost completely blind right now. We have a lot of uncertainty about whether we have 10 times more or 100 times more cases than we know about."[13]

In contrast, in an extraordinary example of digital technology put to use in service of a nation's citizens, VOA (Voice of America) News reported that South Koreans in hot zones received personalized text messages showing new coronavirus cases nearby. They could then click a link that provided detailed information about where the infected patients had traveled.[14] As for testing, South Korea quickly created a network of 96 public and private laboratories to perform coronavirus tests. The process of analysis took about six hours.[15]

Time and Temperature

Across the globe, the response to the emergence of COVID-19 ranged from highly aggressive (China, South Korea) to sluggish (Italy, United States). The results varied accordingly. But in hindsight, the question in front of us is this: Could even the best response have been far better?

The answer is yes.

To dig deeper, let's analyze how the very best responses worked in practice. There were two ways the virus was identified and treatment initiated.

In the first scenario, the constituent became infected. Five days later (on average) the constituent began to feel symptoms: fever, shortness of breath, cough. Particularly in the early stages of the pandemic (December 2019 through February 2020), the constituent was likely to brush off these symptoms as a touch of the flu or ordinary aches and pains. He or she might have waited several days before going to, or calling, the doctor. Eventually, the constituent received a diagnosis and treatment, which if the case were mild may have consisted of nothing more than quarantine. But between the time of infection and the time of quarantine—a week or more—the constituent was freely interacting with others and spreading the disease.

In the second scenario, the constituent became infected. Five days later (on average) the symptoms appeared. At roughly the same time, the constituent was intercepted by a government tester and tested. This may have happened at a drive-by roadblock or by some other method of intervention. In the most aggressive programs (in China), if the constituent showed a fever, he or she was immediately sent to a triage hospital for further tests to determine if the virus was present.

One of the very first symptoms of COVID-19 is a fever. As a result, many nations, including China, India, South Korea, and Russia, made extensive use of temperature screening checkpoints. These were set up at airports, outside apartment buildings, and even at stores. In some other nations, including Germany, health authorities did not place much faith in temperature testing. Why not? Because they believed that testers may have used the wrong instruments or used the appropriate instruments incorrectly, leading to inaccuracies. "We are seeing photographs of people using industrial grade infrared thermometers to measure the temperature of people," said Jim Seffrin, an expert on infrared devices at the Infraspection Institute in New Jersey, to the *Washington Post*, "but these instruments are not meant to measure human body temperature." Using them to measure human skin temperature can lead to inaccurate readings. Taking a reading outside on a cold day could miss a fever, while taking a reading just after the constituent has exercised could give a false positive.[16]

Yanzhong Huang, a senior fellow for global health at the Council on Foreign Relations, told *Post* reporter Emily Rauhala that temperature checks might flag someone with a fever caused by ordinary influenza, while overlooking an infected constituent who isn't showing symptoms. "Screening can be partially effective, but won't be effective for asymptomatic carriers," he said.[17]

Some researchers doubted the effectiveness of airport screening. As Billy J. Quilty and others wrote in their report, "Effectiveness of Airport Screening at Detecting Travellers Infected with Novel Coronavirus (2019-nCoV)," they evaluated the effectiveness of thermal passenger screening for 2019-nCoV infections at airport exit and entry points. "In our baseline scenario," they wrote, "we estimated that 46 percent of infected travellers would not be detected, depending on incubation period, sensitivity of exit and entry screening, and proportion of asymptomatic cases. Airport screening is unlikely to detect a sufficient proportion of 2019-nCoV infected travellers to avoid entry of infected travellers."[18]

Even in the most effective response scenarios, there were significant gaps in knowledge and lags in time. They included:

1. **Depending on the constituent to self-report.** This was the old diagnose-and-treat model in which the healthcare provider was forced to wait until the infected constituent sought help. In a case of a virulent and rapidly spreading disease, this is clearly the worst possible strategy.

2. **Depending on random chance to intercept and test constituents.** Even with aggressive interventional testing, only a portion of the population can be screened. By mid-March 2020, only about 1 in 250 South Koreans, or about 0.4 percent of the population, had been tested. This was one of the highest rates of testing in the world.[19]

3. **Depending on temperature screening.** As noted, "field testing" of constituents with portable electronic thermometers was not a fully reliable method.

The CHOS System in Action

Let's revisit our friend Roberta. At age 70, she would be in the highest-risk demographic for COVID-19. Fortunately, because she was a part of the Big Shift in healthcare from diagnosis and treatment to anticipation and prevention, Roberta has no underlying conditions—diabetes, obesity, heart disease, cancer—that would put her at even greater risk of death.

Her CHOS biomonitor, which she wears during all her waking hours, provides a detailed, real-time picture of her current health. Aside from taking her four primary vital signs—body temperature, blood pressure, heart rate, and respiratory rate—it also connects to other body sensors, providing streaming predictive data. It reports on many of the factors that once had been determined only by blood tests, including the basic metabolic panel, the lipid panel, and various hormones including cortisol, insulin, melanin, and serotonin.

Her data, of which she retains ownership, is streamed in real time to her healthcare provider, which serves two purposes:

1. Roberta's primary care physician no longer needs to rely on Roberta to report symptoms of an emerging disease. While Roberta is, of course, free to consult her physician about any concerns she may have, we know that human beings are often

reluctant to see their doctor about little things they assume will pass quickly, such as a mild fever accompanied by a cough and the sensation of being out of breath. We are likely to shrug off such obvious symptoms, especially if getting sick means losing time at work. With the CHOS in place, Roberta's physician can proactively contact her, inquire about her sudden symptoms, and ask her to go for testing if necessary.

2. In terms of identifying infectious diseases such as COVID-19, Roberta's CHOS can provide the earliest possible warning signs: if she develops a fever, if there is a change in her breathing pattern, and if she starts to cough regularly. These are easy measurements to make, and we already have that capability. When a contagious disease emerges, the symptoms can be programmed into the system so that anyone showing the matching symptoms can be flagged. For example, in March 2020 it would have been incredibly valuable for the CDC to know, in real time, who among our nation's 327 million people were exhibiting those three symptoms. Science fiction? No. The technology is within reach.

Roberta's data, while protected in terms of her privacy, will be invaluable to public health officials as they strive to identify emerging viral threats. Imagine a healthcare provider who suddenly sees an increase in unexplained fevers among his or her constituents. He or she can contact them (just as the South Korean government did in March 2020), ask relevant questions including their recent travel history, and create a pattern or map of an emerging disease. The healthcare provider can then use that same database to track the efficacy of the healthcare system's response.

Imagine not one Roberta but 200 million or more, all plugged into a comprehensive healthcare system. When another virulent disease like COVID-19 breaks out—which we know it eventually will—then we will have no need for inaccurate, clumsy, and time-consuming airport or roadside tests. The data will come streaming in from millions of constituents. A massive disruption to our economy by shutting down public businesses, including theaters, schools, restaurants, and sporting events, may not be necessary because we'll know exactly who has the disease.

Let's say, for example, a new virus was introduced from the tropics to Florida. The very first unexplained set of symptoms would be flagged by the system for special attention. As the matching set of symptoms affected more people, an alarm would be sounded. The CDC would be alerted, as well as the political leadership, both nationally and at the local level. A massive effort could be organized long before the problem would have been recognized under the old self-report system. This would be an example of pinpoint healthcare targeting. We'd know from day one exactly who was affected and, because the constituents' travels were also recorded as part of their data set, where they had been. The historic travel data will serve as a guide to search for other infected people.

The CHOS system is a simple, elegant solution to the problem of managing the outbreak of infectious diseases. The technology is within reach. All that is needed is the national will to make it a reality.

TAKE ACTION!

- Each and every healthcare provider can, and should, express support for a comprehensive national program to launch the CHOS, get constituents plugged into the system, and use the data to predict and prevent the kind of pandemic we saw in 2020.
- Healthcare policy makers need to recognize that the old system is broken, and our slow response to COVID-19 illustrates how desperately we need the Big Shift to a system based not solely on diagnosis and treatment but on anticipation and prevention as well, through a vast national network of constituents and their CHOS modules.

Artificial Intelligence and Gamification

A major theme of this book is how the healthcare industry will leverage the exploding power of digital technology to make the Big Shift from diagnosis and treatment to anticipation and prevention.

Two key elements of digital technology the industry will use to help constituents lead healthier lives are artificial intelligence and gamification, or game mechanics.

Artificial Intelligence: From Science Fiction to Everyday Fact

In the old days (meaning 50 years ago), computers were "dumb" machines capable only of executing a narrowly defined task. You input the problem to be solved, such as a math equation, and the machine solved the problem. Hence the well-known expression "garbage in, garbage out," which meant that you had to be very careful what data you put into the machine because the machine was incapable of interpreting possible variations.

Thanks to massive innovation and increases in processing power and memory, computers are now able to make deductions—that is, choose the *most likely* answer from a set of possible answers. In 1997, the concept of artificial intelligence took a big leap forward when IBM's supercomputer Deep Blue defeated the reigning world chess champion, Garry Kasparov, in a game requiring players to think many moves ahead and choose the best one out of the available possibilities. Then in 2011, during a special *Jeopardy!* TV quiz show exhibition match, IBM's Watson defeated two of the greatest *Jeopardy!* champions, Brad Rutter and Ken Jennings. If you've watched the show, you'll know it's not just a trivia quiz; contestants must often deduce the answers by working backward from the carefully worded clues.

As anyone in the healthcare profession knows, perfect information is not always available. Of course, if the patient arrives with a broken leg after having slipped on the ice, you don't need to go much further to make a diagnosis and treatment decision. But all too often, the patient will arrive complaining of stomach pains or difficulty breathing, and from there the detective game begins. Symptoms may overlap between various diseases, or may seem relevant when they're not, or may be inconsistent. Especially when treating diseases of the mind, such as depression, you often must choose the most likely cause of the patient's discomfort, and if that produces no results, you move on to the next most likely cause.

Increasingly, computers are able to make these kinds of judgment calls, which, combined with their growing data storage capabilities and ability to operate 24 hours a day, 7 days a week, makes them very useful in the healthcare industry.

As Fei Jiang and others noted in their paper, "Artificial Intelligence in Healthcare: Past, Present and Future," a computer capable of AI can use sophisticated algorithms to recognize and learn relevant information from a large volume of healthcare data and then apply those insights to assist clinical practice. These learning and self-correcting abilities can use feedback to improve diagnostic accuracy. The computer can extract useful data from a large patient population to assist making real-time inferences for health risk alerts and predictions of health outcomes. To inform proper patient care, an AI system can assist healthcare providers by searching and presenting the most recent medical information from journals, textbooks, and clinical practices. It can help reduce the diagnostic and therapeutic errors that are inevitable in human clinical practice.[1]

For example, consider strokes.

The vast majority of strokes, also called cerebral infarctions, are caused by thrombus (blood clot) in blood vessels in the brain. However, detection of thrombus in its earliest stages has traditionally been difficult, and oftentimes the constituent is well into the event before the warning symptoms appear with enough force and clarity to cause alarm. But in 2015, José R. Villar and others developed a movement-detecting device for early stroke prediction. It was based on human activity recognition software, a key component in developing a tool that would diagnose strokes early.

For the model-building solution, they inserted into the device two machine learning algorithms—a genetic fuzzy finite state machine and principal component analysis (PCA). The detection process included a stroke-onset detection stage and a human activity recognition stage. Basically, the software tracked the everyday movements of the constituent—hands, arms, legs—and built up an inventory of normal ranges. If the movement of the patient suddenly varied significantly from the normal pattern, an alert of stroke would be activated, and the patient would be evaluated for treatment as soon as possible.[2]

Similarly, for stroke prediction, Andrea Mannini and colleagues proposed a wearable device for collecting data about normal-to-pathological gaits. The data would be extracted and modeled by hidden Markov models and a support vector machine (SVM). Tests revealed the algorithm could correctly classify 90.5 percent of the subjects to the right group.

It does not take much imagination to envision Roberta's CHOS module having stroke detection capabilities, so that if she were to show any of the signs of stroke—especially those in alignment with the FAST acronym of facial drooping, arm weakness, speech difficulties, and time to call emergency services—*even before Roberta herself found them alarming*—she could get immediate medical attention. Once a stroke begins, the patient loses almost 2 million brain cells every minute. Time is of the essence, and a technology that can shave even a minute or two from the onset of treatment could help save millions of lives.

Another example is the use of a convolution neural network—a form of deep learning—to detect diseases that are visible on the body. Researchers have used it to diagnose congenital cataract disease by having the computer learn the ocular images of healthy eyes and then compare the range of normal eyes with the constituent's eye (which is pretty much what a human doctor does). Using the same method of learning and comparing, computers can identify skin cancer from clinical images and detect referable diabetic retinopathy through retinal fundus photographs.

A support vector machine approach is used to identify imaging biomarkers of neurological and psychiatric disease. A combination of SVM and other statistical tools has achieved early detection of Alzheimer's disease, while other researchers have used SVM to test the power of an offline human-machine interface that controls upper-limb prostheses.[3]

Given the rate of technological innovation, it's only a matter of time before all these functions—and many more—are folded into one small device that Roberta can wear in her ear or even on her wrist. The question is, will those in the existing professional healthcare industry be the owners/operators of this vast emerging data and informational network, or will it be in the hands of a technology company concerned first and foremost with profits? Leaders of the healthcare industry stand at a crossroads. One path leads to the same old places and the decline of the industry as outside actors muscle their way in, while the other path leads to innovation, growth, and the Big Shift that will usher in a new era of proactive healthcare.

Gamification: The Winner Lives Longer

Gamification is based on the very simple premise that human beings are much more likely to engage in an activity when it's perceived as fun and leads to an outcome or goal. This includes activities that are not trivial, such as adopting healthier eating habits or getting more exercise, which can result in longer life and fewer visits to the doctor. The willingness of your constituents to participate in gaming comes from several sources: the desire for independence or autonomy, the desire to escape a boring or unpleasant reality, the desire to achieve a skill followed by affirmation of that skill, and the desire to socially relate to others as provided by multiplayer games and the communities that support them.

Gamification can be used as a direct therapeutic tool. As Carecloud.com reported, children with cerebral palsy or spina bifida undergoing physical therapy and diagnostic testing were helped by playing a video-game system consisting of Wii Balance Boards arranged between handrails and a screen. Designed by a group of engineering students at Rice University, the game consisted of the kids shooting at approaching monsters, only instead of using the customary handheld toggles, they used their feet to hit specific spots on the boards. As they improved, the game became more challenging and the gamers accumulated points. The game helped improve balance and coordinated movement, as well as incorporated feedback from the handrails.[4]

In another physical therapy application, the University Orthopedic Center in Salt Lake City utilizes Wii games as physical therapy. Physical therapist Patty Trela says the Wii gets results unobtainable with a standard hospital kit. "The one thing I like," she told VG247.com, "is that the Wii can detect changes in body movements and body-positioning orientations—kind of a three-dimensional picture. We really don't have that in any of the tools in the clinic."[5]

In the area of anticipation and prevention, San Francisco–based HopeLab.org developed a program called Zamzee, which was subsequently acquired by Welltok. Based in Colorado, the company is a data-driven, enterprise SaaS company offering solutions that empower its clients—health plans, employers, providers, and public entities—to connect consumers with personalized health improvement resources, making it "easy and rewarding for consumers to complete actions that optimize their health and wellbeing."[6]

Designed by behavioral scientists, Zamzee seeks to curb childhood obesity by using a motivational website and an activity meter to get children to move more. The goal of the Zamzee website is to initiate behavior change and sustain it in the long term. The site provides children with information on their physical activity levels and lets them achieve goals, earn points, and get rewards for making healthy choices.[7]

In Phase II of the CHOS implementation, digital systems will leverage gamification to significantly improve compliance to disease management and preventive health and wellness. The use of game mechanics will be intensified with new third-party payer incentives. These incentives will encourage constituents by providing them with financial benefits when they save money and make better health choices. Conversely, the games will have disincentives that create punitive measures for noncompliance of preventive health, diet, physical activity, and other determinants. The measurements will be linked to key biomarkers—all accessed through the constituent's CHOS module—and constituents who stay within biomarker ranges will "win" the game, and those who do not will ultimately "lose."

TAKE ACTION!

- Given the rate of technological innovation, it's only a matter of time before microcomputers have sufficient powers of artificial intelligence to anticipate emerging disease. Your organization needs to be an owner/operator of this vast emerging data and informational network, which means investing now before others take the lead.
- Gamification is a highly effective therapeutic tool. In Phase II of the CHOS implementation, digital systems will leverage gamification to significantly improve compliance to disease management and preventive health and wellness. You need to ensure that your healthcare organization is investing in game-based therapies to help keep your constituents on the road to good health.

The Carrot
and the Stick

T he Healthcare Mandate represents a sweeping transformation not just of the healthcare industry, which is populated by many professionals and workers whose job it is to innovate, but of the behavior of our constituents, of whom we are asking something novel. We are asking them to allow their primary care physician to connect them digitally to a 24/7 health monitor and to trust their healthcare provider to keep their personal data safe and confidential.

Of course, many people now use digital health wearables; in 2019, an estimated 60.5 million Americans wore some sort of digital personal data device. Interestingly, the most rapid expansion of the wearables market is in the demographic of people 55 and older, who in 2019 numbered 8.2 million users.[1] But only a few of these are digitally connected to a system like the CHOS module; most keep their data to themselves.

As anyone who has studied the psychology of consumers knows, people approach change with varying degrees of interest. Healthcare constituents see themselves as consumers. And as consumers, they are driven solely by self-interest, which is perfectly normal for consumers.

Marketers generally divide consumers into "adopter" categories based on the individual's appetite for change. The adopter categories were first named and described in 1962 in the book *Diffusion of Innovations* by sociologist Everett Rogers. According to his research, there are five adopter categories—innovators, early adopters, early majority, late majority, and laggards.

1. **Innovators.** They're interested in anything risky and new, and they take pleasure in trying innovative products and services. For example, the very first person in your neighborhood to buy an electric car was an innovator. If you ask an innovator to wear a CHOS sensor connected to a module, he or she will say, "Of course I will!" No incentive will be needed.

2. **Early adopters.** They are opinion leaders who see what the innovators have discovered, buy one for themselves (or wrangle it for free), and then communicate to their followers the usefulness of the new product. They will need little incentive to try the CHOS sensor system.

3. **Early majority.** They carefully observe the early adopters, but they wait to try innovative products until they are certain they will get value from them. Members of this group will need some incentive to try the system, such as a lower healthcare rate and assurances their data will be secure.

4. **Late majority.** They are more conservative and are liable to say, "If it ain't broke, don't fix it." But eventually they go along with what everyone else is doing, as long as the carrot is as good as the stick.

5. **Laggards.** This group is last to adapt to new ideas or technology. They may be suspicious of the new system, wary of being encumbered by a device, and reluctant to surrender their personal data at any price. They require the most blatant use of the carrot and the stick.

To the five categories elucidated by Rogers, in this case we need to add a sixth: the never adopters. These people are the conspiracy theorists and lone wolves who view any community program with deep suspicion and who will adamantly stay off the grid. They also include those who view the healthcare industry with animus, and who, if they got cancer, would rather seek the advice of a gemstone healer than a real doctor. Sadly, they are beyond the reach of real medical knowledge and proven practice.

To achieve any kind of change in human behavior requires a combination of incentives for compliance and penalties for noncompliance.

Unlike smoking cigarettes or eating too many doughnuts, which in self-reporting is subject to deliberate deception and/or personal interpretation, compliance with the CHOS is plainly obvious: Either you're wearing the CHOS medical sensor device, or you're not. If you take it off, the computer at the other end of the CHOS module will know. While wearing it, you cannot fool it, because it's extremely sensitive to all your bodily functions, including those that are involuntary, such as your heart rate and blood hormone levels.

Therefore the goal is simple: to convince as many constituents as possible to plug into the CHOS network and tilt the thrust of our healthcare system from diagnosis and treatment to anticipation and prevention. To convince the early majority, late majority, and finally the laggards to participate will require a very simple system of incentives and penalties. The service must be low cost and easy to deal with.

A Sliding Scale for Insurance Premiums? Not a New Idea

The idea that constituents who make poor health choices will pay more is not revolutionary. Under the Patient Protection and Affordable Care Act, health insurance premiums can vary from person to person, based on the following five variables. The first four are:

1. **Age.** The older the customer, the more the customer will be charged for health insurance. HealthCare.gov notes that older

people often pay premiums that are three times higher than those charged to younger people. This is the only category over which the customer has no control. People cannot change their age!

2. **Location.** States and municipalities can influence insurance rates, as can the level of competition in a particular market. Less competition means higher rates. In theory, the customer could move to an area with lower rates.

3. **The number of people.** The more people covered by the customer's plan, the higher the cost.

4. **The type of plan the customers choose.** They can buy a basic plan or step up to a Cadillac plan.

Smoking: Just Plain Bad—and Expensive

The fifth variable that insurance companies use to determine the rate a customer pays is cigarette smoking. Through a "tobacco rating," the ACA allows for insurance companies to charge smokers up to 50 percent more than nonsmokers. The amount of the allowable surcharge is left up to each state to decide, and therefore tobacco ratings vary from state to state. While most states allow the full 50 percent surcharge, other states, such as California, prohibit the tobacco rating, and some permit a smaller charge, such as Colorado, which allows a 15 percent smoker's surcharge.[2]

Smoking is not considered a preexisting condition, which in the old days was a big problem for many insurance customers. Prior to 2010 and the passage of the ACA, an insurance company would review a customer's application for enrollment, and if the company determined the customer had a preexisting condition such as diabetes or cancer, it could deny the customer coverage or offer coverage at inflated rates. The ACA made it illegal for health insurance companies to deny a customer medical coverage or raise rates due to a preexisting condition.

Even though it's a serious chemical addiction, smoking is considered a *behavioral choice*. If you choose to smoke, which is demonstrably bad for your health and brings a high likelihood of increased healthcare costs for diseases including emphysema and cancer, then you will pay more for your health insurance. Because of the irrefutable scientific evidence that (1) smoking provides no benefit and (2) smoking brings serious health risks, policy makers generally support the tobacco rating.

The insurance industry standard for identifying a smoker is based on two questions the insurance company typically will ask: (1) Are you a smoker? (2) Have you used tobacco products in the last six months?

"Tobacco use" is defined as "any tobacco product, including cigarettes, cigars, chewing tobacco, snuff, and pipe tobacco, used four or more times a week within the past six months."[3]

Because the system relies on self-reporting, why don't people just lie and say they don't smoke? Because if you get caught, that's insurance fraud. And if the applicant lied on a life insurance policy and then were to die within two years of policy issuance, the life insurer would normally do a claims investigation to determine if the statements the insured made in the application were truthful. The insurer is likely to deny claims in which the applicant made a material misstatement of fact, such as claiming to not smoke.[4]

Obesity: Also Bad—and Expensive

The question is, would policy makers and voters accept a broadening of this approach to include other behaviors that are deemed to be injurious to one's health?

For example, obesity is a growing health crisis. If you Google "What's worse, smoking or obesity?" you'll get thousands of results and a spirited discussion.

According to a study in the *Journal of Occupational and Environmental Medicine*, the official publication of the American College of Occupational and Environmental Medicine, obesity is more costly to society than smoking. Dr. James P. Moriarty and colleagues at the Mayo

Clinic found that among more than 30,000 Mayo Clinic employees and retirees, both obesity and smoking were associated with excess costs for healthcare. For smokers, average annual health costs were $1,275 higher than for nonsmokers. For obese individuals, annual healthcare costs were $1,850 higher than for those of normal weight. For those with morbid obesity, the additional costs were up to $5,500 per year.[5]

In the Reuters report "As America's Waistline Expands, Costs Soar," writer Sharon Begley noted that because obese individuals have a higher risk of medical conditions from heart disease to chronic pain, they are absent from work more often than people of average weight. The most obese men take 5.9 more sick days a year; the most obese women, 9.4 days more. Health economists led by Eric Finkelstein of Duke University have calculated that obesity-related absenteeism costs employers as much as $6.4 billion a year. There's also the problem of "presenteeism," or lowered productivity. Finkelstein found that the most obese lose one month of productive work per year, costing employers an average of $3,792 per most obese male worker and $3,037 per female. The total annual cost of presenteeism due to obesity is estimated to be $30 billion.[6]

Obesity shortens life. According to a study published in *JAMA Cardiology*, researchers examined data for 190,672 participants from the Cardiovascular Disease Lifetime Risk Pooling Project and found that people who were either obese or overweight lived shorter lives and lived with more chronic diseases. Those with BMIs higher than 24.9 increased their risk for heart disease, developed heart disease earlier in life, and were more likely to die from a cardiovascular event when compared with those with lower BMIs.[7]

It would appear that while insurance companies are allowed to charge more to offset the costs of smoking (and to provide another incentive for smokers to quit), the costs of obesity are actually *greater*, and yet there's no "obesity rating."

From the perspective of an insurance surcharge, the billion-dollar question is this: Is obesity a preexisting condition, like diabetes, or is it a behavioral choice, like smoking? Should obese individuals pay more for healthcare?

The fundamental problem is that people who are obese are in that condition because they *eat too much food*. The *reasons* why they eat too much can be complicated. An overweight person may have a thyroid condition, or be genetically predisposed to retain fat, or eat to relieve depression or anxiety. And unlike smoking, food is good for you. You must have food to survive—just not too much of it. Eating doughnuts is not illegal. Doughnuts are not considered to be addictive (though many dietitians believe sugar is). One doughnut a week is not going to harm your health.

The question of how to encourage healthy eating and discourage excessive eating, while offering treatment to those who need it for psychological issues, needs to be settled with tough but fair discussions among healthcare professionals.

Player Personas

To optimize compliance to the system, this carrot-stick approach will address a range of player personas. As is true with any other consumer marketplace, some constituents are "drivers" who like to take charge, while others are "followers" who prefer to go at a slower pace. Remember that in our hyperconsumerized culture, it's both necessary and possible to design a customer experience that conforms to the expectations of a wide range of constituent types.

The community is important too. Recent studies show that using communities to support behavioral change significantly improves the outcome. Organizations including Patientslikeme.com provide a safe space where participants can "ask questions, find answers from others who have gone before you, and thrive in a community of people who are helping each other live their best every day."[8]

The Car Insurance "Safe Driver Discount" Monitor

Car insurance is a major cost of car ownership, and it's considered so important that 48 out of 50 states require coverage by law. (Only New Hampshire and Virginia don't require car insurance. In both states, drivers are responsible for damages resulting from a car accident.) Most states require liability insurance, which means that if you cause an accident, the driver you hit is guaranteed to receive compensation from your insurance company.

For decades, it's been a standard feature of car insurance policies that if you're a bad driver who has caused accidents or has received tickets for moving violations, you'll pay a higher rate than if you've got a clean record. States also penalize bad drivers, and they typically use a point system based on "surchargeable incidents" over a six-year period. In California, for example, the points are tracked and can produce penalties levied by the state. California tracks the level of unsafe and risky driving behaviors based on:

- The number of tickets you receive.
- The number of accidents for which you are at fault.
- Reckless driving.
- Driving while under the influence of drugs or alcohol—this is a serious offense.
- A hit-and-run or driving over 100 mph.

When you receive a ticket, drive recklessly, or have an accident, you can face various penalties, including the addition of points against your driving record. Your insurance company will see these points and almost certainly raise your rate.

Remember, the point system reflects the choices you make as a driver *right now*; there's no factor that corresponds to a "preexisting condition."

For years, the auto insurance companies piggybacked off the states' point systems because that was the only yardstick available by which to gauge driver behavior. That is, until the advent of digital data sensors.

The idea of a "black box" that recorded vital statistics of a vehicle or aircraft—speed, braking, and so forth—was nothing new, but traditionally investigators could access these recording devices only after the fact, such as after an accident.

But in the twenty-first century, auto insurance companies began promoting tracking devices, known in the industry as "telematics devices," to follow the driving habits of their customers. Most telematics devices are small pieces of hardware that plug into your car's on-board diagnostics port (OBD-II port). It's the same port on the dashboard that your mechanic uses to plug in a handheld scanner to read error codes and identify problems.

Newer cars, including those equipped with updated versions of the OnStar system, don't need an OBD-II device. Instead they use the car's own data connection to communicate with insurance companies. Moving into the future, this will become the standard system.

When the telematics device is installed in your car, it taps into the vehicle's various computer systems to capture, store, and transmit data. The real-time data is sent back to your insurance provider. When linked to mapping data that shows the speed limits and other traffic controls on the streets on which you drive, the data from the device can indicate whether you are rolling through stop signs or speeding. If your insurer believes you're driving safely, it will reduce your premiums or give you credits on your auto insurance.

With its Snapshot program in 1998, Progressive was the first auto insurance company in the United States to roll out telematics-based tracking. At first, the company used the program to incentivize good driving habits by offering discounts to safe drivers. However, in 2013, the company started using collected data to penalize bad drivers.[9]

The use of telematics in motor vehicles closely parallels the use of the CHOS in human constituents. From the point of view of the customer, there are three benefits to agreeing to use a telematics device:

1. **Rewards for safe driving.** Generally, if the vehicle use data shows you're a safe driver, you'll be eligible for car insurance discounts or earn rewards. You may be rewarded for avoiding risks such as traveling late at night, making hard stops, and driving at high speeds.

2. **Advice on how to be a better driver.** Telematics data can provide useful information about your driving habits, which you can then review with the twin goals of becoming a safer driver and thereby lowering your insurance premium. Some insurers' programs offer you the opportunity to go online or use a safe driving app to track the data your telematics device collects about your driving habits, which can help you improve your driving record.

3. **Usage-based insurance.** In the old days, it didn't matter if you drove your car every day and racked up thousands of miles or if you just drove it on Sundays to go to church. All that mattered was your driving record and your points. With telematics, your insurer will know if you're a road warrior or a homebody. Some insurers offer options on how you use and pay for your insurance, including programs that allow you to pay per mile driven. Your insurer may charge you a daily rate and a per-mile rate for each mile you drive, and allow you to review your trips and daily costs via a mobile app or website.[10]

Some insurers offer telematics services that go beyond tracking how you drive to track how your kids drive. For example, IntelliDrive from Travelers Insurance is a smartphone app that captures and scores the driving behavior of drivers covered on your policy. You can receive email or text alerts to let you know if the vehicle is being driven outside of your safe driving guidelines. GPS also lets you know where your car is being driven. Information tracked includes mileage, time of day, speed, braking, and acceleration.[11]

Why am I talking about car insurance telematics? For two reasons:

1. Your constituents are becoming comfortable with the idea of their behavior being monitored by a corporate entity in exchange for a lower price on the product they're buying. We are seeing this with health insurance, where smokers pay more for choosing to smoke, and with driver's insurance, where drivers who choose to drive aggressively will pay more than drivers who drive safely.

2. The rapid rate of technological innovation all but assures the day is coming when microsized devices will collect and transmit enormous amounts of data—enough to make real-time health monitoring an everyday reality.

The question is this: Is your healthcare organization going to be ahead of the wave or behind it?

Rewards for Making Good Choices

Let's be blunt: if a constituent makes choices that result in a decline in health and increased expense for treatment, and over time does nothing to improve their choices, should that person pay more for health insurance?

When it comes to smoking and reckless driving, there is widespread agreement: the answer is yes.

The Big Shift will expand this concept to include other unhealthy, costly choices.

Obesity and Knee Replacement Surgery

The older you get, the more likely you are to have knee and other joint problems. But it's a statistical fact that if you are overweight or obese, your joints will degrade much more rapidly, and will more likely require surgery than if you were not obese.

As the Arthritis Foundation reports, obesity makes arthritis worse. One in five Americans has been diagnosed with arthritis, but according to the CDC, among obese people that number jumps to more than one in three, and two-thirds of Americans are either overweight or obese.

Osteoarthritis (OA), the most common type of arthritis, is characterized by the breakdown of cartilage. Age, injury, heredity, and lifestyle factors all affect the risk of OA. Obesity is a factor, because the more weight that's on a joint, the more stressed the joint becomes, and the more likely it will wear down and be damaged.

"Weight plays an important role in joint stress," said Eric Matteson, MD, chair of the rheumatology division at the Mayo Clinic, "so when people are very overweight, it puts stress on their joints, especially their weight-bearing joints, like the knees and the hips."[12]

When the knee joint is worn or damaged so that the patient's mobility is reduced and the patient is in pain even while resting, knee replacement surgery is usually necessary. The most common reason for knee replacement surgery is osteoarthritis.[13]

In 2019, the average hospital charge for a total knee replacement (TKR) in the United States was $49,500. A partial knee replacement typically costs about 10 to 20 percent less than a TKR.

In addition to the basic hospital charge for the procedure, inpatient charges from the surgeon and other healthcare providers may add an average of $7,500, bringing the average total charges for a TKR in the United States closer to $57,000. And hospital charges don't reflect the amount the patient pays out of pocket.

Of course, with obese patients the question is, should the patient lose weight before the surgery, or will having the surgery relieve the pain and help the patient move more and lose weight?

Studies suggest it doesn't matter when you do it—weight loss is a positive thing. J. W. Pritchett and D. T. Bortel wrote in "Knee Replacement in Morbidly Obese Women," that in a comparison of obese and nonobese patients, 86 percent of nonobese patients had excellent or good results from knee replacement surgical treatment, while only 57 percent of morbidly obese patients had excellent or good results. They concluded, "Total knee replacement is safe and reasonably effective in the morbidly obese. However, the results are not comparable with those achieved in nonobese patients, and knee replacement should not be expected to facilitate weight loss."[14]

Alcohol Abuse

As AlcoholPolicyMD reported, up to 40 percent of all patients in US general hospital beds (not in maternity or intensive care) are being treated for complications of alcohol-related problems. Annual expenditures for alcohol-related healthcare total $22.5 billion, and in comparison with moderate and nondrinkers, constituents with a history of heavy drinking have higher healthcare costs.[15]

Hypertension

An analysis led by Elizabeth Kirkland, MD, MSCR, an assistant professor of internal medicine at the Medical University of South Carolina, found that in comparison with patients with normal blood pressure, those with hypertension had an estimated $2,000 more in healthcare expenditures annually, equating to an adjusted national expenditure of $131 billion. Patients with hypertension had approximately 2.5 times higher annual inpatient costs, almost double the outpatient costs, and about triple the prescription medication costs.

"Hypertension is the costliest of all cardiovascular diseases, and thus a huge health issue for patients of those practicing cardiology and metabolic health," Kirkland told *MD Magazine*. She added, "The cost burden of hypertension on both population-level and patient-level expenditures is undeniable and highlights an ongoing need to remain vigilant in prevention, early detection, and treatment."[16]

As everyone knows, if you've been diagnosed with high blood pressure, the first advice your doctor gives you is to make lifestyle changes. Your doctor may recommend you eat a heart-healthy diet with less salt, get regular physical activity, maintain a healthy weight or lose weight if you're overweight or obese, and limit the amount of alcohol you drink. These are all things that constituents can do on their own while being monitored by their CHOS module.

Cardiovascular Disease

As the American Heart Association (AHA) reports, in the United States cardiovascular disease is both the number one killer and the most expensive disease, costing nearly $1 billion a day. It tops the list of disease burdens, and this grim situation is only expected to get worse. Projections show that 45 percent of the US adult population will live with cardiovascular disease by 2035, at an annual cost of more than $1 trillion. The AHA points to the "ABCS" as the most effective way to prevent cardiovascular disease: aspirin as appropriate, blood pressure control, cholesterol management, and smoking cessation.[17]

The CDC says that each year in the US, nearly one in three deaths is caused by heart disease and stroke—and "at least 200,000 of these deaths could have been prevented through changes in health habits, such as stopping smoking, more physical activity, and less salt in the diet; community changes to create healthier living spaces, such as safe places to exercise and smoke-free areas; and managing high blood pressure, high cholesterol, and diabetes."[18]

If your constituents are willing to pay higher auto insurance rates to drive recklessly and pay more to be smokers, it's not such a great leap for them to understand that if they aren't at least *trying* to avoid lifestyle diseases, they're going to have to pay more for the privilege.

TAKE ACTION!

- Your goal will be to convince as many of your constituents as possible to do themselves a favor, join the CHOS network, and help tilt the thrust of our healthcare system from diagnosis and treatment to anticipation and prevention.
- The innovators and early adopters will be the first to embrace the Big Shift. In contrast, the never adopters will take pride in refusing to take part, and they will pay more.
- When talking about the CHOS network to those who are skeptical, use the examples of lower insurance rates for nonsmokers and safe drivers as examples of consumers earning lower rates by reducing their own risky behavior. There are many other ways that your constituents engage in self-harming behavior, and if they want to do that, they need to be prepared to pay more for their healthcare.

The Healthcare
Analytics Marketplace

Having come this far, let's take a step back and look at how Roberta's health management system will work.

Some studies suggest that as many as 50 percent of all primary care visits result in an inaccurate diagnosis. The problem isn't that we don't have well-trained caregivers; as you know, they are generally highly trained and qualified. The problem is that the caregivers often don't have enough data or time. The constituent comes to them, they're presented with incomplete information, and with the patient suffering, they feel as though they need to quickly provide answers.

This is where the integrated CHOS sensor comes into play. Roberta's sensor will monitor head movement, total body movement, core body temperature, and many other biological data points through external skin sensors. This technology will be connected to other noninvasive wearable sensors that will monitor virtually every aspect of her body functions and blood chemistry.

This information will be gathered and sent through either her smartphone or a separate data integrator/transceiver that sends a continuous stream of massive health data to her CHOS module, linked to a central server. The module will evaluate the data for accuracy, and then by using machine learning, diagnostic databases, artificial intelligence, predictive analytics, and many other data evaluation methods, it will continuously determine her state of health.

The module will feed Roberta's health information to a real-time health dashboard that shows her risk profile at any given time throughout the day for virtually all disease processes. Her physician will set up her health profile based on her genomic and current health data. Roberta's health profile will also include current medications and all other vital statistics.

The module will not just diagnose her every minute of the day to find the earliest signs of disease processes; it will also leverage game mechanics, social engagement, geofencing, and other systems to encourage Roberta to strive for positive health behaviors. When she walks into a doughnut shop, she may receive a gentle haptic vibration from her CHOS module reminding her that high carbohydrates and sugar will impact her overall health. It may also identify other risky locations and send her notices that will range from a slight vibration from the in-air technology to a range of tones and even voice notifications.

The system will also remind Roberta about opportunities to optimize her health, and it will use game mechanics to incentivize her for taking healthy options. If Roberta requires medications, her CHOS module may also use a dispensary pod to deliver her prescriptions at the right times every day. The system will also work like air traffic control to direct Roberta to specialists as they are needed.

This ubiquitous system of passive information collection combined with active (but gentle) intervention could save millions of lives each year while concurrently significantly reducing the cost of healthcare delivery. This is particularly good news for underserved populations, as historically they have not had good access to preventive care.

Human Health Data Is Worth Big Money

One of the features of the CHOS module is the massive amount of Roberta's personal data it will generate. This data will not only be sourced from her internal vital statistics and therefore be strictly health related; it may also be external and geospatial—that is, showing her physical location and movements throughout the day.

If you multiply that by millions of constituents, you'll have a massive flood of personal digital data. And as we know, any type of information about people and what they do is valuable to both corporations and policy makers. Key users of human health data include healthcare providers, medical device and pharmaceutical companies, patients, payers, marketing firms, and governments. They use health and behavioral data for medical research, marketing, strategizing, and forecasting. Non-healthcare companies can use Roberta's data too, to track which retail stores or service providers she visits, and the ones she *doesn't* visit.

From the health data of large numbers of people, public health patterns can be discerned and emerging diseases identified. This is how John Snow identified London's Broad Street cholera epidemic in 1854 and traced it to the infamous water pump. It's how public health authorities can identify "clusters" of cancer that might signify environmental pollution. It's how pharmaceutical companies can decide which device or drug is worth a billion-dollar investment.

A medical device or pharmaceutical company may license or purchase patient data from a healthcare provider in order to understand prescribing patterns, long-term efficacy trends, patient demographics, and potential market opportunities.

This growing flood of data has a name: the healthcare analytics market. It's the collection of data from all sources that's bought and sold and then subjected to analytical analysis, resulting in improved and efficient healthcare services.

In the healthcare analytics market, human health data is worth money. Big money.

As MarketsandMarkets reported, the overall market for healthcare analytics is expected to mushroom from $14.0 billion in 2019 to $50.5 billion by 2024, at a compound annual growth rate of 28.3 percent during the forecast period. Growth in the market is being driven by the emergence of big data in healthcare, growing venture capital invest-ments, government initiatives to increase the adoption of electronic health records, and growing pressure to curb healthcare spending and improve patient outcomes.

Mordor Intelligence points to factors driving the healthcare analytics market that also include the growth of the Internet of Things, increased focus on collection and analysis of data from different sources for better customer service, technological advancements, and the advent of social media and its impact on the healthcare industry.[1]

According to MarketsandMarkets, the biggest single player in the healthcare analytics market is computer giant IBM, which has a strong presence in the commercial and government healthcare payer markets, as well as a robust sales and distribution network across more than 175 countries. Since 2005, the company has invested $24 billion in the devel-opment of its big data and analytics software and services capabilities and has 6,809 patents to its name.[2]

Other key players include Allscripts Healthcare Solutions (a pub-licly traded American company that provides physician practices, hos-pitals, and other healthcare providers with practice management and electronic health record technology), Cerner Corporation (an American supplier of health information technology solutions, services, devices, and hardware), Philips Healthcare (a division of Koninklijke Philips N.V., a Dutch multinational conglomerate corporation headquartered in Amsterdam), and McKesson Corporation (an American company dis-tributing pharmaceuticals and providing health information technology, medical supplies, and care management tools).

How Personal Health Data Can Be Marketed

The laws surrounding the acquisition, sale, and distribution of personal health data are numerous and vague. Generally they operate more for the benefit of ensuring the flow of information throughout the healthcare industry than ensuring the privacy of individuals.

The single most authoritative regulation is the federal Health Insurance Portability and Accountability Act of 1996 (HIPAA), which protects the privacy of patients and sets forth guidelines on how private health information can be shared. It focuses on three areas:

1. It creates a legal structure for how personal health data may be disclosed and establishes the rights of individuals concerning their health information.
2. It describes security standards for maintaining and transmitting electronic patient information.
3. It specifies a common format and data structure for the electronic exchange of health information.

The fact that HIPAA was passed in 1996, before the vast increase in Internet-based digital data and inexpensive genetic sequencing, should be enough to indicate its limitations. HIPAA only regulates the health industry, and thus only applies to what the law considers "covered entities" and their "business associates." Covered entities include healthcare providers, health plans (health insurers or HMOs), and healthcare clearinghouses. Business associates include any person or organization that creates, receives, maintains, or transmits protected health information (PHI) on behalf of a covered entity.

The key aspect of the legal marketing of personal health data is the degree to which it has been "de-identified." No covered entity can sell data that has not been de-identified, which means that 18 "identifiers" have been removed. They are:

1. Name
2. Address (all geographic subdivisions smaller than state, including street address, city county, and zip code)

3. All elements (except years) of dates related to an individual (including birthdate, admission date, discharge date, date of death, and exact age if over 89)
4. Telephone numbers
5. Fax number
6. Email address
7. Social Security number
8. Medical record number
9. Health plan beneficiary number
10. Account number
11. Certificate or license number
12. Vehicle identifiers and serial numbers, including license plate numbers
13. Device identifiers and serial numbers
14. Web URL
15. Internet Protocol (IP) address
16. Fingerprint or voiceprint
17. Photographic image (Photographic images are not limited to images of the face.)
18. Any other characteristic that could uniquely identify the individual

If a communication contains any of these identifiers, or parts of the identifier, such as initials, the data is to be considered "identified." To be considered "de-identified," each and every one of the 18 HIPAA identifiers must be removed from the data set.

Much can remain. Following these regulations, a packet of personal data could be identified as "African American female, age 34, unmarried, resident of Michigan, weight 180 pounds, carrier of sickle cell disease, elevated level of lead in blood. . . ." You might know someone who fits that description, especially if you lived in the city of Flint.

And if the de-identified data contains a reference to a rare condition such as Abruzzo Erickson syndrome, Gamstorp disease, Rasmussen encephalitis, Weber-Christian disease, or many thousands more diseases that may be of great interest to pharmaceutical companies, then identifying the patient would be very easy.

How about data that has *not* been de-identified?

The HIPAA privacy laws stipulate that covered entities should adhere to the "Minimum Necessary Rule," which states the disclosure of PHI should only be the minimum necessary to achieve the stated purpose. According to the *HIPAA Journal*, the HIPAA privacy laws concerning PHI apply to every covered entity and every third-party service provider or business associate with whom the covered entity does business. These are the *only* parties who should have access to PHI unless authorization is given *by the patient* for it to be disclosed for research, marketing, or fund-raising purposes.[3]

The problem is with the requirement for authorization.

Many corporations and healthcare providers ask their patients or customers to sign routine-looking consent forms that are deliberately dense and unlikely to be carefully read by the signer. As researcher Christine J. Manta wrote in "From the Patient Perspective, Consent Forms Fall Short of Providing Information to Guide Decision Making," after a series of interviews with patients she found that "consent forms are too complex and fail to achieve comprehension."[4]

For example, the personal genetics service 23andMe offers a privacy statement that, in its version of September 30, 2019, ran 8,800 words in length. The accompanying terms of service (TOS) statement ran 10,300 words.

The company explicitly says, "In order to use the Services, you must first acknowledge and agree to the Privacy Statement. You may not use the Services if you do not accept the Privacy Statement." And "In order to use the Services, you must first agree to the TOS. You may not use the Services if you do not accept the TOS."[5]

Combined, the privacy statement and terms of service are the length of a novella. "The problem with a lot of these privacy policies and terms of service is that no one really reads them," Tiffany C. Li, a privacy expert and resident fellow at Yale Law School's Information Society Project, told *Tom's Guide*. "You are paying to help the company make money with your data."[6]

In the 23andMe terms of service, the company says, "If you have given consent for your Genetic Information and Self-Reported Information to be used in 23andMe Research as described in the applicable Consent Document, we may disclose your information to third parties as described in the applicable Consent Document. 23andMe Research may be sponsored by, conducted on behalf of, or in collaboration with third parties, such as non-profit foundations, academic institutions or pharmaceutical companies."[7]

According to the company, 23andMe Research is an ongoing research program aimed at publication in peer-reviewed journals and research funded by the federal government (such as the National Institutes of Health). The consent form cautions the participant, "There is a very small chance that someone with access to the research data or results could expose personal information about you. 23andMe has policies and practices in place to minimize the chance of such an event."[8]

The consumer genetics testing service Gene By Gene Ltd. offers this terse privacy (which it calls "Privacy & Security") statement: "Gene By Gene, LTD. will handle all sample specimens in compliance with all applicable laws and regulations. All data received from the customer and data generated will be created, stored, and transferred according to HIPAA guidelines. The customer understands that Gene By Gene, LTD. is not responsible for misuse, mishandling, or misrepresentation of this data by the customer or other third parties who have been given rightful access to the aforementioned data or materials."[9]

In contrast, MyMedLab.com, based in Joplin, Missouri, which offers a wide variety of blood tests directly to consumers, says flatly: "At MyMedLab, we have a very simple privacy policy. We guarantee your complete privacy by not allowing any third party access to your personal health information. This strict policy is essential to protecting yourself in the new 'information age.' A majority of third parties companies (insurance, employers, benefits, and marketers) are interested in your information for their benefit, not yours. It is important to begin to protect this information and ensure its privacy. MyMedLab guarantees your privacy by reporting your personal health information directly to you."[10]

While the privacy policies and terms of services of healthcare industry data collectors seem to dance around the likelihood of the sale of de-identified data according to the HIPAA guidelines, the law offers *no protection* when you're giving health-related information to a tech company. Tech companies like Fitbit and Apple that work in the health space but aren't officially "healthcare" companies have deliberately avoided HIPAA and operate in the unregulated zone where they can freely gather and trade health-related information.

For example, as TheVerge.com pointed out, if you take an electrocardiogram at your doctor's office, and your doctor puts the results into an electronic health record, then your information is protected by HIPAA because it's within the healthcare system. But if you take an ECG with the Apple Watch and don't share that information with your doctor, that same information is *not* protected by HIPAA. Yet if you take an ECG using the new Apple Watch and share it with your doctor, who puts it into an electronic health record, it is protected by HIPAA. Basically, HIPAA says that if you *choose* to give away your health data to Apple (or Facebook or anywhere else), you forfeit HIPAA protection. Only if you remain within the healthcare system are you protected—at least to a point.[11]

And remember "business associates"? In 2016, IBM acquired Truven Health Analytics, a provider of cloud-based healthcare, analytics, and insights, for the price of $2.6 billion; the intent was for Truven's cloud-based technology, methodologies, and health claims data to be integrated into the Watson Health cloud over time, creating one of the world's largest health-related data collections representing 300 million patient lives.

The Customers Give Their Data, and the Company Then Sells It

Once personal health data became both big enough and manageable enough to be useful to drug companies, it became a valuable commodity on the commercial market. Nowhere was this more clearly demonstrated than the partnership between the British pharmaceutical company GlaxoSmithKline (GSK) and 23andMe. In July 2018, GSK announced it had invested $300 million in the genetics testing company, in part to gain access to customer data. The GSK press release said, "The collaboration will combine 23andMe's large-scale genetic resources and advanced data science skills, with the scientific and medical knowledge and commercialisation expertise of GSK." For her part, Anne Wojcicki, CEO and cofounder of 23andMe, said, "By leveraging the genetic and phenotypic information provided by consenting 23andMe customers and combining it with GSK's incredible expertise and resources in drug discovery, we believe we can more quickly make treating and curing diseases a reality."[12]

Phenotypic data consists of clinical information regarding patients' disease symptoms as well as relevant demographic data, such as age, ethnicity, and sex. In other words, de-identified information.

Many analysts raised concerns about the ethics of asking the company's millions of customers—who in 2020 paid $99 for the basic ancestry report up to $499 for the VIP Health & Ancestry Service—to freely donate their genetic data to 23andMe Research, which means it will be commercially exploited by GlaxoSmithKline, which paid 23andMe $300 million for its use.

"The information that 23andMe is giving to GlaxoSmithKline isn't out of the goodness of the hearts of 23andMe for the public good," said Peter Pitts, president of the Center for Medicine in the Public Interest, to *Time* magazine. "They're making money on this deal. If your data is going to be used for commercial purposes, you should be compensated for that. At minimum, you should be refunded any money you paid to 23andMe to have your genetic test done in the first place" (see Figure 17.1).[13]

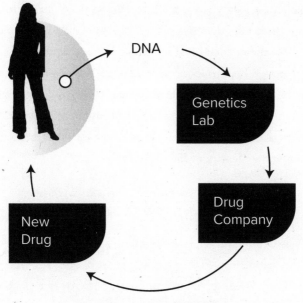

FIGURE 17.1 **The Profit Circle**

Genetics sequencing companies are not alone in leveraging customer and patient data. Throughout the healthcare industry, the problem is pervasive. In 2018, the prestigious Memorial Sloan Kettering Cancer Center came under fire for investing $25 million into a startup company, Paige.AI. Founded by three insiders at Sloan Kettering, the company, dedicated to applying artificial intelligence to healthcare, was granted an exclusive deal to use the cancer center's vast archive of 25 million patient tissue slides, along with decades of work by its world-renowned pathologists. As *The New York Times* reported, hospital pathologists objected to the Paige.AI deal, questioning the use of patients' data—even if it was de-identified—without their knowledge in a profit-driven venture.[14]

It's not just corporations that sell patient data; the states do it also. As the report "Risks to Patient Privacy: A Re-identification of Patients in Maine and Vermont Statewide Hospital Data" by Latanya Sweeney and others revealed, as of 2018, 48 states in the United States collect statewide inpatient discharge data that includes personal health information of each patient's hospital visit. In other words, each time a hospital treats a patient, a data record is sent to the state. A survey found that 33 of those states subsequently sold or otherwise disclosed copies of the data, and 30 of them failed to de-identify data according to the standards established under HIPAA because states are not mandated to follow HIPAA when handling patient data. In many cases, the researchers were able to match these state hospitalization records (which anyone can buy) to newspaper accounts of accidents and other causes of hospitalization and determine the identity of the patients.[15]

TAKE ACTION!

- The healthcare analytics market is growing exponentially and is very loosely regulated. You need to review your policies and business deals to ensure that you're handling patient and constituent data appropriately.
- While being mindful of both present regulations controlling the healthcare analytics market and the likelihood of much tighter controls in the future (as the following chapter will discuss), your organization needs to ramp up its data collection and processing capabilities to meet the demands of the Big Shift toward massive constituent data streams. Constituent data needs to be used to benefit the constituent and *not* as a profit center for the organization, unless— and this is coming!—systems are created for the payment of revenues to the constituents for the lawful sale of their data.

The Big Shift in Healthcare Analytics

A change is coming, and healthcare professionals need to be ready for it. The change is in how we as a society view ownership of personal health information and how such information is exploited.

The notion of ownership is interesting and multifaceted. We all know what it means to own something. If you own something tangible, then you have the exclusive right to use it and even destroy it, like a car that you buy, use, and then send to the junkyard. If another person takes what you own without your permission—such as stealing your car—that person has violated the law.

With tangible objects, ownership is pretty straightforward, except in divorce court, where it can get really messy.

Ownership can also apply to nonphysical things, such as ideas and names. A company can trademark a brand name and own it so that others cannot use it in their market. (For example, you could trademark "Fluffy" as a brand of marshmallows, and no one else could use it to sell marshmallows; but someone could sell a "Fluffy" brand of pillows for the bed.)

As individuals, we each own our name and likeness. That is to say, if you are Joe Smith, a company cannot use your name or likeness to sell its product without your permission. If you happen to be a celebrity, your name and likeness can be extremely valuable. Would you like to name your new line of perfume "Marilyn Monroe" and put her face on the box? Then you'd better be ready to pony up some hard cash, because the name and likeness of the Hollywood icon is owned by Authentic Brands Group (ABG). According to *Forbes*, in 2018 ABG earned a cool $14 million in licensing fees through its ownership of the Marilyn Monroe brand.[1]

But ownership of your personal information, and who has the right to exploit it, can get murky. For example, the home address of most people is public information. Anyone can go to the county courthouse and find out where Joe Smith lives and then use that information to help market products to Joe and to other people. Social media sites vacuum up enormous quantities of data on the habits and choices of their users. Political campaigns use sophisticated voter targeting, looking at past voting histories, religious affiliation, demographics, magazine subscriptions, and buying habits to understand which issues and values are driving which voters. They rely on this data to inform key decisions: which states or constituencies to focus resources on, where to hold rallies, and how to personalize communications with supporters, undecided voters, and nonsupporters. It's almost a given that with the input of available public data, any major campaign organization will be able to precisely predict for whom Joe Smith will vote in the election.

Generally, the consensus seems to be that if something is a matter of public record, then it's fair game for exploitation with no compensation to the original source (that is, to Joe Smith). But the lines are getting blurred. With personal medical data becoming increasingly valuable as a commodity, many people are beginning to insist that personal medical data needs to be recognized as being the sole and exclusive property of the constituent, even if the constituent freely provided such data (typically in the form of lab tests or requests for a diagnosis) to a healthcare provider, such as a hospital.

The Patchwork of State Laws

Currently, the laws governing the ownership of patients' medical data vary from state to state.

According to Health Information & the Law, in 21 states the hospital and/or physician owns the patient's original medical records—that is, the actual pieces of paper or film, as well as the electronic versions of those records. These states include California, Florida, Pennsylvania, and Virginia. In those states, if you go to the hospital and have an x-ray, then the hospital owns that x-ray. If you have a blood test, the lab owns the data from that blood test.

In Texas, a patient's medical records may be owned by a physician's employer, including group practices, professional associations, and non-profit health organizations. The only thing constraining their use of the underlying data on those records is the set of privacy provisions under HIPAA.

In 28 states, there are no laws conferring specific ownership or property rights to medical records. In those states there may be court decisions regarding medical data ownership that apply to providers in a particular state under common law even where there is no statute or regulation. But in general, you can interpret "no laws" to mean the hospital can successfully exert ownership rights.

In just one state, New Hampshire, medical information contained in the medical records at any facility licensed under state law shall be deemed to be the property of the patient.[2]

Patients often have difficulty getting copies of their own medical records to which they are legally entitled. As Carolyn T. Lye and others revealed in "Assessment of US Hospital Compliance with Regulations for Patients' Requests for Medical Records," hospitals are not always compliant with federal and state regulations in their medical records request processes. The researchers' cross-sectional study of 83 US hospitals revealed noncompliance with federal regulations for formats of release and state regulations for request processing times. Only 53 percent of hospitals' forms indicated patients could get their complete records. In addition, there was "discordance between information provided on medical records release authorization forms and that obtained directly from medical records departments regarding the medical records request processes."[3]

Google Wants Your Data

On November 11, 2019, *The Wall Street Journal* revealed a massive joint project by Google and healthcare giant Ascension to collect and analyze the detailed personal health information of millions of people in the 21 states served by the nation's third largest healthcare provider. Called Project Nightingale, the project reportedly involves Ascension sharing with Google data including lab results, doctor diagnoses, hospitalization and other records, and even patients' names and dates of birth. In other words, according to the *Journal*, it all "amounts to a complete health history."

Were the reported tens of millions of patients asked for their permission? They don't have to be asked, and they aren't. Nor were their doctors.

On the other hand, the *Journal* reported that about 150 Google employees have access to "much of the data."[4]

It began in early 2019 when the two companies signed a HIPAA business associate agreement, which would allow Ascension to transfer patient data to Google Cloud and would bar Google from using this data for purposes other than providing services to Ascension. As CNBC reported, the deal came as Google sought to enter the $3.5 trillion health sector by also acquiring fitness tracker company Fitbit and announcing a 10-year deal with Mayo Clinic to be the cornerstone of the healthcare company's digital transformation.[5]

"Data-driven medical innovation is growing exponentially, and our partnership with Google will help us lead the digital transformation in healthcare," said Gianrico Farrugia, MD, president and CEO of Mayo Clinic.[6]

In the court of public opinion, Google faced "an uphill battle to prove that it can be trusted when it makes the bulk of its money through advertising, which relies on extensive use of customer data."[7]

Google Gets Sued

Don't think for a moment that your constituents are afraid to take you to court when they believe their data has been unfairly marketed.

On May 17, 2017, the University of Chicago Medical Center released a statement entitled "UChicago Medicine collaborates with Google to use machine learning for better healthcare," in which the university announced it was collaborating with Google "to study ways to use data in electronic medical records to make discoveries that could improve the quality of healthcare." The press release also noted that the partnership was using Google Cloud's "state-of-the-art infrastructure to keep digital health records stored securely with the highest level of protections and strictly following HIPAA privacy rules . . ."[8]

The program got under way. In a January 2018 research paper published by Google entitled "Scalable and Accurate Deep Learning for Electronic Health Records," the company verified it had used electronic health record data of patients at University of Chicago Medicine from 2009 to 2016. Alvin Rajkomar and coauthors wrote, "We validated our approach using de-identified EHR data from two US academic medical centers with 216,221 adult patients hospitalized for at least 24 hours. . . . We included EHR data from the University of California, San Francisco (UCSF) from 2012–2016, and the University of Chicago Medicine (UCM) from 2009–2016."[9]

In June 2019, the University of Chicago, the medical center, and Google were sued in a potential class-action lawsuit. The allegation was that the deal violated patient privacy because the patient records included date stamps of when patients checked in and checked out of the hospital. As *The New York Times* reported, this was seen to be a problem because Google could combine the dates with other information it already possessed, including location data from smartphones running its Android software or Google Maps and Waze, which would allow the company to establish the identities of the patients in the medical records. The lawsuit accused the university of consumer fraud and fraudulent business practices because it neither sought nor received express consent from patients to disclose their medical records to Google.[10]

Thieves Love Healthcare Data

We often think of cybercriminals stealing social security numbers and credit card account information because it's easy to imagine those being easily converted to cash. But the market for stolen medical records is becoming just as big.

Data breaches are becoming an increasingly critical issue for the healthcare industry. In the first six months of 2019 alone, nearly 32 million records were exposed, more than double the total number for 2018.

"Health information is a treasure trove for criminals," Tom Kellermann, chief cybersecurity officer of Carbon Black, told HealthTech. "By compromising it, by stealing it, by having it sold, you have 7 to 10 personal identifying characteristics of an individual."

Reports indicate that the high value of medical records on the dark web has surpassed that of social security and credit card numbers, which, according to Experian, can sell for up to $1,000 online, depending on the completeness of the information contained within.

Criminals can use personal medical data to create fake IDs, with which they can buy medical equipment or drugs. They can combine a false provider number with a real patient number and file phony claims with insurers.

From a thief's point of view, one of the advantages of medical records is that they cannot be changed. For example, if your bank suspects your credit card has been compromised, your bank simply cancels the card and issues you a new one. Problem solved! But if your medical records are stolen, the thief may have personal information about you that isn't going to change.

Part of the problem is that unlike banks and credit card companies, in the area of cybersecurity, healthcare companies are novices with outdated ideas. "Organizations are far too reliant on firewalls and encryption, neither of which can stop modern-day cyberattacks," said Kellermann. "The big challenge with the entire governance of the healthcare sector with regards to cybersecurity, is that there are physicians who run the board, who run various departments. And these folks are very astute when it comes to medical knowledge but not quite prepared to handle the risks of IT and IT deployment."[11]

Blockchain Solves Two Big Problems

In the era of massive challenges facing the healthcare analytics market, two concerns are paramount:

1. The healthcare analytics market is porous, meaning the security of personal health data cannot be guaranteed. Computers can be hacked, cozy business deals made, and data mishandled, causing it to fall into the hands of unauthorized third parties. Data can be sold "out the back door" just like any other commodity, and once it's out there, you can't get it back.

2. The original producers of healthcare data—patients, constituents, and customers of healthcare providers and health industry companies—whose data is worth money in the healthcare analytics market, are not compensated. In fact, they *pay* to access

the healthcare system and to have their DNA tested or their disease treated, and then the company takes a double profit by selling their data to a third party.

The Big Shift is providing solutions to both problems.

In regard to data security, the emerging technology of blockchain is providing hope of a solution. Blockchain technology was originally developed to record cryptocurrency transactions—that is, bitcoin. However, as blockchain has matured and has been adopted across unrelated industries, the use of blockchain technology in healthcare is demanding attention.

Briefly, blockchain technology can be seen in the form of a growing list of data records, called blocks, that are sequentially linked using cryptography. Each block contains a cryptographic hash of the previous block, a time stamp, and transaction data. By design, a blockchain is resistant to modification of the data. It is an open, distributed ledger that can record transactions between two parties in a verifiable and permanent way.

Look at it this way: In the old days, a ledger was a physical book that was kept by a record-keeper (such as a bank) in which transactions and contracts were recorded. If you deposited money into your account, it was recorded in the ledger. If you took money out, it was recorded. When you bought a house, the transaction was recorded with the office of the county clerk.

Traditional ledgers—both physical and electronic—have three significant characteristics:

1. **They are inherently private.** The keeper of the ledger has privileged access not available to others.

2. **They can be altered.** Anyone with access to the ledger can change an entry and alter "the facts." This is why transactions recorded in ledgers require a high degree of trust. When you deposit money into your bank, you trust the bank to record it accurately and not alter the data. (If you want to read about

how a big bank can alter customer data for unethical purposes, all you have to do is Google "Wells Fargo Bank fraud.")

3. **They may be difficult to obtain.** Different ledgers are kept by various providers, who may not communicate well and who may seek to protect their turf. Fragmented, siloed patient records create inaccuracies and inefficiencies across the breadth of the healthcare system. If you go to a new specialist, for example, the specialist has to get your records from your primary care physician and any previous specialists.

According to a survey conducted by KLAS Research, in the realm of healthcare data, interoperability—the smooth coordination of independent systems—is rare. KLAS's survey revealed only 6 percent of clinicians found that information from other organizations was easy to obtain without interrupting their workflow, and fewer than one-third said they could easily access data from other electronic health records.[12]

Blockchain technology is fundamentally different. A blockchain ledger in the form of a series of transactions is called a "distributed ledger" because it's not held in one place or on one computer. Instead, it's on an entire peer-to-peer network, which collectively adheres to a protocol for internode communication and the validation of new blocks. This means that once recorded, the data in any given block cannot be altered retroactively without changing all subsequent blocks, which requires the consensus of the network majority. Although blockchain records are not unalterable, blockchains may be considered secure by design. When properly configured to detail the exchange agreement, a blockchain can maintain title rights because it creates a record that compels offer and acceptance.

Data stored on the blockchain is generally considered incorruptible. Without getting too far into the weeds, the system works in a way that's similar to a safe deposit box at a bank, with two keys. The *public key* (actually a string of numbers) is an address on the blockchain. The *private key* is a password that gives its owner access to the owner's digital assets or the means to interact with the features that blockchains now support. No centralized "official" copy of a contract or ledger exists, and no user is "trusted" more than any other.

The breakthrough innovation of blockchain technology is that it solves two problems at once: the problem of security and the problem of ownership.

On the security front, blockchain ledgers are inherently more secure than traditional databases. The decentralization of electronic health record storage through the use of a blockchain could greatly improve the security of health data because if hackers were to gain access to the blockchain, they would only see one or two blocks of data, which are unusable without the context of the rest of the chain. When a constituent's medical information is distributed across many databases, and when, in order to access it, a network of stakeholders needs to give permission, then security is reinforced, as the chances to corrupt all the members of the network and gain access to the data are slim.

Here's how it works, in steps:

1. Patients and healthcare providers produce data from various sources, including the CHOS module data, biological exams, imagery, genetic tests, and treatment records.
2. All the medical data is encrypted, and constituents digitally sign consent forms specifying who has access to the data. If the patient doesn't want Google to have access, it's not granted.
3. Data is stored conventionally in data warehouses owned by healthcare organizations. It is time-stamped and traceable.
4. The blockchain acts like a search engine or catalog, listing the data stored.
5. To gain access to constituent data, qualified healthcare providers query the database and then provide the constituent's key.

The ultimate "keeper of the key" to the set of data built around the constituent *is* the constituent. Under this system, the healthcare providers—who, after all, have been *paid by the constituent* (either directly or indirectly) for their service—do not retain any ownership rights to that data. They cannot sell it, distribute it, or use it for any other purpose without the permission of the constituent.

While to some people the idea that constituents should own their medical data is revolutionary, to many others it's common sense.

Your Constituents Exert Their Rights to Control Their Personal Data

As a result of the Big Shift in healthcare, for constituents like Roberta, the primary product of the CHOS module, as well as conventional tests and treatments, will be a tremendous flood of personal health data.

The competition for a person's medical data could be fierce, and analysts see major conflicts ahead unless the issue of ownership is resolved. Given the robust evolution in consumer protection laws over the past 50 years, it's safe to say that eventually the law will come down on the side of the constituent.

You may have heard of the Universal Declaration of Human Rights, a document adopted by the United Nations General Assembly at its third session on December 10, 1948, at the Palais de Chaillot in Paris, France. The Declaration consists of 30 articles affirming each individual's rights. They were eventually ratified as the International Bill of Human Rights. While not legally binding, they have been elaborated in subsequent international treaties, economic transfers, regional human rights instruments, national constitutions, and other laws.

For example, Article 1 says that all people are born free and equal. Article 17 says we each have the right to own personal property. Article 27 states we each have the right to copyright our creative products.

Today, there is a growing movement to make ownership of your personal data the thirty-first human right. In June 2018, Hu-manity.co, a company designed to create decentralized human rights using proprietary technology and legal innovations on blockchains, declared Article

31: "Everyone has the right to legal ownership of their inherent human data as property."

Hu-manity.co had estimated the size of the global human data marketplace to be between $150 billion and $200 billion annually. The company argues that without having the thirty-first human right declare that a constituent's data is his or her personal property, organizations will buy, sell, and exploit inherent human data, leaving people no choice about or control over where, how, when, or by whom their data is used.

Richie Etwaru, CEO of Hu-manity.co, says his goal is to get away from the current system and make personal medical data a person's legal property.

"The data's being used without being classified as property and without explicit consent and authorization," he told National Public Radio. "And as a result there's really this whole gray area about, 'Can you really make billions of dollars off of a discovery that came from me?'"

Milind Kamkolkar, chief data officer at the drug company Sanofi and an advisor to Hu-manity.co, added that it was difficult to track the many complex transactions involving people's personal medical data. "Sometimes it just feels like it's 'blood diamonds' in the world of data sharing. We can't really track how that data came through, but someone's making money off this, and making an incredible amount of money off this. Personally, I think there are going to be regulations as we start waking up to this phenomenon."[13]

Etwaru and his colleagues at Hu-manity.co aren't just pointing out the problem; they're offering a solution. In 2018, the company introduced an app called #My31 that would let people specify how their medical data can and cannot be used. Individuals' preferences would be added to their electronic medical records and similar data from pharmacies.

In a press release announcing #My31, the New Jersey–based company said, "Hu-manity.co's global inherent Human Data Consent and Authorization Blockchain (HD-CAB) is built on a 'chain of chains' strategy combining Ethereum and other fabrics. Consent and authorization to use inherent human datasets—geospatial data, driver and vehicle history, consumer spending habits, medical history, and recreational habits—can now be managed transparently as legal property on a block-chain. Humans who claim and exercise the new decentralized human right #31 will enjoy the legal characteristics of property ownership for inherent human data, such as involvement in sale, fair market value negotiations, sharing, security, and protection from theft."[14]

Note that Hu-manity.co asserted that people have the right to own and control all their personal data, including not only their medical data but their physical location, where they drive their car, and where they spend their money. The #My31 app allows the constituent to bundle all personal data in one place and then license that data to the organization or buyer the constituent chooses. It's as if the constituent owned a house and decided to rent it or wrote a book and signed a deal with a publisher.

The app sales page said, "Once you claim your 31st Human Right, you will receive a title for your digital data declaring it as your property. While privacy is often misunderstood, property is powerful, well under-stood, and comes with ownership."[15]

With your title, which is just like the title to your house or car, you have the right to either opt in or opt out of the data marketplace.

Hu-manity.co chose Hyperledger Fabric as its underlying block-chain technology running on the IBM cloud. Etwaru told TechCrunch that the company chose IBM for both technical and business reasons: "Launching with IBM brings credibility and validation to the notion that data should be human property."[16]

As of December 2019, Hu-manity.co reported over 100,000 people in 70 countries had downloaded the app, and the company was on target to reach 1 million in 2020.[17]

That may not seem like very much today, but there was a time when Amazon, Google, and Apple each had fewer customers than 100,000. In those early days, it would have been very foolish to bet against them! We are at the beginning of a massive wave of disruption in the area of personal data ownership, and healthcare companies and leaders would be well advised to embrace it.

TAKE ACTION!

- In collecting and maintaining constituent data and making it available to the constituent, ensure that your organization scrupulously adheres to HIPAA guidelines.

- By state law, you may think your healthcare organization owns the records of your patients. At the moment, it might—but that will change. Take heed of the experience of the University of Chicago—if you attempt to sell or otherwise leverage your patients' data, prepare for lawsuits.

- How secure is the healthcare data of your constituents? Doctors and healthcare professionals are not often also data security specialists, and they often make poor security managers. Get a professional to protect your organization's data and the many devices connected to it.

- Blockchain technology is poised to solve two problems at once: the problem of data security and the problem of data ownership.

- Be aware of the growing pressure to create the thirty-first human right: "Everyone has the right to legal ownership of their inherent human data as property." Is your organization ready for this?

- The #My31 app proposes to let your constituents specify how their medical data can and cannot be used. This may not prove to be the ultimate solution, but at the very least it's a clear signal that times are changing, and the Big Shift is upon us.

How We're Going to Pay for Constituent Care

Nothing in this life is free, and that includes healthcare. Someone needs to pay the bills.

In the United States, our constituents pay for their healthcare—meaning treatment for disease or injury—through one or more of three methods.

1. Taxes and Government Borrowing

The more common way to say this is "government programs," including Medicare and Medicaid. But the federal government has to get its money from somewhere, so either it collects taxes, or it borrows. The states are not permitted to run on deficit spending; only the federal government has that right.

In fiscal year 2020, federal revenue was budgeted at $3.64 trillion; state revenue was "guesstimated" at $2.13 trillion; local revenue was "guesstimated" at $1.39 trillion. Total US government revenue, including federal, state, and local, was "guesstimated" to be $7.17 trillion.[1]

As for healthcare, in 2018, the federal government spent nearly $1.1 trillion, of which $225 billion came directly from taxpayers in the form of federal income tax revenues. On an individual basis, more than a quarter of what you pay in federal taxes goes toward Medicare, Medicaid, Affordable Care Act subsidies, and other healthcare programs, according to a Committee for a Responsible Federal Budget analysis for *The Wall Street Journal*.[2] Of the total $1.2 trillion that the federal government spent on healthcare, Medicare took about $644 billion, Medicaid and the Children's Health Insurance Program accounted for about $427 billion, and veterans' medical care claimed about $80 billion.[3]

If you take the US population as 330 million people, federal spending on healthcare per capita was therefore $3,300.

Ask yourself, in 2018, did you consume $3,300 worth of federally subsidized healthcare? If you're in generally good health, probably not.

2. Private Health Insurance Plans

In 2017, spending on private health insurance—for policies from Tufts, Blue Cross, Ascension, and all the others—totaled $1.2 trillion.

As CNBC reported, the average annual health insurance premium for a single American was about $7,188 for 2019, with employers carrying a significantly larger portion of the overall expense. Over half of Americans rely on their employer for health insurance, so typically employees do not pay the full cost. The average American actually paid about $3,400 for insurance. Spending on retail prescription drugs reached $333.4 billion.[4]

With about a 5 percent increase from 2018 to 2019, increases in insurance premiums have outpaced increases in wages.

3. Cash Out of Pocket

According to the Kaiser Family Foundation's annual employer benefits survey, individuals who rely on employer-based insurance benefits are paying an average of $1,242 in out-of-pocket costs. Families are on the hook for an average of $6,015 in out-of-pocket expenses, which is about a 71 percent increase over the past 10 years.

Overall, in 2017, Americans spent $3.5 trillion, or $10,739 per person, on healthcare.[5]

To recap:

- In 2017, federal and state governments paid $1.7 trillion for healthcare, mostly for Medicaid and Medicare. Much of this came from taxpayers.
- Private health insurers (mostly employer plans) paid over $1 trillion. About $765 billion was from premiums employers paid, and $280 billion was funded by the premiums employees paid. But employees are really paying for the whole thing, because they trade lower wages for healthcare.
- In 2016, average out-of-pocket health spending per capita was $1,103.

Who Gets Paid

The vast river of healthcare money goes into the bank accounts of a long list of healthcare providers and related businesses.

For your constituents, the biggest single healthcare expense is the cost of their health insurance. America's Health Insurance Plans asked research firm Milliman to break down healthcare premiums and track where each dollar goes. The results, published in "Where Does Your Healthcare Dollar Go?," show how much of each dollar goes to which expense line in an average health insurance company.[6] You can see the results in Table 19.1.

The first four categories in the table—prescription drugs, doctor services, office and clinic visits, and hospital stays—account for 81.8 percent, or 81.8 cents, of each dollar. So 81.8 percent is spent on diagnosis

PERCENTAGE OF $1	PROVIDER, PRODUCT, OR SERVICE
23.3	Prescription drugs
22.2	Doctor services
20.2	Office and clinic visits
16.1	Hospital stays
4.7	Taxes
3.3	Fees and business expenses
1.8	Customer engagement
1.6	Finance, claims, and special investigations
1.6	Care management
1.6	Technology and analytics
3.5	Admin, provider management, net profit

TABLE 19.1 **What Each Healthcare Dollar Pays For**

and treatment, along with the prescription drugs that are commonly prescribed as part of the treatment or recovery process.

What would the state of our nation's health be if this ratio were adjusted so that just 10 percent of this treatment cost was directed instead toward anticipation and prevention, leaving 71.8 percent for diagnosis and treatment? Or even better, if the ratio were 20 percent anticipation and prevention, with 61.8 percent for diagnosis and treatment?

That would be a Big Shift.

Once we recalibrate our healthcare system to focus on anticipation and prevention, the costs of diagnosis and treatment would decline, because people who get sick would be treated earlier in the disease process, at a lower cost.

Obviously, little would change in the diagnosis and treatment of accidental injuries. If you fall and break your arm, that's an event that cannot be anticipated. But it's precisely that kind of mechanical repair that our nation's healthcare system does so beautifully. We are very good at fixing people who have been injured. We can even give them new limbs and other body parts.

The healthcare problems that we are *not* very good at are lifestyle diseases. We spend trillions of dollars attempting to treat heart disease and obesity, but they are not solved by surgery, MRIs, or prescriptions.

If you want to see a microcosm of how lifestyle diseases can negatively impact a population, look no further than the island of Okinawa.

Okinawa: A Mini-America

It's well known that the people of Okinawa, Japan, once had exceptionally long lives and a high number of centenarians. This was largely due to their active lifestyle and the local diet, which was low in red meat and high in vegetables, including the Satsuma sweet potato, the bitter goyain melon, and seaweed, particularly *konbu*.

But with the growing influence of American fast food, that has changed. During the time the United States administered the island from the end of World War II until 1972, American culture seeped into the island. In 1963, Okinawa got the very first fast-food outlet in Japan, and those fast-food places kept coming. Today it has more fast-food outlets per capita than anywhere else in the country. Since 2000, as a percentage of their overall diet, Okinawans have been consuming as much fat as Americans.

As the *Telegraph UK* reported, the generation that grew up eating American food is now reaching middle age, and people are increasingly overweight and at risk from diabetes. "Research shows that Okinawans consume more fat, smoke more, and drink more than the average Japanese. We use cars instead of walking or cycling," said Yoko Asato, a spokesperson for the local health department.

Nearly half of men in their forties are obese, and almost 30 percent of Okinawan men die before reaching 65. In the census of 1995,

Okinawa had the highest longevity of all 47 prefectures of Japan. By 2000, it was twenty-sixth. As the old people—who lived most of their lives eating seaweed and *goya*, the local vegetable—die off, the legendary life expectancy will plummet.[7]

Meanwhile, the rate of hip fractures on Okinawa is rising. As H. Arakaki and others reported in "Epidemiology of Hip Fractures in Okinawa, Japan," statistics show that between the years 1988 and 2004—only 16 years—people 50 years of age or older became more susceptible to hip fractures. After analyzing the data, they concluded, "The accretion of the hip fracture incidence rate was greater than that which could be explained purely by changes in population size and structure."[8]

Heart disease is increasing. As S. Miyagi and others reported in "Longevity and Diet in Okinawa, Japan: The Past, Present and Future," as late as 1990 the age-adjusted death rates of the three leading causes of death were lower in Okinawa than the Japanese national averages, and people were living longer than the average. But only 10 years later, the standard mortality ratios of heart disease and cerebrovascular disease for both sexes in Okinawa had increased over their 1990 levels. The standard mortality ratios of ischemic heart disease for men in Okinawa exceeded that of mainland Japan.[9]

There could not be a more stark—and sad—example of what lifestyle diseases can do to a population in a short amount of time.

Okinawa is a mini-America. There, the health crisis is clear, and the cause is obvious.

The solution?

If the island were ruled by a king, it would be easy. The king would decree:

1. Tear down all the fast-food restaurants. Outlaw them. Get people back on the traditional diet.
2. Get people out of their offices and back to working outdoors.
3. Get people out of their cars and make them walk.

Within a generation, the life expectancy and overall health of Okinawans would rebound to their early twentieth-century levels.

Is this going to happen? No. Japan is a free society, and there will not be a Communist China–style Cultural Revolution dictated by the government.

Just like in America—and around the world—the people in Okinawa will have to *choose* to be healthy, and what the government can do is encourage—or even pressure—its citizens to work toward better health.

If the Japanese government could act freely to solve the problem, it would invest in better health through physical fitness and better eating habits. It might impose a stiff tax on junk food, which in most markets is priced low, making it particularly attractive to low-income people. Such a tax would both raise revenue for health programs and discourage consumption of the foods being taxed.

Tax Sugary Drinks

Imposing a tax on cigarettes to both raise revenue and discourage consumption has been done for many years. Many government entities are looking to do the same thing with another clearly identifiable health culprit: sugary drinks.

As the World Health Organization reports, sugary drinks are linked to diabetes and obesity. People who consume sugary drinks regularly—one or two cans a day or more—have a 26 percent greater risk of developing type 2 diabetes than people who rarely consume such drinks. Diabetes brings a high cost to society; from 2011 to 2030, losses in gross domestic product worldwide due to diabetes, including both direct and indirect costs, are expected to total $1.7 trillion—$900 billion in high-income countries and $800 billion in low- and middle-income countries.

In its 2017 report "Taxes on Sugary Drinks: Why Do It?," WHO reveals taxes on sugary drinks help reduce consumption and prevent obesity. Statistics show that a tax on sugary drinks that raises prices by just 20 percent can lead to a reduction in consumption of around 20 percent, thus helping to reduce obesity and diabetes. Estimates suggest that, over 10 years, a tax on sugary drinks of just 1 cent per ounce in the United States would result in more than $17 billion in healthcare cost savings.

WHO proves its case by citing the example of Mexico, where in January 2014 the government added an excise tax of 1 peso (about 5 cents) per liter on any nonalcoholic beverage with added sugar to the country's Special Tax on Production and Services, which is paid by the producer and represents about a 10 percent increase in price for the consumer.

After just two years of implementation, a study conducted by the Mexican National Institute of Public Health and the University of North Carolina showed an average reduction of 7.6 percent in the purchase of taxed sugary drinks, with a corresponding increase of 2.1 percent in purchases of untaxed beverages, particularly bottled water. Over $2.6 billion in new tax revenues had been raised during those first two years of implementation, and some of this revenue was earmarked for installing water fountains in schools across Mexico.[10]

Obesity and the Airlines: Is It Time to Weigh Passengers?

While the growing obesity epidemic may impact healthcare most directly, other industries are impacted as well. As recently as the turn of the twenty-first century, the airline industry thought it had found a path to greater profits by making airplane seats smaller and closer together. But now this strategy is colliding head-on with the reality that passengers are getting bigger. Many major airlines have been forced to adopt policies that state if the passenger cannot comfortably lower both armrests, he or she must buy a second seat or upgrade to business class, where seats are wider.[11]

The idea has been floated that airline passengers should be weighed before boarding. Fuel Matrix, a British firm involved in airline fuel-saving software and technologies, has proposed weighing passengers before boarding a flight. The idea is not to charge obese customers more, but to allow airlines to calculate the exact "zero-fuel weight" of the aircraft, which is the weight of the plane itself plus all cargo and passengers, and load the exact amount of fuel needed for the flight.

The company says that weight capture for passengers will be automatic and confidential and causes no issues with the UK General Data Protection Regulation or the Data Protection Act 2018, because biometric data is already widely used by airlines and airports. The software, Fuel Matrix says, will integrate readily with modern self-actuated passenger systems to further enhance the speed and smoothness of the passengers' journeys through an airport.[12]

Does this sound like an invasion of privacy and a violation of personal rights?

Actually, there was a time when weighing passengers was routine. The *Economist* has pointed out that in the early days of commercial air travel, passenger aircraft were less powerful and carried less fuel and consequently had strict weight limits. For instance, in 1933, on the inaugural flight of the Boeing 247 airliner from San Francisco to New York, the plane could not carry more than 16,805 pounds including fuel. The 10 passengers with tickets had to get on the scale, as did their flight attendant, who could not weigh more than 135 pounds.[13]

While the practice was phased out as planes got bigger, it's coming back. In November 2012, Samoa Airlines, a regional carrier using small aircraft, announced a policy of charging passengers not by the seat but by the total weight of the passenger and his or her luggage. "The next step is for the industry to make those sort of changes and recognize that 'Hey, we are not all 72 kilograms [about 160 pounds] anymore, and we don't all fit into a standard seat,' Chris Langton, Samoa Air chief executive told CNN. 'What makes airplanes work is weight. We are not selling seats, we are selling weight.'"[14]

In August 2015, Uzbekistan Airways, the flag carrier of Uzbekistan, announced it would charge passengers according to how much they weighed. The airline said its passengers would be weighed on scales in airport departure zones.[15]

Airline number crunchers say that additional savings can be made by allocating heavier passengers in the optimum areas of the plane to ensure that the aircraft is properly balanced. At present, pilots sometimes need to apply "trim" during level flight to counter an imbalance, which adds to the fuel burn.

While first-class passengers are unlikely to appreciate being told where to sit to balance the plane, basic economy travelers can be assigned to the ideal locations to ensure the aircraft is well balanced.[16]

Deciding Who Pays

Today in America, we have a healthcare revenue stream with three tributaries forming the main river, from which the healthcare provider is paid. These three streams are the government, private health insurance companies, and individual personal payments. When you trace the revenue streams back to their sources—the spots high up in the hills where the flow begins—you find the individual constituent who is simultaneously the taxpayer, the employee, and the patient. He or she pays the taxes, takes less salary, and pays out of pocket. The only other entity creating money to pay for healthcare is the government, which can borrow; but even borrowing must be paid back by the taxpayer.

At the end of the day, constituents pay for the entire system. Then the only question becomes, how do we decide how much each person has to pay?

In today's system, if you assumed that the sicker you were, the more you paid, you'd be wrong.

As we've discussed in earlier chapters, since the passing of the Affordable Care Act, our nation has been moving toward a "no-fault" health insurance market where insurers cannot base their rates on whether the applicant has a preexisting condition. Insurance companies can charge you more if you smoke cigarettes, but that's just about the only discriminatory criterion left over from the old days when they could pick and choose whom they wanted to cover.

This has helped create a situation in which the money spent by private insurers and the government (Medicare and Medicaid) to treat sick people is skewed heavily toward a small percentage of constituents.

As HealthSystemTracker said, "In a given year, a small portion of the population is responsible for a very large percentage of total health spending. . . . In 2016, 5 percent of the population accounted for half of all health spending. The 5 percent of people who spend the most on healthcare spend an average of around $50,000 annually; people in the top 1 percent have average spending of over $109,750. At the other end of the spectrum, the 50 percent of the population with the lowest spending accounted for only 3 percent of all total health spending; the average spending for this group was $276."[17]

Let that sink in for a moment: 5 percent of the population, or 16.5 million people, accounted for 50 percent of all healthcare spending, or $1.75 trillion.

But these aren't just "freeloaders"—they pay more in out-of-pocket fees too. In 2016, just 1 percent of the population accounted for nearly 20 percent of all out-of-pocket spending on health services, and the top 5 percent of spenders accounted for 46 percent.

In the Medicare population, 1 percent of the patients are responsible for 15 percent of spending. There are two patterns typical of highest-cost patients: those who cycle in and out of the hospital with preventable conditions and those who have a single catastrophic event. In "The Most Expensive Patients in the Hospital," Karen E. Joynt and others report the mean Medicare payment for prolonged mechanical ventilator patients in 2010 was $61,995, with a maximum of $1.3 million, making them the costliest to treat.[18]

A 2016 Canadian study by Wodchis and others found that one-third of high-cost users (individuals in the highest 5 percent bracket of costs) remained in that same category during the subsequent two years. Most spending among high-cost users was for hospitalization, in contrast to lower-cost users, among whom spending was predominantly for ambulatory care services. The most common reasons for hospital admissions among high-cost users were chronic diseases, infections, acute events, and palliative care.[19]

A 2019 study by Kaiser Permanente arrived at similar conclusions. KP looked at internal studies of utilization and detailed information on care given its 4 million patients in Northern California, which had been captured by its electronic health record system. Researchers made two conclusions.

1. The makeup of the most expensive 5 percent was much more heterogeneous than has been assumed. "The group comprises three roughly equal segments of patients with very different medical needs," wrote study authors Robert Pearl and Philip Madvig. These patients are "people with one or more chronic medical conditions that could be improved or kept under control; people who suffer a onetime catastrophic health problem; and people with severe chronic conditions who can't be returned to good health and require expensive treatment continually."

2. The constituents in the first two segments of the top 5 percent vary from year to year. To the authors, this explained that disease-management programs haven't delivered positive returns because they aren't designed to address the heterogeneity and unpredictability of expensive patients.[20]

The Solution? The CHOS Module

This brings us back to the core of the Big Shift: delivering personalized health maintenance to all constituents with the CHOS module that will monitor their physical condition in real time and allow their primary care physician to anticipate and prevent disease—whether minor or major—as well as receive instant notification of an acute event.

A wealth of data shows that the Big Shift from a focus on diagnosis and treatment to one on early detection (driven by digital wearables) and prevention demonstrates a clear path toward reducing the cost of healthcare while improving the quality of clinical care. In other words, not only is there no cost increase in this new approach, but the cost savings is significant and will provide the following key benefits:

- Early detection provides far greater interventional options for the patient.
- Real-time continuous patient monitoring combined with game mechanics and social engagement will deliver the behavioral changes necessary to address obesity, one of the major cost centers driving chronic disease.
- Shifting economic incentives for both patients and the healthcare industry will significantly change marketing and innovation targets, driving significant reductions in cost.
- Continuous patient monitoring can be achieved with extremely low-cost wearable technologies that deliver major returns on investment.
- Financial transparency through a new level of value-based healthcare will require that interventions provide a significant benefit in cost when compared with the cost of lifestyle changes.
- Sharing costs and savings with patients will have a major impact on patient care selection.
- Some healthcare rationing will occur. (For example, you may be required to lose weight prior to being approved for a knee replacement.)
- In the next 10 years, disincentives will become rather punitive for noncompliant patients. This will be not unlike the disincentives that we currently have in place for cigarette smoking and that are being introduced for the consumption of sugary drinks.

- Significant new resources will be made available to drive and incentivize prevention, wellness, and overall health.

The Big Shift Will Save Money

While economic incentives such as the sugary drink tax will provide additional revenues for government subsidies, studies have shown that personalized preventive medicine saves money.

In "The Impact of Personalized Preventive Care on Health Care Quality, Utilization, and Expenditures," Shirley Musich, PhD, and colleagues report on their study of MD-Value in Prevention (MDVIP), a network of affiliated primary care physicians who utilize a model of healthcare delivery based on an augmented physician-patient relationship and focused on personalized preventive healthcare. The national network consists of 900 physicians serving over 300,000 patients in 45 states and the District of Columbia,

Among 10,186 MDVIP constituent members and randomly selected, matched nonmembers, the researchers found that when compared with nonmembers, MDVIP members experienced reduced utilization of emergency room and urgent care services. Members also achieved program cost savings, and older age groups were more likely to realize savings in the early years with preventive activities indicating condition management. "These results," they wrote, "indicate that a primary care model based on an enhanced physician-patient relationship and focused on quality and personalized preventive care within a time frame of three years can achieve positive healthcare expenditure outcomes and improved health management."[21]

And in "How Preventive Healthcare Services Reduce Spending for Payers," Thomas Beaton explained how care that's focused on prevention can help keep patients from developing costly chronic conditions and save money. According to the CDC, chronic diseases that are avoidable through preventive care services drive 75 percent of the nation's healthcare spending and reduce economic output in the United States by $260 billion a year.

Reducing the prevalence of hypertension in the United States by just 5 percent would save the economy $25 billion in treatment costs, said the surgeon general's National Prevention Strategy. Preventing long-term, debilitating diseases like HIV/AIDS will reduce the cost of treatment. "For every HIV infection prevented, an estimated $355,000 is saved in the cost of providing lifetime HIV treatment," said the surgeon general's report.[22]

As any hospital administrator knows, unnecessary emergency room visits by uninsured constituents are a huge driver of healthcare costs. Parkland Memorial Hospital in Dallas had a particularly high rate of uninsured ER visits, with almost 85 percent of its patients either uninsured or on Medicaid. With 872 beds, it's one of the 10 biggest hospitals in the United States. In 2016, the hospital spent over half its budget—$871 million—on uncompensated care.

In response, in 2015 Parkland instituted the "frequent flyer" program, called the Parkland Center for Clinical Innovation (PCCI). It focuses on the patients who had visited the hospital at least 10 times in the previous month. Many were homeless, and some of them had annual unpaid bills of up to $100,000. The goal of the program was to build a network of hundreds of community-based social services around Dallas County, with Parkland Memorial at the center of it, all knitted together by a computer network.

As *Politico* reported, while the frequent fliers haven't yet been fitted with wearable monitors (that will come in the near future!), a sophisticated software platform enables the hospital to, upon their discharge from its emergency room, refer these uninsured homeless people to appropriate shelters, pantries, and other social services providers. There, social workers monitor their clients' efforts to maintain their health: getting healthy food, filling their prescriptions, finding a place to sleep, or having money for the bus. It's much cheaper to meet the needs of these constituents outside the medical system, and anticipate and prevent, rather than pay when they get sick.

As Benjamin Franklin said over 200 years ago (and as we noted earlier in the book), an ounce of prevention is worth a pound of cure.

TAKE ACTION!

- Is there an Okinawa in your community? Are your constituents becoming more sedentary and obese, and are they dying at a younger age? Then you need to think about massive intervention and how to anticipate and prevent the snowballing health crisis.
- Is there a movement in your community or state to tax sugary drinks? If so, are you on board with it? And if not, can you start a ballot initiative?
- Most disease management programs haven't delivered positive returns because they aren't designed to address the heterogeneity and unpredictability of expensive patients. But with today's technology, your organization can deliver personalized health monitoring that recognizes and embraces each person's individual health profile.
- Early detection provides a wealth of interventional options for the patient. Is your organization ready and equipped to anticipate and prevent disease?
- Ensure that your organization has studied the Parkland Memorial Hospital's PCCI program, and will go the extra mile to help your uninsured constituents where they live, thereby reducing their visits to the emergency room.

The Prescription for Healthcare Leaders

I n this book we've covered a lot of ground very quickly. We started with the premise that while our current healthcare industry does some things very well—the development of treatments for HIV/AIDS is just one example—overall, we know there's a lot of room for improvement. Compared with other industrialized nations, while we spend more than they do, we don't get comparable results. No system is perfect, but in the United States we've become accustomed to occupying a position of world leadership in many areas, and you could say that in the field of healthcare the United States was once the global leader. But today it would be difficult to make that argument.

There is no single threat or imperfection that's preventing the US healthcare industry from achieving its full potential. You can't point to just one thing and say, "Ah! If we could only fix *that*, then we'd be back on track!" There are many obstacles and problem areas, requiring a wide variety of fixes.

There is no single savior who will come along and transform the industry. Even the president of the United States has limited power to effect widespread change. Returning our healthcare system to a position of world leadership requires the combined talents of every stakeholder, from healthcare organization CEOs and Washington politicians to the frontline healthcare providers in every hospital and clinic in the nation.

Our task is made greater and more urgent by the fact that disruption—technological, social, and political—is impacting the industry at an increasing rate and with increasing force. It's like a dam on a river with a small crack in it. At first the water trickles through the crack, and you might be lulled into believing it's not a threat. But over time the water keeps eating away at the crack, making it wider and wider. Soon the trickle becomes a stream and eats away more forcefully at the crack, becoming stronger still. The rate of flow keeps increasing, and the gap gets wider more quickly, until the water is gushing through. New cracks appear, and it won't be long before the dam collapses and the valley below is flooded.

If you identify the crack in the dam early enough, you can take the necessary steps to reinforce the dam and keep it strong. But the longer you wait, the more difficult and expensive the task will be.

Healthcare professionals may take some comfort in knowing that the challenges facing the healthcare industry are some of the same ones facing other industries. They include the accelerating pace of technological disruption, the growing expectations of consumers to get what they want *right now*, and the fragmentation of the concept of the professional expert together with the proliferation of consumer-friendly, unregulated advice and treatment services.

Obesity is a growing health problem. Among all the disruptive forces at work in the first half of the twenty-first century, it has affected the healthcare industry more than any other. It's part of the rise of lifestyle diseases—those adverse health conditions brought about not by an external threat such as a virus or an accident, but by how we live our lives.

The Big Shift in Personal Responsibility

Lifestyle diseases raise the difficult subject of personal responsibility that is much less of a factor in traditional diseases. If a mosquito bites you and you get malaria, few people would say it was your fault. If you slip and fall on an icy sidewalk and break your leg, it's not your fault—and the jury in your civil suit against the property owner will agree.

A genetic disorder is not your fault, and you should not be penalized for it. We believe that diseases such as Alzheimer's that are associated with aging are not your fault, and the rise in the rate is unavoidable. The Alzheimer's Association has said, "The number of Americans surviving into their eighties, nineties, and beyond is expected to grow dramatically due to medical advances, as well as social and environmental conditions. Additionally, a large segment of the American population—the baby boom generation—has begun to reach age 65 and older, ages when the risk for Alzheimer's and other dementias is elevated."[1]

These are not forces within a constituent's direct control.

But what has been particularly vexing for the healthcare industry is the rise of deadly lifestyle diseases that, at least on the surface, appear to be within the direct control of the individual. They are diseases directly related to the three big disruptive forces in modern life: our predilection and ability to overeat; the overabundance of nonnutritive foods such as sugar, corn syrup, and refined flour; and our increasingly sedentary lifestyle. We are eating more and moving less, and the result is a suite of diseases, including diabetes, arthritis, and heart disease, that are resistant to the types of external "fixes" in which Western medicine excels. We try to treat these diseases with conventional methods, including medications, but we're not getting to the root of the problem, which is human behavior.

The good news is that we now have the tools to get the job done.

We have the technology—imperfect today, but improving exponentially—to anticipate emerging health issues in each and every individual constituent, even before these issues rise to the level of "disease." We presently have rudimentary digital sensors that can detect, capture, and digitally transmit various vital signs; and given what we're experiencing right now, we can fully expect such devices to become smaller, more powerful, and more versatile every year. It will not be long before a personal health monitor will be able to detect the early signs of a wide range of diseases and alert the CHOS module even before the constituent becomes aware of any symptoms.

The Big Shift and the Way Ahead

In my practice, I find that while many healthcare leaders are aware that massive disruption is happening, they are not often clear on the size, speed, and depth of change. Meanwhile, other healthcare organizations—the leaders—are already developing a range of new practices that will ensure their success in the near and long terms. The laggards need to follow suit or risk being left behind.

In our dynamically changing healthcare landscape, healthcare organizations need to embrace these emerging drivers of market strength.

Master Change Management

The term "change management" was made popular decades ago when organizations needed to restructure their enterprises to address market and economic change. Unfortunately, most organizations see change management as a way of emotionally dealing with changes that have already happened rather than leveraging oncoming change as an opportunity. To drive sustainable growth and marketplace relevance, as a leader you need to embrace change and make it work *for* your company, not against it.

Innovate or Perish

If you are dealing with a new marketplace—and in many ways, with healthcare you are—you have two choices: *react to it* or *invent it*. Needless to say, inventing it is the smarter strategy, as it adds more enterprise value and allows you to lead your marketplace. Ask yourself these three very basic questions: "Have we evaluated our innovation readiness? Have we built a comprehensive innovation strategy? Have we empowered our organization to take smart risks?" If the answer is no to any of these questions, you could be at risk of slipping into the abyss.

Become a Customer Experience Superstar

In other industries, we see an intense focus on what used to be called "customer service" but what is now more precisely referred to as the "customer experience."

Like it or not, your constituents—including the ones with self-inflicted lifestyle diseases—are becoming accustomed to a seamless and positive customer experience. In the healthcare universe, their experience includes every interaction with a healthcare services provider, from the ads they see on TV or in magazines to the bedside visit by their doctor after inpatient surgery. Of course, while physicians and nurses will need to keep putting their energies into the treatment of the patient, the Big Shift, with its technological data collection capabilities, data safety guarantees, and emerging penalties for noncompliance, will usher in a new era of connectivity and communication. The constituent and healthcare provider will be brought closer while making non-medically qualified health information providers less attractive.

Get Agile and Lean

Leading healthcare organizations are throwing bureaucracy and sluggish processes overboard in favor of Scrum, Agile, and Lean best practices. These practices, which are being imported into healthcare from the manufacturing and software industries, are supported by a culture of innovation and foresight, all targeting the quality of patient care and enterprise success and sustainability.

Hire and Promote Future-Forward Leaders

The future belongs to those who prepare for it and embrace it. This requires a cultural shift of leaders who are willing to build out future-casting activities, look at all the disparate trends affecting the enterprise, and shape the *future* healthcare organization *today*.

Embrace Technology

At a recent major conference of the College of Healthcare Information Management Executives, during my keynote presentation I observed that hospitals and clinics are technology organizations that happen to deliver exceptional clinical quality, patient safety, and exquisite human experiences. To my pleasant surprise, among the audience members I found tremendous support for this reality, and in fact most of the best hospitals had already begun the process of building their technology infrastructure for the future.

Support Enterprise Excellence

Sluggish, layered, hierarchical enterprises that have committed to managing by looking in the rearview mirror will fail with mathematical certainty. Enterprise excellence requires that an organization set aside its legacy view of the universe in order to leverage new best practices. These new best practices include the way healthcare providers leverage data to glean better key performance indicators, allowing them to quickly identify and address both problems and opportunities to thrive. These organizations encourage a culture of collaboration. They don't cling to what was; they focus on what is possible, and they built fast, agile approaches toward delivering exquisite patient value while concurrently reducing cost and improving efficiency.

Take Innovation Seriously

In my work as a management consultant, my colleagues and I spend a great deal of our time mopping up after failed innovation initiatives. In fact, you could say that we function as an innovation and strategy hazmat team. In doing this work, we have discovered that the leaders within these organizations invariably treated strategic excellence and innovation as a bumper sticker. With a few celebratory meetings, the opening of a so-called innovation center, and some other forms of window dressing, they were sure that they were on their way to innovation excellence. But the innovations didn't come, and they concluded that innovation was either impossible or irrelevant. Not only is innovation both possible and relevant; it is a healthcare mandate.

To have a place in the future, you need to shoulder the burden of helping invent it. Innovation is your future, but like any protocol backed by research, you must follow the protocol. In other words, as a healthcare leader and stakeholder, you must create a comprehensive innovation road map that ensures that all the working parts are in place. When done properly, your organization should expect multiple returns on innovation.

Ensure Your Place in the Future with "Future Casting"

The Big Shift has many facets: the consumer shift, the technology shift, the economic shift, the human shift, and the research shift, all of which must be managed through durable systems. Artificial intelligence, 5G, the learning machine, the Internet of Things, connection architecture, anticipatory/predictive analytics, quantum computing, data analytics, wearables, body sensors, automated drug dispensers, and hospital command centers will all come together to significantly reduce the cost of healthcare, identify disease processes early, and work in concert with wellness and prevention programs to transform healthcare.

The best organizations in healthcare are putting together teams of subject-matter experts to drive their organizations forward in the context of known and likely trends. These efforts will result in significant opportunities to anticipate and prevent disease, expand revenue, reduce cost, improve clinical care, broaden access, and ensure stakeholder/patient safety.

Future casting can ensure your organization is on the proper trajectory. While developing a future-casting program and team seems like an obvious investment, too many organizations are in disruption denial, suffering from a condition I call "disruption dysphoria." In other words, they are reluctant to recognize the changes happening around them.

Too many healthcare executives make slight and insignificant changes to their strategies each year. They keep the format that was created at the turn of the century. Tearing up your strategy and taking a completely fresh look at your core mission may be painful, but in a time of massive change with new tools, technologies, customers, stakeholders, and a massively disrupted healthcare ecosystem, it may be required.

TAKE ACTION!

If you were to create a healthcare system from scratch, or create your own organization all over again, what would it look like?

Recall Roberta, whom we met in the first chapter of this book. Given the technology available today and likely to be available in the future, what system would you design to anticipate and prevent disease—or from another point of view—to help Roberta stay healthy?

You'd want to:

- Design a system that preserves our best strategies for curing diseases and fixing broken body parts while focusing strongly on anticipation and prevention.
- Connect Roberta to her doctor with real-time diagnostic technology, so that—just like the car dealership would be alerted to a problem in your car—her doctor would be alerted to a problem even before Roberta reported symptoms.
- Help Roberta feel confident and secure about sharing her personal data, so you'd support the thirty-first human right, giving Roberta ownership of her data.
- Reward Roberta for good health choices and gently penalize her for consistently poor choices. After all, the rate of lifestyle diseases is increasing, and personal responsibility is becoming increasingly important.

You'd find that some constituents—possibly Roberta—will be early adopters and will embrace these new initiatives with enthusiasm. Others will come around once they become comfortable with change, while some will resist because they don't like any form of change.

The same will be true of your colleagues in the healthcare industry, stakeholders, and politicians. Some will embrace innovation and a bright future, while others will resist. That's just the way of the world. The task is formidable, but together we can get it done.

Notes

Chapter 1

1. The Harris Poll, https://theharrispoll.com/only-nine-percent-of-u-s
   -consumers-believe-pharmaceutical-and-biotechnology-companies-put
   -patients-over-profits-while-only-16-percent-believe-health-insurance
   -companies-do-according-to-a-harris-pol/.
2. https://www.westhealth.org/press-release/survey2018/.
3. https://ftp.cdc.gov/pub/Health_Statistics/NCHS/NHIS/SHS/2014_
   SHS_Table_A-18.pdf.
4. https://www.health.harvard.edu/blog/why-men-often-die-earlier-than
   -women-201602199137.
5. https://www.orlandohealth.com/content-hub/why-avoiding-the-doctor
   -is-mens-number-1-health-problem.
6. https://www.tesla.com/service.
7. https://www.onstar.com/us/en/support/advanced-diagnostics/.
8. http://compositesmanufacturingmagazine.com/2017/11/lamborghini
   -terzo-millennio-can-store-electric-energy-heal/.
9. YiNa Jeong, SuRak Son, EunHee Jeon, and ByungKwan Lee, "An
   Integrated Self-Diagnosis System for an Autonomous Vehicle Based on
   an IoT Gateway and Deep Learning" (2018).
10. https://www.ncbi.nlm.nih.gov/pmc/articles/PMC6480663/.

Chapter 2

1. https://www.ststworld.com/trepanation-unusual-medical-procedure-of-
   drilling-hole-in-the-skull/.

2. https://www.nlm.nih.gov/exhibition/lifeandlimb/maimedmen.html.

3. https://www.cartercenter.org/resources/pdfs/news/health_publications/ itfde/updated_disease_candidate_table.pdf.

4. https://medicalxpress.com/news/2018-09-drug-resistant-superbug -hospitals.html.

5. https://www.cdc.gov/drugresistance/about.html,

6. https://www.thebalance.com/causes-of-rising-healthcare-costs-4064878.

7. https://www.cnbc.com/2019/02/11/this-is-the-real-reason-most -americans-file-for-bankruptcy.html.

8. https://jamanetwork.com/journals/jama/fullarticle/2720029.

Chapter 3

1. UNAIDS.org, https://www.unaids.org/en/resources/fact-sheet.

2. Cleveland Clinic, https://health.clevelandclinic.org/causes-u-s-deaths -changed-greatly-infographic/.

3. CDC, https://www.cdc.gov/nchs/fastats/leading-causes-of-death.htm.

4. PHM, https://www.ncbi.nlm.nih.gov/pmc/articles/PMC5278808/.

5. CDC, https://www.cdc.gov/media/releases/2017/p0718-diabetes-report .html.

6. PMC, https://www.ncbi.nlm.nih.gov/pmc/articles/PMC2828342/.

7. ADA, https://www.diabetes.org/resources/statistics/cost-diabetes.

8. http://worldpopulationreview.com/states/gdp-by-state/.

9. https://www.genengnews.com/topics/drug-discovery/novartis-kymriah -wins-fda-approval-as-first-car-t-cancer-therapy/.

10. WAPO, https://www.washingtonpost.com/outlook/2018/11/26/why -prescription-drug-prices-have-skyrocketed/.

11. PolicyMed.com, https://www.policymed.com/2014/12/a-tough-road -cost-to-develop-one-new-drug-is-26-billion-approval-rate-for-drugs -entering-clinical-de.html.

12. https://www.goldsteinresearch.com/report/global-hypertension-drugs -market-size-outlook.

13. https://www.mayoclinic.org/diseases-conditions/high-blood-pressure/ in-depth/diuretics/art-20048129.

14. https://www.rxlist.com/ace_inhibitors/drugs-condition.htm.

15. https://www.healthline.com/health/heart-disease/arbs#side-effects-and -risks.

16. https://www.mayoclinic.org/diseases-conditions/high-blood-pressure/ in-depth/calcium-channel-blockers/art-20047605.

17. https://www.medicinenet.com/beta_blockers/article.htm#what_are_the_ side_effects_of_beta_blockers.

Chapter 4

1. https://www.endocrineweb.com/news/obesity/20229-being-obese-can -lead-weak-bones.

2. https://www.ncbi.nlm.nih.gov/pubmed/24811098.

3. https://www.ncbi.nlm.nih.gov/pmc/articles/PMC5708005/.

4. Darkness to Light, https://www.d2l.org/the-link-between-child-sexual -abuse-and-obesity/.

5. Sycamore Institute, https://www.sycamoreinstitutetn.org/economic-cost -adverse-childhood-experiences/.

6. Mitzi Baker, UCSF.edu/news, https://www.ucsf.edu/ news/2016/10/404446/undoing-harm-childhood-trauma-and-adversity.

Chapter 5

1. https://www.healthline.com/health/nstemi#diagnosis.

2. CDC, https://www.cdc.gov/heartdisease/facts.htm.

3. Rohan Khera, https://www.ahajournals.org/doi/full/10.1161/ CIRCULATIONAHA.117.030128.

4. https://www.reuters.com/article/us-health-heart-income/heart-attack -stroke-tied-to-lost-work-and-wages-idUSKCN1PH2LG.

5. http://www.ushistory.org/tour/philadelphia-contributionship.htm.

6. https://www.aafp.org/news/health-of-the-public/20181210lifeexpect drop.html.

7. https://www.businessinsider.com/cost-of-healthcare-countries-ranked -2019-3.

8. http://worldpopulationreview.com/countries/life-expectancy-by-country/.

9. https://www.medicaldevice-network.com/news/device-predicts-heart -disease/.

Chapter 6

1. MarketWatch, https://www.marketwatch.com/story/did-your-local -primary-care-physician-close-their-practice-heres-why-2019-05-08.

2. Rosser, https://www.ncbi.nlm.nih.gov/pmc/articles/PMC111215/.

3. Basu, https://jamanetwork.com/journals/jamainternalmedicine/article -abstract/2724393?guestAccessKey=1af666c9-8ff4-4da1-bf84 -98ddb3997000&utm_source=JAMA+Network&utm_medium =referral&utm_campaign=ftm_links&utm_content=tfl&utm_ term=21819.

4. Standdesk.com, https://www.standdesk.co/6-dramatic-business-benefits -of-healthy-employees/.

5. Entrepreneur.com, https://www.entrepreneur.com/article/309685.

Chapter 7

1. https://www.hta.gov.uk/law-cryonics.

2. Ellison, https://www.beckershospitalreview.com/finance/11-hospitals -closed-so-far-this-year-here-s-why-060619.html.

3. Toyota, https://www.businessinsider.com/innovate-or-die-a-mantra-for -every-business-2013-7.

4. https://www.cancerresearch.org/immunotherapy/what-is-immunotherapy.

5. https://www.cdc.gov/ehrmeaningfuluse/introduction.html.

6. https://www.sciencedaily.com/releases/2018/05/180504103811.htm.

7. https://www.genome.gov/about-genomics/fact-sheets/Sequencing -Human-Genome-cost.

8. Ira Kalb, "Is Apple Becoming More Like Toyota in Its Approach to Innovation?" *Huffington Post*, January 27, 2016, https://www .huffingtonpost.com/ira-kalb/is-apple-becoming-more-li_b_9085164 .html.

9. ANA Awards, https://www.nursingworld.org/news/news-releases/2019 -news-releases/2019-ana-innovation-awards-winners-announced/.

10. https://www.statista.com/statistics/265645/ranking-of-the-20 -companies-with-the-highest-spending-on-research-and-development/.

11. Vijay Govindarajan and Srikanth Srinivas, "The Innovation Mindset in Action: 3M Corporation," *Harvard Business Review*, August 6, 2013, https://hbr.org/2013/08/the-innovation-mindset-in-acti-3.

Chapter 8

1. https://www.ccsinsight.com/press/company-news/2332-wearables -market-to-be-worth-25-billion-by-2019-reveals-ccs-insight/.

2. https://www.idc.com/getdoc.jsp?containerId=prUS44930019.

3. Ibid.

4. https://support.apple.com/en-us/HT204666#sensors.

5. https://www.temptraq.com/Home.

6. https://www.medicalnewstoday.com/articles/326096.php.

7. https://www.aarp.org/home-family/personal-technology/info-2018/ wearable-tech-health.html.

8. *New York Times*, https://www.nytimes.com/2002/01/18/world/arne-h-w -larsson-86-had-first-internal-pacemaker.html.

9. https://www.polymersolutions.com/blog/implantable-medical -monitoring-device/.

10. Mayo Clinic, https://www.mayoclinic.org/tests-procedures/implantable -loop-recorder/pyc-20384986.

11. MobiHealthNews, https://www.mobihealthnews.com/content/fda-clears -abbott%E2%80%99s-smartphone-compatible-cardiac-monitor-implant.

12. EMBS.org, https://www.embs.org/about-biomedical-engineering/our -areas-of-research/wearable-implantable-technologies/.

13. Computerhistory.org, https://www.computerhistory.org/timeline/ computers/.

14. Verdict Media, https://www.medicaldevice-network.com/news/biotronik -fda-injectable-cardiac-monitor/.

15. https://www.ncbi.nlm.nih.gov/pmc/articles/PMC4751024/.

16. http://www.automotivesensors2017.com/.

17. Kang et al., https://www.ncbi.nlm.nih.gov/pubmed/26779949.

Chapter 9

1. RIAA, https://www.riaa.com/u-s-sales-database/.

2. Billboard, https://www.billboard.com/articles/news/1048045/update -madonna-confirms-deal-with-live-nation.

3. BusinessInsider, https://www.businessinsider.com/2008/4/jay-z-gets-150 -million-what-does-live-nation-get-lyv-.

4. *Fortune*, https://fortune.com/2017/04/06/fda-23andme-genetic-tests/.

5. NEJM, https://www.nejm.org/doi/full/10.1056/NEJMp1316367.

6. NIH, https://ghr.nlm.nih.gov/primer/dtcgenetictesting/ directtoconsumer.

7. Symptomate, https://symptomate.com/diagnosis/en/#0-668.

8. Symptomate, Terms of service.

9. WebMD.com, https://www.webmd.com/about-webmd-policies/about -privacy-policy11.

10. Essilor, https://www.essilor.com/en/.

11. Babylon Health, https://www.babylonhealth.com/us/about_us.

12. TechCrunch, https://techcrunch.com/2017/04/25/babylon-health-raises -further-60m-to-continue-building-out-ai-doctor-app/.

13. Ibid.

14. Frost & Sullivan, https://ww2.frost.com/news/press-releases/600-m-6 -billion-artificial-intelligence-systems-poised-dramatic-market-expansion -healthcare/.

15. Wicklund, https://mhealthintelligence.com/news/mhealth-researchers -turn-the-smartphone-into-a-diagnostic-device.

16. Smartphone, https://mhealthintelligence.com/news/can-smartphones -help-diagnose-skin-cancer.

17. Amanda Montell, https://www.byrdie.com/self-diagnosis-internet.

18. Bloomberg, https://www.bloomberg.com/news/features/2018-09-20/ orthodonists-aren-t-smiling-about-teeth-straightening-startups.

19. https://www.alliedmarketresearch.com/orthodontics-market.

20. CrowdMed, http://blog.crowdmed.com/when-crowds-are-smarter-than -doctors/.

21. NME, https://www.nme.com/photos/30-biggest-selling-cds-of-the-past -30-years-1435853.

22. WebMD, https://www.comscore.com/Insights/Market-Rankings/ comScore-Ranks-the-Top-50-US-Digital-Media-Properties-for -December-2015/.

Chapter 10

1. Doctor on Demand, https://www.doctorondemand.com/.

2. Fast Company, https://www.fastcompany.com/3019564/the-mental -health-advocate-talksessions-melissa-thompson.

3. Fitbit, https://investor.fitbit.com/press/press-releases/press-release-details/ 2018/Fitbit-Inc-to-Acquire-Twine-Health/default.aspx.

4. Babalola, http://health-medical-economics.imedpub.com/consumers -and-their-demand-for-healthcare.php?aid=21061.

5. Gallup, https://news.gallup.com/poll/145025/americans-doctor-advice -without-second-opinion.aspx.

Chapter 11

1. USDA, https://www.ers.usda.gov/webdocs/publications/82220/eib-166 .pdf?v=42762.

2. Yang et al., https://jamanetwork.com/journals/jama/article-abstract/ 2731178.

3. Reuters, https://www.reuters.com/article/us-health-sitting/americans-get -more-sedentary-as-computer-use-surges-idUSKCN1RZ2BD.

4. Qiushi Chen et al., "Prevention of Prescription Opioid Misuse and Projected Overdose Deaths in the United States," https://jamanetwork .com/journals/jamanetworkopen/fullarticle/2723405.

5. https://www.mbahealthcaremanagement.org/topics/the-societal-cost-of -obesity/.

6. https://www.pharmaceuticalprocessingworld.com/rfid-in-pharmaceuticals-market-projected-to-grow-10-percent-this-year/.

7. https://www.statista.com/statistics/543070/number-of-wearable-users-in-the-us/.

Chapter 12

1. Statista.com, https://www.statista.com/statistics/638613/worldwide-data-center-storage-used-capacity/.

2. https://www.networkworld.com/article/3325397/idc-expect-175-zettabytes-of-data-worldwide-by-2025.html.

3. https://www.gizmodo.co.uk/2016/12/every-book-ever-published-would-fit-on-to-one-hard-disk/.

4. IDC Report/Seagate, https://www.seagate.com/our-story/data-age-2025/.

5. https://www.statista.com/statistics/471264/iot-number-of-connected-devices-worldwide/.

6. IDC; also https://med.stanford.edu/content/dam/sm/sm-news/documents/StanfordMedicineHealthTrendsWhitePaper2017.pdf.

7. https://khn.org/news/death-by-a-thousand-clicks/.

8. https://www.ghx.com/the-healthcare-hub/2017/healthcare-transformation-clean-data-at-the-center/.

9. https://healthlinkdimensions.com/solutions/hcp-data-hygiene-services/data-cleansing/.

Chapter 13

1. NIH, https://ghr.nlm.nih.gov/primer/consult/treatment.

2. https://www.mphonline.org/worst-pandemics-in-history/.

3. https://www.infoplease.com/math-science/health/diseases/epidemics-of-the-past-smallpox-12000-years-of-terror.

4. https://www.sciencedirect.com/topics/neuroscience/smallpox-epidemics.

5. https://www.cdc.gov/smallpox/prevention-treatment/index.html.

6. NPR, https://www.npr.org/2011/04/05/135121451/how-the-pox-epidemic-changed-vaccination-rules.

7. Wendy K. Mariner, George J Annas, and Leonard H. Glantz, "Jacobson v Massachusetts: It's Not Your Great-Great-Grandfather's Public Health Law," *American Journal of Public Health.* 95(4): 581–590 (April 1. 2005), doi:10.2105/AJPH.2004.055160, ISSN 0090-0036, PMC 1449224, PMID 15798113.

8. https://annals.org/aim/fullarticle/2727726/measles-mumps-rubella-vaccination-autism-nationwide-cohort-study.

9. Chung, https://www.ncbi.nlm.nih.gov/pmc/articles/PMC3890451/.

10. CDC, https://www.cdc.gov/diabetes/pdfs/data/statistics/national
    -diabetes-statistics-report.pdf.

11. https://www.heart.org/en/news/2018/08/29/smoking-in-america-why
    -more-americans-are-kicking-the-habit.

12. Ibid.

13. https://www.nerdwallet.com/blog/insurance/life-insurance-savings
    -quitting-smoking/.

14. https://www.cdc.gov/media/releases/2019/p1114-smoking-low.html.

Chapter 14

1. https://www.thelancet.com/action/showPdf?pii=S0140-6736%2820%
    2930183-5.

2. Ibid.

3. https://www.nytimes.com/2020/01/10/world/asia/china-virus-wuhan
    -death.html.

4. https://www.nytimes.com/2020/01/21/health/cdc-coronavirus.html.

5. https://www.who.int/docs/default-source/coronaviruse/situation-reports/
    20200121-sitrep-1-2019-ncov.pdf?sfvrsn=20a99c10_4.

6. https://www.who.int/docs/default-source/coronaviruse/situation-reports/
    20200315-sitrep-55-covid-19.pdf?sfvrsn=33daa5cb_6.

7. https://www.bloomberg.com/graphics/2020-coronavirus-pandemic
    -global-economic-risk/.

8. https://www.cnbc.com/2020/03/13/sp-estimates-the-new-coronavirus
    -could-cost-us-insurers-90-billion-in-medical-expenses.html.

9. https://www.cdc.gov/coronavirus/2019-ncov/downloads/2019-ncov
    -factsheet.pdf.

10. https://www.who.int/news-room/q-a-detail/q-a-coronaviruses.

11. https://www.cdc.gov/coronavirus/2019-ncov/symptoms-testing/
    symptoms.html.

12. https://www.propublica.org/article/how-south-korea-scaled-coronavirus
    -testing-while-the-us-fell-dangerously-behind.

13. https://www.npr.org/2020/03/13/815522836/u-s-coronavirus-testing
    -gets-a-breakthrough.

14. https://www.voanews.com/science-health/coronavirus-outbreak/south
    -korea-shows-world-how-slow-spread-coronavirus.

15. https://www.bbc.com/news/world-asia-51836898.

16. https://www.washingtonpost.com/world/coronavirus-temperature
    -screening/2020/03/14/24185be0-6563-11ea-912d-d98032ec8e25_
    story.html.

17. Ibid.

18. Quilty et al., https://www.eurosurveillance.org/content/10.2807/
    1560-7917.ES.2020.25.5.2000080#abstract_content.

19. https://www.washingtonpost.com/world/asia_pacific/coronavirus
    -test-kits-south-korea-us/2020/03/13/007f14fc-64a1-11ea-8a8e
    -5c5336b32760_story.html.

Chapter 15

1. Jiang et al., https://svn.bmj.com/content/2/4/230.full#ref-48.

2. Ibid.

3. Jiang et al., https://svn.bmj.com/content/2/4/230.full#ref-49.

4. Carecloud, https://www.carecloud.com/continuum/gamification
   -healthcare-game-changer/.

5. VG247.com, https://www.vg247.com/2011/01/04/motion-control
   -debunked-as-fitness-aid/.

6. Welltok.org., http://www.welltok.com/differentiators/.

7. https://www.fitness-gaming.com/news/health-and-rehab/hopelabs
   -games-turn-technology-into-a-powerful-tool-for-health.html.

Chapter 16

1. Wearables, https://www.emarketer.com/content/older-americans-drive
   -growth-of-wearables.

2. Smokers surcharge, https://www.healthmarkets.com/content/smoking
   -and-health-insurance.

3. Healthmarkets, https://www.healthmarkets.com/content/smoking-and
   -health-insurance.

4. https://law.freeadvice.com/insurance_law/life_insurance_law/insurance_
   lie_smoke.htm.

5. ISHN.com, https://www.ishn.com/articles/92739-study--obesity-more
   -costly-than-smoking.

6. Reuters, https://www.reuters.com/article/us-obesity/as-americas
   -waistline-expands-costs-soar-idUSBRE83T0C820120430.

7. PCRM.org, https://www.pcrm.org/news/health-nutrition/overweight
   -and-obesity-shorten-lifespan.

8. https://www.patientslikeme.com/about.

9. https://cars.usnews.com/cars-trucks/car-insurance/how-do-those-car
-insurance-tracking-devices-work.

10. https://www.allstate.com/tr/car-insurance/telematics-device.aspx.

11. https://www.travelers.com/car-insurance/programs/Intellidrive.

12. https://www.arthritisfoundationasia.com/arthritis-obesity.html.

13. https://www.nhs.uk/conditions/knee-replacement/.

14. Prichett, https://www.ncbi.nlm.nih.gov/pubmed/1925861.

15. http://www.alcoholpolicymd.com/alcohol_and_health/costs.htm#_edn1.

16. https://www.mdmag.com/medical-news/hypertension-costs-patients
-additional-2000-annually-estimated-131b-nationally.

17. AHA, https://www.heart.org/en/get-involved/advocate/federal-priorities/
cdc-prevention-programs.

18. CDC, https://www.cdc.gov/vitalsigns/heartdisease-stroke/index.html.

Chapter 17

1. https://www.mordorintelligence.com/industry-reports/global-healthcare
-analytics-market-industry.

2. https://www.marketsandmarkets.com/Market-Reports/healthcare-data
-analytics-market-905.html?gclid=EAIaIQobChMIwJqv25-n5gIVEIiG
Ch3keA0pEAAYAiAAEgKd5fD_BwE.

3. https://www.hipaajournal.com/hipaa-privacy-laws/.

4. Manta, https://www.ncbi.nlm.nih.gov/pmc/articles/PMC5290300/.

5. 23andMe, https://www.23andme.com/about/privacy/.

6. *Tom's Guide*, https://www.tomsguide.com/us/23andme-gsk-dna-data
-deal,news-27685.html.

7. 23andMe, https://www.23andme.com/about/tos/.

8. 23andMe, https://www.23andme.com/about/consent/.

9. Gene By Gene Ltd., https://genebygene.com/terms-of-service/.

10. MyMedLab.com, https://www.mymedlab.com/privacy.

11. TheVerge.com, https://www.theverge.com/2019/1/29/18197541/health
-data-privacy-hipaa-policy-business-science.

12. GSK, https://www.gsk.com/en-gb/media/press-releases/gsk-and
-23andme-sign-agreement-to-leverage-genetic-insights-for-the
-development-of-novel-medicines/.

13. *Time*, https://time.com/5349896/23andme-glaxo-smith-kline/.

14. *New York Times*, https://www.nytimes.com/2018/09/20/health/
memorial-sloan-kettering-cancer-paige-ai.html.

15. Sweeney et al., https://techscience.org/a/2018100901/.

Chapter 18

1. *Forbes*, https://www.forbes.com/sites/zackomalleygreenburg/2018/10/31/the-highest-paid-dead-celebrities-of-2018/#3874c427720c.

2. http://www.healthinfolaw.org/comparative-analysis/who-owns-medical-records-50-state-comparison.

3. *JAMA*, https://jamanetwork.com/journals/jamanetworkopen/fullarticle/2705850.

4. *The Wall Street Journal*, https://www.wsj.com/articles/google-s-secret-project-nightingale-gathers-personal-health-data-on-millions-of-americans-11573496790.

5. CNBC, https://www.cnbc.com/2019/11/12/google-project-nightingale-hospital-data-deal-raises-privacy-fears.html.

6. Mayo Clinic, https://newsnetwork.mayoclinic.org/discussion/mayo-clinic-selects-google-as-strategic-partner-for-health-care-innovation-cloud-computing/.

7. CNBC, https://www.cnbc.com/2019/11/12/google-project-nightingale-hospital-data-deal-raises-privacy-fears.html.

8. University of Chicago, https://www.uchicagomedicine.org/forefront/research-and-discoveries-articles/2017/may/uchicago-medicine-collaborates-with-google-to-use-machine-learning-for-better-health-care.

9. Google, https://www.researchgate.net/publication/322695006_Scalable_and_accurate_deep_learning_for_electronic_health_records.

10. *The New York Times*, https://www.nytimes.com/2019/06/26/technology/google-university-chicago-data-sharing-lawsuit.html.

11. HealthTech, https://healthtechmagazine.net/article/2019/10/what-happens-stolen-healthcare-data-perfcon.

12. KLAS, https://klasresearch.com/resources/press-releases/2016/10/11/do-clinicians-have-the-interoperability-they-need.

13. NPR, https://www.npr.org/sections/health-shots/2018/10/15/657493767/if-your-medical-information-becomes-a-moneymaker-could-you-could-get-a-cut.

14. https://www.businesswire.com/news/home/20180605005581/en/New-Company-Hu-manity.co-Blockchain-Declare-31st-Human.

15. https://techcrunch.com/2018/09/06/hu-manity-launches-app-giving-consumers-legal-control-over-medical-data/.

16. TechCrunch, https://techcrunch.com/2018/09/06/hu-manity-launches-app-giving-consumers-legal-control-over-medical-data/.

17. Email from Richie Etwaru, December 15, 2019.

Chapter 19

1. https://www.usgovernmentrevenue.com/current_revenue.

2. *The Wall Street Journal*, https://www.wsj.com/articles/how-100-of-your-taxes-are-spent-8-cents-on-national-parks-and-15-on-medicare-1492175921.

3. https://www.taxpolicycenter.org/briefing-book/how-much-does-federal-government-spend-health-care.

4. CNBC, https://www.cnbc.com/2019/10/09/americans-spend-twice-as-much-on-health-care-today-as-in-the-1980s.html.

5. CNBC, https://www.cnbc.com/2018/12/06/americans-shelled-out-10739-per-person-on-healthcare-last-year.html.

6. https://www.ahip.org/wp-content/uploads/2017/03/HealthCareDollar_FINAL.pdf.

7. *Telegraph UK*, https://www.telegraph.co.uk/news/health/news/3342882/Japanese-get-a-taste-for-Western-food-and-fall-victim-to-obesity-and-early-death.html.

8. Arakaki et al., https://www.ncbi.nlm.nih.gov/pubmed/20814705.

9. Miyagi et al., https://www.ncbi.nlm.nih.gov/pubmed/18924533.

10. WHO, https://apps.who.int/iris/bitstream/handle/10665/260253/WHO-NMH-PND-16.5Rev.1-eng.pdf;jsessionid=8EB115B97B24B2AC48001A2353D589F3?sequence=1.

11. https://www.smartertravel.com/airline-obesity-policies/.

12. http://www.fuelmatrix.co.uk/.

13. Ibid.

14. CNN, https://www.cnn.com/2013/04/02/travel/samoa-air-fare-by-weight/index.html.

15. http://www.travelstart.co.za/blog/these-are-the-airlines-who-charge-passengers-by-their-body-weight/.

16. https://www.independent.co.uk/travel/news-and-advice/airlines-weigh-passengers-check-in-baggage-cargo-balance-a8860071.html.

17. https://www.healthsystemtracker.org/chart-collection/health-expenditures-vary-across-population/#item-start.

18. Joynt et al., https://www.ahajournals.org/doi/abs/10.1161/circ.130.suppl_2.17306.

19. Wodchis et al., "A 3-Year Study of High-Cost Users of Healthcare," https://www.ncbi.nlm.nih.gov/pubmed/26755672/.

20. *Harvard Business Review*, https://hbr.org/2020/01/managing-the-most-expensive-patients.

21.   Musich et al., https://www.ncbi.nlm.nih.gov/pmc/articles/ PMC5296930/.

22.   Beaton, https://healthpayerintelligence.com/news/how-preventive -healthcare-services-reduce-spending-for-payers.

Chapter 20

1.   https://www.alzheimers.net/alzheimers-is-on-the-rise-in-these-states/.

Index

Thank You

Thank you for reading *The Healthcare Mandate*.

For additional free resources on how to lead your organization in a time of massive disruption in the healthcare industry, please visit thehealthcaremandate.com.

About the Author

Nicholas **J. Webb** is a preeminent healthcare futurist, professional speaker, award-winning inventor of medical devices, and
author. He works with some of the top healthcare organizations—including Pfizer, Blue Cross, Siemens Healthcare, the American
Hospital Association, and the American Academy of Dermatology—to
help them lead their market in enterprise strategy, patient experience,
and innovation. He has been awarded over 40 patents by the US Patent
and Trademark Office, and he has invented one of the first wearable
technologies and one of the world's smallest medical implants. He is
the founding Chief Innovation Officer of the Center for Innovation at
Western University of Health Sciences in Pomona, California, where he
also serves as an adjunct professor of health sciences.

For more information visit nickwebb.com/healthcare.